*The Truth about William Shakespeare*

For Shakespeare biographers, [the Manningham anecdote] is one of those unverifiable vignettes too good to discard on the grounds of merely dubious provenance.
Anthony Holden, *William Shakespeare: His Life and Work*


Toutes choses sont dites déjà; mais comme personne n'écoute, il faut toujours recommencer.
André Gide, *Traité du Narcisse*

# The Truth about William Shakespeare

## Fact, Fiction and Modern Biographies

David Ellis

EDINBURGH
University Press

For Michael Irwin

© David Ellis, 2012, 2013

Edinburgh University Press Ltd
22 George Square, Edinburgh EH8 9LF

First published in hardback by Edinburgh University Press 2012

www.euppublishing.com

Typeset in 11.25/13 New Baskerville
by Servis Filmsetting Ltd, Stockport, Cheshire, and
printed and bound in Great Britain by
CPI Group (UK) Ltd, Croydon, CR0 4YY

A CIP record for this book is available
from the British Library

ISBN 978 0 7486 4666 1 (hardback)
ISBN 978 0 7486 4667 8 (paperback)
ISBN 978 0 7486 4668 5 (webready PDF)
ISBN 978 0 7486 5388 1 (epub)

The right of David Ellis
to be identified as author of this work
has been asserted in accordance with
the Copyright, Designs and Patents Act 1988.

# Contents

*Preface* vii
*Acknowledgements* x

## PART I
1  Rules of the game   3
2  How to make bricks without straw   12
3  Forebears   21
4  The female line and Catholicism   29
5  Boyhood and youth   39
6  Marriage   47
7  The theatre   55
8  Patronage, or who's who in the Sonnets   64
9  Shakespeare and the love of men   74
10  Shakespeare and the love of women   81
11  Friends   89
12  London life   100
13  Politics   109
14  Money   117
15  Retirement and death   126
16  Post-mortem   134

## PART II
17  Gossip   145
18  The post-modernist challenge   152
19  The argument from expertise   161
20  Final thoughts   170

| | |
|---|---:|
| *Notes* | 178 |
| *Index* | 193 |

# *Preface*

THIS IS A BOOK as much about biography as Shakespeare. My interest in biography began when I was asked to write the third volume of the Cambridge life of D. H. Lawrence, and it continued with a short biographical study of Byron. Lawrence and Byron are, in many ways, ideal subjects for biography. Both of them left behind hundreds of letters (eight volumes in one case, and twelve in the other), and from time to time Byron also kept a private diary. They both lived in periods when it had become acceptable to lay bare one's private feelings in poetry or fiction, an opportunity neither of them passed up. Prominent and controversial, they made strong impressions on the people they met, many of whom rushed to record what it was like to be in their company and thereby spawned a huge literature of memoir and reminiscence. But what often struck me while working on these two authors, was how many moments in their lives there were when, despite the mass of documentation available, the biographer could have no idea of their location, of what they were doing and of how they felt.

While I was involved with Lawrence and Byron, I was also busy teaching Shakespeare and trying to think about his plays. What first alerted me to the problem of his biography was the revised edition of Samuel Schoenbaum's *Shakespeare's Lives* (1991). This survey of attempts to write a life of Shakespeare from the earliest times up to the 1980s is one of the few academic books in this area which deserves to remain on the shelves. A distinguished scholar with an incisive mind, who also wrote with great panache, Schoenbaum surveyed his chosen field in a memorable way. Yet when I put together the knowledge his book gave me with my experience of working on Lawrence and Byron, what became puzzling was why and how biographies of Shakespeare could continue to appear. It seemed a problem which might be as much sociological as literary, but one I felt it important to address.

As long ago as 2001, I debated some of the major issues raised by any life of Shakespeare with Katherine Duncan-Jones, in a seminar room of the Globe theatre in London; and during the course of the last decade I tried to review as many of the new biographies as I could. My first, preliminary attempt at establishing a position on the subject came in 2005 when I published *That Man Shakespeare*. This was almost wholly an anthology of texts which illustrated how, over the centuries, writers had tried to construct a life of Shakespeare, in biographies certainly, but mainly in novels, poems and plays. There was, however, included in the book a chapter in which I tried to analyse the methods modern biographers use to escape the limitations of their data. The arguments adumbrated in this chapter are much expanded, developed and (I hope) refined in what follows; and since 2005 by no means marked the end of the constant stream of new biographies which were then appearing, I have been able to include reflections on recent works by Stephen Greenblatt, James Shapiro, René Weis, Jonathan Bate and several others. This has not always been a joyful task and I have approached it with considerable hesitation. Of all the various clans which make up the tribe of 'academic English', the one devoted to Shakespeare studies is the most numerous and powerful. Often riven by internal disputes, nothing is more likely to unite it than criticism from outside, but in any case, and more generally, I am conscious from my own experience, on both sides of the fence, that nobody likes a party-pooper. From time to time I have felt I knew what the little boy must have experienced when he said the Emperor had no clothes. If, however, the Emperor was indeed walking about with nothing on, somebody needed to say so. Opinions will differ as to how far this analogy holds. Many will no doubt feel that writing a Shakespeare biography is a perfectly viable and respectable occupation. I am very far from being the first to declare the opposite (every new biography has been greeted by at least one sceptical review); yet as far as I know, no one recently has been willing to make that declaration in an expanded form, and to back it up with examples. In doing this, I hope to show some of the ways in which biography usually functions and demonstrate, if not what it should be then at least how it ought not to be written. People sometimes talk airily of a 'theory of biography' without having any clear idea in their heads of what such an animal would look like. It has seemed to me that moves in that direction yield less understanding of what is now often called 'life-writing' than thinking in a concrete way about biography's traditional staging-posts and practices.

# Acknowledgements

ARTHUR MALTBY READ A draft of this book and gave me some sound advice, as did John Worthen, an ever-present friend in need. I have learnt a lot from Robert Bearman's rigorous attention to facts. For help in my thinking about Shakespeare, I am grateful to two former colleagues at the University of Kent, Reg Foakes and Molly Mahood, and to a present one, Marion O'Connor. Ken Fincham has always been available to put me right on matters historical and I have gained a great deal from the conversation of Edward Greenwood. As always, I need to record my warm thanks to my friend Frank Cioffi for many years of sage counsel and good cheer. Angela Faunch and her colleagues in the Document Delivery department of the Kent library have never let me down and I am grateful to Gill Tobin for printing out numerous early versions of what follows.

# PART I

# 1

## *Rules of the game*

WHAT DO WE MEAN when we say that we have *known* someone? On what is our claim to knowledge based? Among the strongest claimants to accurate understanding of another person must be members of the subject's family, those who, over a long period, have enjoyed daily contacts and a shared environment. These are the people with the authority to describe certain habits or gestures as characteristic and even predict how the subject would have behaved in certain circumstances. Almost equally strong as their claim is the one that can be made by a husband, wife or sexual partner. They have the shared environment and daily contact but also that more intimate knowledge which comes from physical contact. If they have a disadvantage, it is that they often have no personal knowledge of the subject's early or so-called formative years, but also that the kind of relationship they enjoyed will sometimes have had an intensity which leads to warped judgement. 'I can read him like a book,' said the first girlfriend of D. H. Lawrence, to which he later replied that the book was in several volumes, strongly implying that there were some of these she had never opened.[1]

People who have worked with the subject are also reliable witnesses. Standing next to a person on the factory floor, or sitting by them in an office, can yield information not necessarily accessible to a family member or sexual partner. Different kinds of work environment can be more or less revealing. A soldier, for example, might well feel that nothing teaches us more about another human being than shared danger. Yet if we accept that view, it may largely be because courage happens to be very high on our scale of values.

Eating out with people every week gives us a knowledge of them which is very different from that which can be acquired on the battlefield, but which may, in some respects, be just as valuable.

This last comparison dramatises the obvious truth that all eye-witness reports are partial, which does not, of course, deprive them of their value and authenticity. Compared with the evidence provided by a sibling, sexual partner, work colleague or close friend, the position of biographers will seem very weak, especially when they have never met the subject or, as in the most common of cases, that subject is long dead. And yet they do have certain advantages. If they are not eye-witnesses themselves, they can put themselves in a position to compare different eye-witness reports and thereby produce what might hopefully be described as a more 'rounded picture'. Working as they so often do with letters, they can deal with the fact that a letter-writer will tend to adopt a different persona for the different people addressed by surveying a whole range of correspondence. In the most favourable of cases, they will also have access to a diary or journal in which the subject has recorded thoughts and feelings not revealed to the closest of his or her intimates. It is evident that these have to be treated with great caution. People do not always tell the truth about themselves, as Freud was by no means the first to have demonstrated. But if what they say cannot always be taken at face value, it at least provides the biographer with a starting point. Where, after all, would Freud have been if his patients had never even spoken to him?

Although nothing can replace one individual's intimate knowledge of another, there are ways in which biographers can 'know' their subject. Compared with the understanding which can come from personal contact, these may seem artificial, mediated as they so largely are through the written word. Although for some this is a fatal limitation, the written word is still the major resource of most historians, and there is an obvious sense in which anyone who offers to tell the story of another person's life has to become a historian. This simple truth ought to serve as a reminder that writing biography should be subject to strict conditions and that (to come rapidly to the point) none of these is met in the case of Shakespeare. Most biographers, for example, rely very heavily on letters and not one of those which Shakespeare must have written has survived. This might seem mildly surprising but less so is that he left behind no diary or journal since the habit of keeping these only became common long after his death.

The question of eye-witness reports appears at first more promising. In the second volume of his magisterial *William Shakespeare: A Study of Facts and Problems*, E. K. Chambers lists *fifty-eight* contemporaries of Shakespeare who made allusions to him, a number of them on more than one occasion. This seems like an embarrassment of riches until the reader discovers that the vast majority of these witnesses refer only to Shakespeare's writings (usually in the most cursory and unilluminating fashion), and no more than six of them have anything of any potential biographical significance to say. Six is a disappointingly low number and it is only reached by counting in Anthony Scoloker who, in an epistle which accompanied his poem *Diaphantus*, refers to '*Friendly* Shakespeare's Tragedies'.[2]

A single word, without illustration or corroboration, is hardly enough to tell us whether Shakespeare was indeed a friendly man, especially when, as Ernst Honigmann has pointed out, the tone of the Scoloker epistle is playful and ironic;[3] and the remaining five reports or allusions are only slightly more informative. The best known of them is the attack traditionally attributed to the dramatist Robert Greene. 'For there is an upstart Crow', the author of *Greenes Groats-worth of Wit* famously complains (echoing a line from the third part of Shakespeare's own *Henry VI*),

> beautified with our feathers, that with his 'Tygers hart wrapt in a Players hyde', supposes he is as well able to bombast out a blanke verse as the best of you: and being an absolute *Johannes fac totum*, is in his owne conceit the onely Shake-scene in a countrey.[4]

No complete consensus yet exists as to whether Shakespeare is being accused of plagiarism here, or criticised for being a mere actor who had not been to university and yet still had the temerity to write. The attack is significant because it shows that by 1592, when it was first published, the 28-year-old Shakespeare must have already been well established in the world of the London theatre; and it is interesting because it suggests that there was at least one person from that world who did not think much of him.

Whether that person was in fact Greene has been much disputed recently.[5] *Greenes Groats-worth of Wit* appeared after its supposed author's death and the heavy involvement of Henry Chettle in its publication has favoured an assumption that he must himself have written much of it. In his epistle to *Kind-Harts Dreame*, also published in 1592, Chettle writes (in apparent reference to what Greene is purported to have said of Shakespeare): 'I am sory as if the orginall fault had beene my fault, because myselfe have seen his demeanor no lesse civill than he excelent in the qualitie he professes.' That he is speaking here of having observed Shakespeare's demeanour *since* the attack is confirmed by his having previously said that he was acquainted with neither of the two people (usually thought to be Shakespeare and Marlowe) *Greenes Groats-worth* had offended. Chettle follows his apology with: 'Besides, divers of worship have reported his uprightnes of dealing, which argues his honesty, and his facetious grace of writing, that approves his Art.'[6] Some still doubt that Chettle is here referring to Shakespeare rather than (for example) to Peele;[7] but on the assumption that he is, what he says could initially seem like a rich haul. He has complimentary things to say about Shakespeare's demeanour, as well as reports from others ('divers of worship') about his 'uprightnes of dealing'. His words provide a striking contrast with Greene, although, if Greene is to be absolved of responsibility for what was said in his name, they also indicate Chettle's capacity for a rapid change of mind. What is clear is that he cannot have known Shakespeare long enough to comment on anything *but* his demeanour, and that otherwise he is reliant on the testimony of others. The common suggestion that these others were powerful friends of Shakespeare, who had put pressure on Chettle to apologise, only reduces the authority of his remarks. These are certainly more interesting than the single word 'friendly', but not for that reason any more reliable. They hardly take us very much further towards discovering – to use the common phrase – what Shakespeare was really like.

'What was he like?' is a loose phrase to apply to Shakespeare but it suggests what a reader of his biography would like to know. On one level, it means no more than what did he look like?, how did he dress?, was he loquacious or silent in company?, did he like to drink?, and so on. These may seem relatively trivial matters but they help to give the 'feel' of a subject. None of the witnesses in Chambers's section of 'Contemporary Allusions' records any details of what Shakespeare was like to be with which would give us that feel. On this last matter of drink, a few phrases are often quoted from the notes John Aubrey made when he was preparing his 'brief life' of Shakespeare. These are to the effect that Shakespeare was 'not a company keeper', that he 'wouldnt be debauched', and that if invited out he would write to say he could not come because he was in pain.[8] The notes belong to a period around 1681 and Aubrey's major source for them was William Beeston, son of the Christopher

Beeston who, for a relatively short period between about 1598 and 1602, was a member of the same theatre company as Shakespeare. What Aubrey is reporting, therefore, is an impression or anecdote which refers to events which are eighty years in the past and which he garners not at first, but at second hand. This means that the possibility, always strong in these cases, of the reporter having remembered one incident and then generalised from it in a way which is distorting, cannot be explored. One could easily imagine that when the members of the Lord Chamberlain's Men went drinking in one of the few islands of free time available to them between performing and learning new parts, Shakespeare (whose responsibilities to the company exceeded theirs) declined to join them; and even that from time to time he avoided a social obligation by saying he was not well. But the evidence is too flimsy to be certain that this was so, and even if it were, our knowledge of Shakespeare would hardly be much advanced.

How sociable Shakespeare was with his colleagues will seem a minor issue but it slides easily into a clearly more significant category of 'what was he like' because it concerns his attitudes, and between his attitudes to drink and (for example) noise, foreigners, pets, cruelty and women, there is a short step to his beliefs in the realms of politics and religion. The witnesses have next to nothing to say on these crucial matters, being only slightly more forthcoming when it comes to general questions of what we call character. Scoloker holds his place among them because of that single word 'friendly'; but one might also ask whether Shakespeare was cheerful, resolute, moody, vengeful, reliable, or a host of other adjectives habitually used to define character. Of course, many will feel that they know the answers to questions like these, as well as to those which concern attitudes, because they have read or seen his works; but there are major problems in taking that view which will emerge as this book proceeds. Other character-defining adjectives, apart from 'friendly', can be found in the reports of those in Chambers's list of those claiming to have known Shakespeare, who is referred to in at least one of them as 'honest' and 'gentle'. But those words alone tell us very little and they call out for some illustration or gloss which is invariably lacking.

Without letters or diaries, and with no eye-witness reports of any substance, the private life of the biographical subject becomes inaccessible. Yet not all of life is private. Human beings perform actions in the world that are easier to trace than their thoughts and feelings and, in relation to these, the outlook in Shakespeare's case is a little less gloomy. His biographers are fond of observing that he is very well known to us in comparison with playwrights of roughly the same period (Marlowe and Jonson excepted); but since our knowledge of the private lives of writers such as George Peele, Thomas Kyd or Anthony Munday is practically non-existent, that is hardly an impressive claim. They are nevertheless quite right to imply that our ignorance is far from complete. There are surviving records which refer to the dates of Shakespeare's baptism, marriage and death, as well as to the christening of his children, and numerous documents relating to his financial or legal affairs. From these, it has become possible to construct what might be called a rough *chronicle* of his life (of the kind, for example, in Peter Holland's excellent entry on Shakespeare in the 2005 edition of the *Dictionary of National Biography*), although it remains very rough indeed. For long stretches we have very little idea where he was or how he was passing his time so that what cannot be established is that basic tool of all biography: an accurate chronology. Between the christening of Shakespeare's twins, Hamnet and Judith, in 1585, for example, and that public attack on him in 1592 as a brash newcomer on the London theatrical scene, there is only one surviving record.[9] It has therefore become customary for biographers to refer to this seven-year period as 'the lost years'. This is an instinctively cunning move in that it implies that all the others have been found. In fact, if one thinks of biography as an attempt to describe what the subject was like, to recover details of tastes, behaviour, friendships, temperament or character, all Shakespeare's years might accurately be described as lost; but even on the bread-and-butter questions of where he was when, how he passed his time and whom he knew, the record remains very sparse indeed. There is more about the public than the private man but even that does not (one would have thought) take us very far.

One response to our ignorance of Shakespeare's life is to say it does not matter. Why should we care when we already have his writings? There is a hard-line position according to which all biographical information is distracting and our ignorance of Shakespeare is therefore a good rather than bad thing in that it leaves us freer to appreciate his poems and plays. Whether or not one adopts this view must be chiefly a matter of taste, but there is at least one argument against it. Shakespeare is our national Bard and everyone is therefore expected, through exposure during childhood and youth, to understand what he has to say. But the insufficiently acknowledged truth is that he is often a difficult writer who can, on occasion, be impenetrably obscure. That knowledge of the biographical as well as historical circumstances in which certain of his more difficult lines were written would clarify them is a likelihood which applies particularly to his sonnets. In the 1890s, A. E. Housman wrote a poem about a young man who is being dragged off to prison because of the colour of his hair: 'But they pulled the beggar's hat off for the world to see and stare, / And they're taking him to justice for the colour of his hair.'[10] The naïve reader of the day must have felt that persecuting people for their hair colour indicated a pretty poor state of affairs, the less naïve one that the colour of the young man's hair must have been intended by Housman to stand for something else. For those who first read the poem without knowing anything about its author and then learnt that he was a homosexual, dismayed by the punishment meted out to Oscar Wilde, every line in it would have undergone a radical and irreversible change. It is quite possible that many of the more difficult lines in Shakespeare's sonnets would be not only clarified but also radically altered if we knew to whom they were addressed, when precisely they were composed (or revised), the circumstances of their composition, and whether Shakespeare himself approved or supervised their publication: all questions to which centuries of scholarly enquiry have failed to provide definitive answers.

This intellectual justification for knowing more about Shakespeare is probably only a minor component in the appetite which exists for details of his life. In many cases, as John Updike has been one of many to point out, people are anxious to learn about the life of a writer in order to prolong the pleasure which that writer has given them, 'to partake again', as he puts in, 'from another angle, of the joys ... experienced within the author's oeuvre'.[11] They can, on occasion, be disappointed as when, for example, someone they have admired for his depictions of domestic harmony turns out to have been a wife-beater; but, in general, they are able to continue through biography an acquaintance they have first formed through poems, novels or plays. Any discordance between life and art is, in any case, often overborne by the strong curiosity which exists about anyone who has achieved something remarkable in life. It is no doubt this, rather than any more specifically literary feeling, which takes thousands to Stratford every year, keen to see precisely where the great man was born and grew up. There is perhaps here a satisfaction in discovering that, allowing for the difference in period, Shakespeare was, in his origins, much like the rest of us, but perhaps also amazement that an apparently ordinary human being could have gone on to achieve so much that was exceptional.

Whatever the reasons for wanting to know about Shakespeare, that desire certainly exists, so that those proud to be without it must be conscious of belonging to a minority. It is an appetite which began to grow fifty or so years after Shakespeare's death and has been on the increase ever since. Great scholars, such as Edmond Malone in the eighteenth century, J. Halliwell-Phillipps in the nineteenth, or E. K. Chambers in the twentieth, dedicated many years of their lives to satisfying it, and not without some modest results. It was Malone, for example, who succeeded in clarifying the question of Shakespeare's brothers and sisters, and who found what is still the only extant letter written to him (though there is some considerable doubt whether it was ever sent). Many advances of this kind were made but all three men had ways of acknowledging, more or less implicitly, that none of these was of crucial biographical significance. Malone's way was the most implicit of all, in that he died with only a fragment completed of the biography on which he had spent over twenty years (it took the story up to 1592). Halliwell-Phillipps lived to publish the results of his researches in 1881, but he then called them *Outlines of the Life of Shakespeare* and they obstinately remained what this title suggests through many subsequent editions. Nearer to our own time, E. K. Chambers was surely warning his readers not to expect miracles by entitling his major contribution to Shakespeare biography *William Shakespeare: A Study of Facts and Problems*, and by then making clear that, in any attempt to reconstitute the details of Shakespeare's life, there were far more of the latter than the former.

By temperament and training, these three towering figures were inclined to tread warily but they all had contemporaries, and then successors, who were more fancy-free. Less inhibited biographies than theirs began to appear regularly in the nineteenth century, increasing in number as time passed. They were nourished by the occasional minor discovery, usually associated with Shakespeare's parents or his Stratford background rather than the man himself. The last significant documents with a direct relation to his life were unearthed in 1909. It was then that two Americans (a husband-and-wife team called Wallace), working away in the Public Records Office, came across the transcripts of a civil suit brought by Stephen

Belott against his father-in-law, Christopher Mountjoy, and discovered that Shakespeare had been one of those required to testify. Because nothing of similar importance has been found since then, one might expect the supply of biographies to have tapered off. Rather the opposite is the case and there was a particular glut of them at the beginning of this century, with biographical studies of Shakespeare by (amongst many others) Katherine Duncan-Jones, René Weis and Jonathan Bate on one side of the Atlantic, and Stephen Greenblatt and James Shapiro on the other. Previously, the authors of lives of Shakespeare had largely been professional writers or 'men of letters', but these five authors confirmed a trend whereby biography became a prize for those Shakespeareans from the Academy who had become eminent in their profession. Given the limitations of data with which they then had to deal, this was as if highly trained athletes were required to qualify at international level so that they could then participate in an annual British sack race. The puzzle was how they could participate at all when the information with which they had to deal was not only so limited but had been in the public domain for so long. What resources of intelligence, scholarship or ingenuity did they possess that allowed them to make bricks without straw?

# 2

## *How to make bricks without straw*

THE WIDE VARIETY OF methods which Shakespeare's biographers have developed over the years in order to overcome the inevitable disadvantages of their position will be amply illustrated in what follows, but it will be useful here to give a brief indication of the major ones. Because so little is known about Shakespeare, and all authors of his 'life' are obliged to speculate, one of their problems is how to acknowledge this uncomfortable fact without giving their readers the impression that they might just as well have opened an historical novel. Part of the solution lies in phraseology: finding the right expressions and knowing how to put them in the right places. Those weasel words 'perhaps', 'if', 'probably', 'could have', 'may' and so on are difficult to avoid when the subject has left behind diaries or letters, and there are numerous eye-witness reports; but, deprived of these resources as Shakespeare biographers inevitably are, they become essential. Skilfully handled, they can function to recall that moment in many an American courtroom drama when the handsome defence attorney suddenly suggests to his hostile male witness the scenario which makes him responsible for the murder of which his own female client stands accused (the genders are interchangeable). Although the prosecuting counsel then leaps to his feet with an objection, the idea of that witness as the real culprit is firmly lodged in the jury's mind well before the judge can say 'Sustained'. The weasel words I mention have this same function of 'sustained' in that they acknowledge the rules in the very moment when they are being broken. They announce an intellectual responsibility which would make writing

## How to make bricks without straw

yet another life of Shakespeare very difficult while at the same time presiding over what is – if the work is to get written – its very necessary abandon. What is particularly distinctive about their use in the case of Shakespeare is that they tend to accompany speculative answers to questions which have always proved unanswerable – how he managed to become an actor, for example, or the number of times he returned to Stratford once he was settled in London – and then vanish on the subsequent occasions these answers are taken for granted as essential narrative building blocks. One can see why this must be so. What might perhaps have been has to become what certainly was the case if the biography in which this transformation takes place is not to suffer a life-threatening loss of weight.

Even when the weasel words of qualification are not simply dropped, and the mood covertly changed from the conditional to the assertive, the English language is full of devices which help hard-pressed Shakespeare biographers to make what is speculative sound certain, or build into an apparently definitive statement touches which give it what has come to be widely known as plausible deniability. But logic can come to their aid also. Over the years, a technique has been developed for solving some of their difficulties, which could be termed the argument from absence. This consists in making the lack of information with which Shakespeare biographers have to deal work for them, in turning a negative into a positive.

The most familiar way this method operates can be seen in general statements about Shakespeare's character. If there is one word in these which now appears more often than any others it is 'discreet': here was someone, the impression usually is given, who steered clear of trouble and liked to keep his head down, a man who (as Jonathan Bate has recently put it) had 'an instinct for caution' and a 'track record of staying out of trouble'.[1] It will be obvious immediately how this way of presenting Shakespeare transforms the fact that we know virtually nothing about him from a weakness into a strength. Viewed from this perspective, the absence of information is not so much a result of the passage of time, accident or Shakespeare's social status (whether or not aristocrats wrote more letters than ordinary people, those they did write were more likely to be preserved), but of particular patterns of behaviour. If, in his private capacity, Shakespeare left so little mark on his age, it is because it was in his nature to do so. This conclusion is open to challenge from those who say that it cannot be drawn without reference to some standard of comparison, but that is not far to seek. In his *Shakespeare: A Life,* Park Honan is one of many to indicate what the standard is when he insists that,

> As a man [Shakespeare] would lack a quirky egotism, as seems clear from his relatively peaceful career in the theatre, a hive of tension. He was not involved in Ben Jonson's kind of embroilments, or Marlowe's. He has a calm, fine control of emotive materials, and his Sonnets, in the artfulness of their structures, reveal a lordly, easy play over feelings.[2]

The final phrases in this extract may be especially questionable but what the whole of it illustrates is the freedom for calling Shakespeare discreet, or peace-loving, which can be derived from the fact that he did not leave a conspicuous trail in the law courts, and was never arrested for counterfeiting or murder, as Marlowe and Jonson were. However true it may be that not all manifestations of violence, aggression and unpleasantness end up in the courts, the failure to uncover a trace of any legal difficulties comparable to those suffered by his two great contemporaries has allowed biographers to arrive at conclusions about his character which are otherwise hard to draw.

The argument from absence works best when the reader can be persuaded that a gap for which there might in reality be many different reasons has only one explanation. A slightly more specific illustration of it involves the vexed question of Shakespeare's religious views. Since his was a period of violent religious controversy, nothing could seem more biographically significant than some clear indications of where he stood on religious matters. In recent times, it has become fashionable to suggest that he was a Catholic, not merely sympathetic to the old faith but rather someone willing to support those working to restore it. Since this was a dangerous position to hold, it is clear that, as a covert Catholic, Shakespeare would not have been keen to advertise. It is this which leads the well-known Shakespearean scholar, Gary Taylor, to write, 'I can't prove Shakespeare was a Catholic. But then, if he were one, he would have had strong incentives to prevent *anyone* from being able to prove it.'[3] It is not difficult to see how this has encouraged some to imply that it is precisely because Shakespeare never reveals he was a Catholic that we know he probably was one. Useful as this move may be, it leads to an absurdity which has been well described by Robert Graves in his novel, *They Hanged My Saintly Billy.* This tells the only lightly fictionalised story of Dr William Palmer, who was executed in 1856 for the murder by strychnine of his betting partner, John Cook. There was strong circumstantial evidence to suggest that Palmer had committed this crime but nothing of a more definite variety, so that at one point the prosecution's chief pathologist appeared to be arguing that, since strychnine is very rapidly absorbed into the body, the absence of any hint of it in Cook's showed that Palmer must certainly have used it to poison him.[4]

Several pertinent instances of the argument from absence will be illustrated later, but like the use and misuse of words which imply doubt or uncertainty, it is a relatively minor resource for Shakespeare biographers in comparison with two other, major ones. The first of these could be summed up briefly as making historical background stand in for an absent biographical foreground. In the writing of a biography of someone whose life has been written many times before, there is always an initial difficulty. Theoretically speaking, there are as many possible biographies as there are people willing to write them – new perspectives on the same old material – but in practice the public like to be given the impression that their biographers have been driven to composition by material which is new. This is perhaps why the blurb for Michael Wood's 2003 life of Shakespeare talks of 'a wealth of unexplored archive evidence' and 'fascinating new discoveries'. Since the only recent discovery about Shakespeare which can be described as fascinating dates back (as I have said) to 1909, the new material Wood refers to here must be of an historical rather than strictly biographical nature: more information, that is, on Stratford, the rise of the commercial theatre, Court politics, or Elizabethan and Jacobean life in general. It is this which many biographers use to compensate for their inevitable ignorance of the details of Shakespeare's life; though there is little to say about the man himself, the supply of information about his times is ever increasing and inexhaustible. According to Samuel Schoenbaum, it was the Victorian biographer Charles Knight who was the first person properly to 'associate Shakespeare with the circumstances around him' and thus triumph over the 'limitations of his data'.[5] This method of dealing with their difficulties is one which Knight's successors have been employing ever since, yet whether it is really the triumph Schoenbaum calls it must be considered doubtful. One of the exciting historical events which took place while Shakespeare was still a boy, for example, was the 'mission' of Edmund Campion to England in 1580. A member of a small group of Jesuits who came from the continent with the intention of reconverting as many English people as possible to the old faith, the charismatic Campion is thought by some to have passed through Warwickshire; yet whether he met Shakespeare's parents or, as at least one biographer would have it, Shakespeare himself, is unknown and remains unknown, however many details of Campion and his sad fate are provided (he was arrested and executed in 1581). Much later in Shakespeare's life, an episode of similarly intrinsic, historical interest was the effort made by the out-of-favour Earl of Essex in 1601 to defeat his enemies at Court. Shortly before he launched what was later interpreted as the beginnings of an unsuccessful attempt to seize and perhaps murder the Queen, a group of his followers went to the Globe and commissioned a special performance of *Richard II*, a play in which a monarch is deposed. As I shall show, Shakespeare's biographers have given increasingly detailed and interesting accounts of this episode but without being able to establish how far Shakespeare himself was involved (if, indeed, he was involved at all), or where his sympathies lay. This is because, although historical background may be essential for a full understanding of an individual's thoughts, feelings and actions, it can never compensate for an initial lack of information on those three matters. To think it can is to be like a man who takes a cart, carefully refurbishes or paints its structure, and then expects the horse suddenly to materialise, panting between the shafts.

The method Charles Knight inaugurated has become increasingly popular in recent times, as Shakespeare biography has been more and more the preserve of academics who have often spent many years accumulating background knowledge. Their specialist interests have strengthened the tendency for a life of Shakespeare to be a history book, and often a very interesting history book, which is only disguised as biography. A particularly successful example of this tendency was James Shapiro's *1599: A Year in the Life of William Shakespeare*. None of the reviewers who welcomed this work commented on the ambiguity of its title, which would have led ordinary readers to expect some account of how Shakespeare passed his time in the Spring, what he did in the Summer, and how he fared in the Autumn and Winter of 1599. What they, in fact, were offered was something much more like a narrative of various important happenings in 1599, one of the years in which Shakespeare happened to be alive. Even more than in many other comparable works, that is, history (cultural, social or political) was made to do the work of life-writing. Nearly always doing that work also, however, is the second major resource of the Shakespeare biographer, the one which consists in inferring the details of his life from his writing, or seeing those details reflected in it. T. S. Eliot once warned us against this habit when he famously claimed that 'the more perfect the artist, the more completely separate in him will be the man who suffers and the mind which creates'; but he had been anticipated in this view by Halliwell-Phillipps who, in a preface to his *Outlines* of Shakespeare's life, wrote that

> it must surely be admitted that the exchange of the individuality of the man for that of the author is the very essence of dramatic genius, and, if that be so, the higher the genius the more complete will be the severance from personality.[6]

These are two statements the full implications of which most people quite reasonably find difficult to accept. It is hard not to believe that, as Stephen Greenblatt puts it in the preface to his biography, the words Shakespeare wrote 'contain the vivid presence of actual, lived experience'.[7] The difficulty is that connections between those words and the 'lived experience' must often have been extremely indirect and subtle, so that there have to be strict criteria which govern any attempt to establish them. To understand how the life of any author is made manifest in his writings, the biographer needs to know both a great deal about that life and the particular circumstances in which individual works were composed. To say these criteria are not met in the case of Shakespeare would be the understatement of the year. 'We know more about the life of Shakespeare than about that of any of his literary contemporaries bar Ben Jonson,' Anthony Holden blithely declares, and he goes on, 'And the rest is there for all to see, in and between every line he wrote.'[8] But deciphering the plays in the way this suggests is not as easy as he implies. Many people might agree that, when Hamlet talks about acting to the players who visit Elsinore, we are hearing Shakespeare's own thoughts (although, since Hamlet is a character in a drama, these might also have been intended as the thoughts of a typical aristocratic patron of the Elizabethan theatre); but does that then mean we have direct access to his own views or feelings when Falstaff pronounces on honour, or Othello on women? Searching for characters in the plays who can be taken as articulating Shakespeare's own thoughts is the simplest and perhaps crudest method for helping the biographer to make bricks without straw. The reader of what follows will encounter several more, as well as the special and delusively promising case of the Sonnets with their apparently autobiographical 'I'. But as an introductory example of the general difficulty, and of how Shakespeare's biographers overcome it, the fate of his son Hamnet will serve as well as any.

Hamnet died in August 1596, when he was eleven, and the loss of his only male heir must, one imagines, have been a blow to Shakespeare. Any serious student of his life would like to know how it affected him. Since there are no private documents which tell us this, his biographers have traditionally found his reaction to the event in the words of Queen Constance in *King John*, after her young son Arthur has been captured and she rightly fears his life will be in danger:

> Grief fills the room up of my absent child,
> Lies in his bed, walks up and down with me,
> Puts on his pretty looks, repeats his words,
> Remembers me of all his gracious parts. (3.iii)[9]

Biographers have found it reasonable to believe that what we hear in these moving lines is Shakespeare lamenting the death of his own son because Hamnet and the Arthur of the play would have been pretty much of an age, and *King John* is usually assigned to early 1597, when the memory of Hamnet's death would still have been fresh. Unfortunately for them, at least two distinguished scholars have argued strongly for a date which is much earlier, and it is clear that Shakespeare could not have been mourning Hamnet's loss long before it took place.[10] Chronology of composition is a remarkably tricky business in Shakespeare studies. Duncan-Jones describes *The Merry Wives of Windsor* as a play which 'can be dated with unusual precision' and she goes on to say that, in his representation of young William Page in that play, Shakespeare was assimilating his dead son 'into what he happened to be writing in the spring after his death'. For her, therefore, William may be the nearest Shakespeare ever came to providing for Hamnet 'a public memorial'.[11] Her book bears the Arden imprint but when Giorgio Melchiori came to edit *The Merry Wives* in Arden's 'Third Series', he decided it belonged to 1599, or later.[12] This lack of consensus as to when the plays were written (as opposed to registered or performed) is a considerable inconvenience to those looking for the man in his work; but that activity is too important to the biographers for them to be much troubled by it and, in any event, it is always open to them to say (in relation to *The Merry Wives*) that, although Shakespeare would not have written a memorial to his son while he was still alive, he could still have been remembering him not merely one, but three or four Springs after his death. This is the approach adopted by David Bevington, who, sympathetic to the idea that the effect of Hamnet's death can best be found not in *The Merry Wives* but in *Twelfth Night*, explains away a delayed reaction of four years or so by saying that 'mourning for such an event can take time and patience'.[13]

Most of the recent biographers are quite anxious about chronology but one it seems to leave untroubled is René Weis, who feels he can not only guess when the plays were written but also divine more or less exactly what Shakespeare was doing at the time of their composition. So precise is he on the latter question that he finds Constance's words in *King John* slightly *pre-dating* Hamnet's death; but he then shows the resourcefulness all Shakespeare's biographers require by suggesting they were written when he already knew his son was dying.[14] The play in which he finds a more powerful expression of grief, however, is *Romeo and Juliet*. The sorrow expressed by the Nurse, Capulet and Lady Capulet in that play over Juliet's death is, he says, 'raw and heart-rending', and to him an obvious echo of what Shakespeare must have felt in losing Hamnet.[15] In the course of elaborating this case he finds an alternative answer to an objection to which Duncan-Jones might be said to expose herself in identifying memories of Hamnet in William Page. He is, after all, a character surrounded by cheerfulness and one who certainly does not die. But that, says Duncan-Jones, is inevitable in a 'festive farce, with no scope for any expression of private grief'.[16] In dealing with the comedy in *Romeo and Juliet*, Weis takes a different tack, noting how,

> Shakespeare managed to conjure up a lively, funny maverick like Mercutio, at a time when he was presumably overwhelmed by grief, testimony perhaps to an iron resolve. Perhaps *Romeo and Juliet* was an act of solace and atonement, a determined creation of children in the teeth of adversity and death, children who, unlike his son, would be resurrected every time the Chorus stepped out to launch another performance.[17]

The strategy employed here is of the 'heads-I-win-tails-you-lose' variety, and one which, in this instance, allows Weis to decide that either Shakespeare is directly expressing his grief and sense of loss in the plays he wrote shortly after Hamnet's death, or that the exuberant cheerfulness in many of them represents a compensatory mechanism for overcoming his sorrow. It would be wrong to imagine that arguments of this variety can be countered. What Weis says here may be true, but it may just as well be false. There is nothing which survives that would allow anyone to decide the issue. Nor, if one excludes chronology, is there anything to confirm or deny the effect of Hamnet's death in the very many other places, apart from *Romeo and Juliet*, where it has been found (*Hamlet* is a favourite hunting-ground), or the claims of those who decide to make that effect general. Anthony Holden, for example, attributes to Hamnet's death 'the personal grief which now becomes a recurring strain in [Shakespeare's] work ... lifting his history to quite another poetic plane',[18] while Michael Wood, ignoring the predominantly comic mood of the plays which appear to have been written shortly after 1596, describes the effect on Shakespeare's writing of losing his only son in this way:

> Within the next year or two a change gradually came about not only in Shakespeare's themes but also in his way of writing, in his language and imagery. The great tragedies followed, plumbing 'the well of darkness'. This was not only a personal tragedy but a powerful intimation of mortality.[19]

It stands to reason that Shakespeare must have been affected by the death of Hamnet but it is a smart move to let the reader decide exactly where in the plays this is evident, in case one of the likely candidates was written before it took place, but also because relevant quotations which readers themselves recall have more effect than any the biographer could choose for them. That with the right kind of encouragement (or the wrong one, in my view), any reasonably informed reader can find such quotations ought nevertheless to be a worry. This may be a case where the ability of very many people to come up with different answers to the same question is not significant, since the effect of Hamnet's death on Shakespeare's writing can always be described as *pervasive*. Yet the ease with which the operation may be carried ought surely to be felt disturbing. It is one of which information-starved biographers are none the less fond because the apparent access it gives to Shakespeare's private feelings constitutes, along with the reliance on history, such a major reason why lives of Shakespeare can still continue to appear.

# 3

## *Forebears*

MANY BIOGRAPHERS HAVE WHAT amounts to an obsession with forebears, tracing back their subject's ancestry as far as it will go. That they are wise to do so is suggested by the money people are willing to pay to anyone who will establish their genealogical tree, or the popularity of television programmes such as 'Who do you think you are?' where various celebrities trace their family origins. As this title suggests, the search for ancestors would not be so popular if there were not an assumption that it had some explanatory power for us now: that it can help to throw light on our own character. That is a belief which would seem to be supported by everyday experience. Those who have children are constantly detecting in their offspring mannerisms which they identify as also belonging to their parents or themselves; and no one could count the number of times the expression 'takes after' is used in family discussions.

Yet genetic inheritance is a highly complicated matter, much more so than most biographers seem willing to acknowledge. In his splendid biography of Picasso, John Richardson traces back the painter's lineage to a 'fifteenth century knight of legendary courage', Juan de Leon (d. 1481).[1] There is no reason for thinking that this derivation is dubious, but neither is there a better one for believing that it would matter if it were. More apparently pertinent are Peter Ackroyd's dealings with Charles Dickens's paternal grandparents. Both of them, he explains, were servants and he finds it noteworthy that William Dickens, who died 'long before' his grandson's birth, was a butler because the characters in the novels are 'always being . . . observed by butlers'. More importantly, he believes that Dickens inherited his thrift, conscientiousness and administrative ability from his grandfather William. His paternal grandmother was also 'trusted and competent' but more significant is the reputation she had as a 'fluent storyteller'. 'Towards the end of her life,' Ackroyd writes, 'she gave her grandson a fat old silver watch which had belonged to her husband, but it is also possible that he inherited much more interesting gifts from her.'[2]

If there is less danger of this kind of airy speculation in dealing with Shakespeare's forebears, it is because information about them is so meagre. It is natural to seek some explanation of the unexpected appearance in a Stratford glover's son of abilities which would make him his country's greatest dramatist – 'ex nihilo nihil fit', as Lear more or less says to Cordelia – but in Shakespeare's case there are no surviving records of tale-spinning grandmothers or relations from the distant past with literary talent. At the beginning of her biography, Duncan-Jones has sought to compensate for this lack by suggesting that the West Midlands 'was much the likeliest region of England to produce a major secular poet and playwright'. With strong traditions of drama and civic pageantry, good local grammar schools and generous patrons, it was, she suggests, far enough away from London to enjoy an uninhibited cultural life. The results could be seen in the large number of writers born in the general area while Warwickshire itself was 'an even more fertile breeding ground for men of letters than its neighbouring counties'.[3] Without the usual list of ancestors to explain the phenomenon of Shakespeare, Duncan-Jones has ingeniously switched that responsibility to his home turf. Ackroyd switches it elsewhere in noting that the name of Shakespeare, spelt though it might be in as many as eighty different ways, occurs often in Warwickshire records. 'It was', he comments, 'a family name of long local settlement, in a literal sense part of the landscape. This may help to explain the rootedness of Shakespeare himself within English culture.'[4]

It is hard to make sense of this last sentence but Ackroyd seems driven to it because, in spite of a good deal of industrious ferreting, the first forebear about which anything concrete is known is Shakespeare's grandfather Richard, who farmed in the village of Snitterfield, while the first to emerge clearly from the mist is his father, John. Leaving Snitterfield to make the four- or five-mile transfer to Stratford, John Shakespeare became very active in business there and, as a result, left his mark in the courts, suing or being sued. He did well enough early on to buy at least two freehold properties in the town, including the Henley Street house in which his son William may have been born. These purchases provided a route into Stratford's town council, the oligarchy of prominent citizens who ran most of the town's local affairs. Anyone who holds public office becomes easier to trace and John Shakespeare was elected as an alderman in 1565 and became high bailiff, or what we might call the mayor, in 1568. These facts and others like them tell us something about him, but not very much. The only hint of his character comes from a manuscript note made by a clergyman called Thomas Plume in the 1650s. 'Sir John Mennis', Plume wrote, 'saw once [Shakespeare's] father in his shop – a merry Cheekd old man – that said – Will was a good Honest Fellow, but he durst have crackt a jest with him at any time.'[5] Duncan-Jones agrees with Chambers that because the John Mennis to whom Plume here refers was born in 1599 he could not have known John Shakespeare (who died in 1601); but she nevertheless concludes from this anecdote that Shakespeare inherited from his father a 'strong interest in entertainment and mirth' and says that 'it is entirely believable that Shakespeare's unfailing skill in turning the most solemn language into an instant quibble or bawdy repartee was a skill . . . learned from practice during his early years at home'.[6] Greenblatt goes even further than this in taking the 'merry cheeks' of Shakespeare senior to be a possible indication that he drank too much, noting that if Caesar's 'cold sobriety' makes him seem less appealing than the great-spirited Antony in *Antony and Cleopatra*, then 'John Shakespeare may have never seemed more like a nobleman to his observant, imaginative child than when he was in his cups, *his cheeks burning*.' Yet reviewing other treatments of drinking in the plays, including Hamlet's denunciation of his fellow Danes for their over-indulgence and Falstaff's paean of praise to 'sherry-sack', Greenblatt concludes that what Shakespeare finally inherited from his father was a distaste for the effects of alcohol and that Hal's rejection of Falstaff therefore represents 'an adult son's contempt for the symbolic father who had failed him'.[7] In their reliance on the Plume note these two biographers demonstrate that 'ex nihilo nihil fit' is not perhaps always true after all.

For Greenblatt, John Shakespeare's drinking problem provides an explanation for what are otherwise puzzling aspects of his career in Stratford. From at least January 1577, for example, until he was finally discharged from the council in September 1586, he attended only one meeting. Moreover, although it was customary to fine aldermen for non-attendance, he was exempted, as he was also when in 1578 it was agreed that all aldermen should pay four pence a week towards the relief of the poor. As Robert Bearman has suggested, it is difficult not to interpret these facts, as well as several other, similar ones he has meticulously investigated, 'as evidence of John's financial difficulties',[8] an indication that the glove trade, and the other commercial activities in which he may have been involved, were not going well, whether because he had over-extended himself or (in Greenblatt's view) taken to the bottle. This apparent decline in his fortunes is usually correlated with two other beliefs that are almost universally held about him: that some time after 1568 he made an application for a coat of arms which was allowed to lapse and that in 1596 this application was successfully reactivated. The almost ubiquitous assumption is that this reactivation was only possible because his son had made so much money in the theatre.

In the apparent decline of John Shakespeare's fortunes, biographers, and especially the more recent ones, have found a major key to his son's character. This is in part because, although forebears may not have the biographical significance they are habitually assumed to have, the attitude their descendants adopt to them can be very important. No biographer of Virginia Woolf, for example, can afford to ignore the possible effects on her of having been born into the intellectual purple of English society. So many of the people around her had achieved distinction in various intellectual fields that she must sometimes have felt like the step-sister of Mary Shelley, Claire Clairmont, who, brought up in William Godwin's household, once complained 'in our family, if you cannot write an epic poem or novel that by its originality knocks all other novels on the head, you are a despicable creature, and not worth acknowledging.'[9] Shakespeare certainly did not have this problem but in looking back to his father, nearly all the biographers assume, he saw someone who had fallen from financial grace and was therefore driven in his later life to restore the family fortune, to compensate for his father's failure. 'The dream of restoration', Greenblatt writes, 'haunted Shakespeare throughout his life.'[10] The idea is a comfortingly familiar one and it helps to explain Duncan-Jones's claim that 'Iago's advice "Put money in your pocket" was one of [Shakespeare's] own favourite maxims.'[11] Those business dealings of Shakespeare's which upset so many Bardolaters in the nineteenth century can be acquitted in the twenty-first of being the result of mere acquisitiveness by an appeal to a psychological model in which children are for ever making amends for their parents, or fulfilling their failed ambitions. But since we cannot know whether Shakespeare's investment record would have been any different had his father always remained a prosperous alderman, it is a model which in his case is very difficult to apply.

In the scenario the biographers imagine, it is not, of course, financial security only which Shakespeare spent his life trying to recover, but a lost or diminished social status. There is a broad agreement among them that he had what Peter Ackroyd has called 'an abiding preoccupation with gentility', and hardly any of them would question Greenblatt's assertion that Shakespeare was 'anything but indifferent to being counted as a gentleman'.[12] The main evidence for believing this is the reactivated application for a coat of arms in 1596, but in Greenblatt's account the urge to be a gentleman can be traced much further back. He, in fact, makes it a possible reason why Shakespeare became an actor, suggesting that 'Will may have been attracted to the trade of acting in part because it so centrally involved the miming of the lives of the gentry,' and he adds that with 'his father's faded but still notable distinction, he could have arrived at the sense that he could confidently carry off the role of a gentleman and fulfil his parents' dream'.[13] As Greenblatt himself recognises, this is a strange idea to attribute to a young man starting out in life in the 1580s, given the social status of most actors in that period; but he presumably feels that, leaving aside the danger of Shakespeare turning up at the stage door to find he had been assigned the part of the second ostler, someone whose father had recently slipped down in the social scale preferred being a pretend gentleman to none at all.

There is nothing to make it certain that it was not Shakespeare but his father who reactivated the application for a coat of arms (there are hints in the documents to suggest that the latter's affairs might have improved in the 1590s, perhaps because of his son but maybe because of his own efforts). Nor can it be convincingly shown that Shakespeare had a concern for making money, or acquiring a coat of arms, that had in it any of the excess or abnormality implied by the psychological condition attributed to him. The suggestion that he did care about the arms, and to the extent of being something of a snob, is usually bolstered by a supposed reference to Shakespeare in Jonson's *Every Man Out of His Humour*. A character in that play called Sogliardo, who is described as 'an essential clown

'... so enamoured of the name of a gentleman that he will have it though he buys it', has just acquired a coat of arms. He describes his purchase in some detail to another character called Puntarvolo, who insists that it needs a motto and that this ought to be 'Not without mustard'.[14] The primary reference here appears to be to a moment in Thomas Nashe's 1592 best-seller *Pierce Penniless*, when the 'young heir or cockney that is his mother's darling' vows that, if he is saved from an unpleasant situation at sea, he will never eat dried cod again. Once the danger is over, however, he adds the proviso, 'Not without mustard, good Lord, not without mustard'.[15] Although nobody wants to claim that Sogliardo is in any way a portrait of Shakespeare, and everyone agrees that the coat of arms he describes bears no relation whatsoever to the one secured by Shakespeare's father in 1596, it is felt that 'not without mustard' not only alludes to Nashe but also is a mocking reference to the motto '*non sanz droict*' which had been adopted by the Shakespeare family for their coat of arms. In support of this reading, Duncan-Jones offers what she specifically terms 'an argument from eloquent silence' – a more familiar variation of what I have called the argument from absence. This is that in the 1616 folio of Jonson's works, which very conveniently includes cast lists for the first productions of his plays, Shakespeare is cited as having appeared in *Every Man In His Humour* but not in its successor. Does not this indicate, she implies, that there was something insulting to Shakespeare in *Every Man Out*?[16]

There are all kinds of possible reasons why Shakespeare was omitted from the cast, or cast list, of *Every Man Out*, as Duncan-Jones herself admits, and the speculation (to me an unlikely one) that Jonson was making fun of him with 'Not without mustard' is no more than that. But even if he had been, that would not establish that Shakespeare was someone who 'pursued' status in order to compensate for his father's failures, or that he was in any way a snob. It is true that there are in Shakespeare's plays strong expressions of distaste for the common people. Some of the most striking of these come from Coriolanus who, after he has accused a group of Roman citizens of rubbing the poor itch of their opinion until they make themselves scabs, is ironically told by one of them that they have always his good word (1.i). But Coriolanus is hardly someone who carries authorial authority in any uncomplicated way, and there is a character from another play in whom a striving after gentility, snobbery and a disdain for common folk is remorselessly satirised.

Malvolio is something of a lion in the path for Greenblatt but he walks round him by saying that 'Malvolio serves as the shadow side of Shakespeare's own fascination of achieving the status of a gentleman.' Ackroyd is both more explicit and more ingenious, suggesting it is very likely that Shakespeare himself played Malvolio and that it would have come naturally to him to 'parody pretensions to gentility at the same time as he pursued them with the utmost seriousness, to mock that which was most important to him. It was part of his instinctive ambivalence in all the affairs of the world'.[17] The point here is not that a writer who had himself an unhealthy concern for status would have been incapable of creating a character such as Malvolio, but rather that neither Coriolanus nor Malvolio can provide us with reliable information as to what Shakespeare felt about his father, his status or his coat of arms.

The belief that, throughout his life, Shakespeare was in search of gentility in order to compensate for his father's supposed business failures is one of the master narratives of recent biographies. Even when it is not explicit, it is often apparent as an underlying assumption. The effects it has can be subtle and seem to me evident in the first chapter of Shapiro's *1599*. This is called 'A Battle of Wills' and deals chiefly with the departure from the Lord Chamberlain's Men of its well-known clown, Will Kemp. His eventual replacement was Robert Armin, who specialised in playing witty court fools and who sang well. It was for him that Shakespeare appears to have written roles such as Touchstone, Feste and the Fool in *King Lear*. Kemp had been a very different kind of performer, large and athletic, celebrated for his dancing and, judging from the clown roles in Shakespeare's earlier plays, adept at playing blundering figures from the lower classes. There is documentary evidence to show that he certainly played Dogberry in *Much Ado*, as well as the minor role of Peter in *Romeo and Juliet*. David Wiles has conjectured that he also played Falstaff, although the gap between that role and the two just mentioned is so huge that his claim must raise grave doubts.[18]

Accepting Wiles's claim unreservedly allows Shapiro to assume that if Falstaff did not appear in *Henry V*, even though an epilogue to the second part of *Henry IV* had suggested he would be there, it was because Kemp was no longer a Lord Chamberlain's man. The clown's departure is thus one of the events which make 1599 a crucial year in Shakespeare's career and which justify focusing so exclusively on it. Relying on those words in Hamlet's address to the players in which he criticises clowns for ad-libbing (3.ii),

Shapiro assumes that Kemp left the company because of sharp differences with Shakespeare over 'the role of the clown and the nature of comedy'. Yet the opinions of Hamlet are not necessarily those of Shakespeare himself and, even if they are, there is no certainty they were directed at Kemp rather than at other, inferior performers. Interpreting Kemp's departure as he does, however, is useful to Shapiro because it allows him to develop his idea of 1599 as Shakespeare's breakthrough year, a time when he moved forward to a more sophisticated art. 'As Shakespeare found himself moving steadily at this time towards a more naturalistic drama in which characters like Rosalind and Hamlet feel real', he writes, 'the traditional clown became an obstacle.' He finds in *As You Like It* a more mature treatment of love and in *Hamlet* what everyone else finds, a remarkably enhanced ability to portray the inner life of characters. These, he feels, are advances which accord well with his Whig view of the development of Shakespeare's genius, always progressing forward to greater and greater achievements. Although there is something to be said for this idea, it has disadvantages which I will discuss later. My interest here is rather in how the thesis about Shakespeare's artistic development tends to run parallel with one about his social advancement. Kemp, Shapiro writes, 'loathed social climbers and went out of his way to praise those who didn't stand upon rank. No doubt Shakespeare's pursuit of gentility rubbed [him] the wrong way.'[19] The impression we are given is of a Shakespeare who, as he progressed up the social scale, turned his back on his origins and, in the process, began to despise the 'low comedy' which had been a feature of his early career. And yet there are no genuine, well-founded reasons to suppose that he ever came to regret that he had created a character such as Bottom, for example, or that in becoming a gentleman, he was in any way anxious to forget the time when he had not been one. When Kemp left the Lord Chamberlain's Men (for reasons no one knows), Shakespeare moved away from writing Kemp-like roles in order to accommodate a different actor; but the notion that he was keen to escape 'low comedy' is an invention of nineteenth-century critics uncomfortable with clowns and anxious to maintain the Bard's dignity. That he was also keen to escape his comparatively modest social origins, however, and that (as Michael Wood has put it) he 'craved acceptance and status',[20] is a notion which has been foisted on him by biographers, over-interpreting the small number of available facts and working with well-worn stereotypes.

# 4

# *The female line and Catholicism*

THE KIND OF INFORMATION we have about Shakespeare's father does not tell us much, but it is a goldmine compared with what is available about his mother. She was called Mary Arden before her marriage and was the daughter of a relatively prosperous farmer who came from the village of Wilmcote, close to Stratford. For years, a house in this village where she was supposedly brought up was shown to visitors but in 2000 it was discovered that the real building stood a few hundred yards away. From a strictly epistemological perspective, the shift of attention can hardly have made much difference, although many of the surviving pilgrims from before 2000 might well have felt cheated. When you are holding the tibia of a saint in your hand you have to believe it is authentic even if, for most purposes, one tibia from the right period is likely to be just as good as any other.

The early relationship with the mother has been crucially important for many recent biographers, especially those of a psycho-dynamic tendency. The ones who choose to write about Shakespeare find Mary Arden stony ground, although the ingenuity they display is often surprising. Park Honan's life of Shakespeare was published two years before this present century began and opened with an insistence on the importance of historical background for a proper understanding of his subject. He pointed out that just after Shakespeare was born there was an outbreak of the plague in Stratford. *Hic incipit pestis*, the parish register reads on 11 July 1564, opposite the burial record of an apprentice, and in the following six months a tenth of the town's population died.

Most Shakespeare biographers include this information, using it as an illustration of how different sixteenth-century life was from our own, or pointing out how significant the plague would be for their subject's future career since for long periods it closed the theatres in which he made his living. But Honan's interest is in deducing from it that the infant Shakespeare could only have survived because of the loving attention of his mother and that, in the period of the Stratford plague, 'a pattern of Mary's special care for her son is also likely to have been set'. He finds this significant for the formation of Shakespeare's character, claiming that 'William's confidence cannot be dissociated from the emotional support he must have found at home' and that this is why, in writings such as his Sonnets, he reveals 'a lordly, easy play' over feelings. 'In early life,' Honan continues, 'he must have been the focus of Mary's very urgently watchful, intense love.'[1] The implication in these words about the causal effects of Mary Arden's mothering is entirely unwarranted by anything we actually know, but then so is Honan's initial assumption as to what her mothering was like. Shakespeare's survival cannot be adduced in support of this assumption since it is quite possible that, when the plague was threatening, anxious care was no more effective than benign neglect.

The general feeling is that Mary Arden would have been a good catch for John Shakespeare. This is in part based on Mary's father having owned the house in Snitterfield where John's own father lived; yet Robert Arden was a man with many children and what he left her on his death did not amount to a fortune. It did, however, include a house and land in Wilmcote which, in what is usually taken as a sign of his financial difficulties, her husband mortgaged to a relative for £40 in 1578, twenty-two years after his marriage. There were other, smaller bequests but the notion that John was bettering himself appears to come mostly from his wife's maiden name. This was the same as a rich and influential family of Ardens who lived in Castle Bromwich, not too many miles away. They were fiercely Catholic and came to grief in a spectacular fashion when the unbalanced son-in-law of Edward Arden, John Somerville, set off for London in 1583, letting slip on the way that he was going to assassinate the Queen. In 1599 the Shakespeare family appear to have tried to have the coat of arms they had recently been awarded combined with that of this ancient, if by then discredited, Arden family, but the heralds could find no connection between it and Mary's ancestry. Despite Jonathan Bate's assertion that she had 'a network of associations in the local gentry of the old faith',[2] no one since has been able to find a connection either. The assumption remains that she not only believed she was well born but actually was so, and that this fact has an important bearing on Shakespeare's development. 'It has often been suggested', Peter Ackroyd writes, 'that male actors are prone, in their earliest years, to identify with the mother,' and he sees this as an explanation for 'the overriding concern for nobility and gentility in Shakespeare's plays'. Could Shakespeare's mother also have taught her son, he asks, 'his fastidiousness and disdain'?[3] And yet it is not so much this social aspect of the inheritance from the female line which interests the biographers most but rather the fierce Catholicism she is assumed to have displayed before her son in his early years. The evidence usually adduced for that lies partly in certain Catholic formulations from her own father's will, but chiefly in her supposed connection to the Ardens of Castle Bromwich.

An immense amount of labour has been expended in the last twenty years on trying to show that Shakespeare was, in fact, brought up in a staunchly Catholic household. One of the problems has been the difficulty of knowing precisely what it meant to be 'Catholic' in the second half of the sixteenth century, especially since, during much of its first half, 'Catholic' is what nearly everyone had been. After the death of Henry VIII, Edward VI had pushed forward Protestant reforms but when Mary came to the throne the process went into reverse. In the early years of her own reign, Elizabeth adopted a more live-and-let-live policy, asking only that people should conform in public, whatever they might feel in private. Her chief concern was with those so deeply committed that they were determined to turn back the clock when the only immediately effective way of doing that would be to get rid of Elizabeth herself. The Pope did not help, with a number of pronouncements in 1580 which suggested it would not be sinful to assassinate her. She understandably took a dim view of those on the fringe of the Catholic community who accepted the apparent logic of their situation and became, like John Somerville or his father-in-law, Edward Arden, enemies of the State. The assumption is that, through the relationship with Edward Arden, Shakespeare's mother would have been, in an ideological if not practical sense, on this fringe also and that she transmitted her feelings to her children.

Support for the idea of a Shakespeare who grew up in a fervently Catholic household has been found on his father's, as well as on his mother's, side. This may well seem strange, given that, as a member of the Stratford Corporation, John Shakespeare would have had to declare his adherence to the Protestant order of things; and that he was the official directly responsible in 1564 for seeing that the wall paintings in the local Guild chapel were covered over or defaced (a characteristically Protestant move against the worship of images). He also had all his children christened in the local church and was buried according to its prevailing rites. What radically changed the view of him which these facts suggest was the discovery in the eighteenth century of a document in which he appeared to declare his allegiance to the old religious order. This was the 'Last Will of the Soul, made in health for the Christian to secure himself from the temptations of the devil at the hour of death', composed by a Milanese cardinal in the 1570s during an outbreak of plague. The copies of this document, which Edmund Campion is thought by some to have brought to England on his secret mission there in 1580, had spaces in them where individuals could fill in their own names, before appending their signature or mark. Towards the end of the eighteenth century, it was claimed that one bearing John Shakespeare's name had been found hidden in the rafters of his former house, but the circumstances surrounding this discovery led Edmund Malone to conclude that its associations with John Shakespeare were bogus, and this has been the opinion of many scholars since. There are some, however, who accept that it was genuine (a suggestion hard to explore since the document no longer exists), and then use it as an explanation of the decline in John Shakespeare's fortunes. It was not, they argue, financial embarrassment which led him to absent himself from meetings of the Stratford Corporation but a strengthening of his former Catholic beliefs. Moreover, when he was cited in 1592 for staying away from church, this was not because he was fearful of being arrested for debt, as the citation clearly indicated, but for the more obvious reason that his beliefs no longer allowed him to attend. In this context, the mortgaging of his wife's Wilmcote property for £40 was not part of an effort to raise money but a tactic whereby a Catholic could pass on property to friends or relations in order to be less threatened by the increasingly punitive fines to which failure to attend church exposed him. The biographical consequence of arguments like these is a Shakespeare who grew up in a house where not only one of his parents was a fervent adherent to the old scheme of things, but both of them were.[4]

## The female line and Catholicism

Arguments concerning the religious beliefs of Shakespeare's parents continue to rage, but the important issue for anyone attempting to write his life is what effect it would have had on him if both his mother and father were indeed Catholics: what kind of difference it would have made. There is the beginnings of a possible answer to this question in what can now be called the great Shakeshafte controversy. Alexander Houghton was a rich Catholic landowner from Lancashire, who in 1581 made a will in which he left his musical instruments and 'play clothes' to his half-brother, Thomas, if the said Thomas was 'minded to keep and do keep players'. If he was not so minded, then they were to go to Sir Thomas Hesketh whom Houghton also asked 'to be friendly unto Foke Gyllom and William Shakeshafte, now dwelling with me, and either take them unto his service, or else help them to some good master'.[5] In his *Brief Lives*, John Aubrey claimed that, in the early part of his existence, Shakespeare had been a 'Schoolmaster in the countrey'.[6] The idea that he had gone to Lancashire in that capacity and, having been drawn into either music or acting, is the Shakeshafte referred to in the Houghton will, first emerged in the 1930s but was given a strong boost in the 1980s by Ernst Honigmann. At first sight it might seem absurdly arbitrary, especially given that Shakeshafte was a common name in Lancashire at the time; that if Shakespeare were looking for an alias (as some suggest), he might have done rather better; and that money left to Shakeshafte elsewhere in the will suggests someone who had put in years of service whereas any period Shakespeare might have spent in Lancashire, between his leaving grammar school and getting married, would have had to have been brief. But Honigmann and others have managed to find a large number of circumstantial details to support the identification of Shakeshafte with Shakespeare, the most important of which is that the John Cottam who was the master at Stratford grammar school for two years after 1579, and whose brother was a Jesuit priest, was a neighbour of the Houghtons and went back to live near them in Lancashire after his brother was arrested. The suggestion is that Cottam recommended Shakespeare to the Houghtons as a young (very young) schoolmaster, one who was not licensed by a local bishop as schoolmasters usually were, and had not been to university as Cottam and all the other masters at Stratford grammar school had, but who shared their own strong Catholic beliefs and could therefore be trusted with their children. This would mean that Shakespeare had not only inherited his parents' faith but was also willing to enter into a network of semi-secret contacts, taking the considerable risk of associating himself with what became, as the century advanced, an increasingly threatened Catholic underworld.[7]

Any attempt to give the essentials of the 'Shakespeare and Catholicism' issue runs the risk of drastic simplification, but the alternative is to be dragged into a quagmire of speculation where one possibility is continually balanced against another and there is no dry ground. Ten or fifteen years ago, the topic was on the front page of Shakespeare Studies, when the effect of Honigmann's work was being felt and there were very energetic interventions from Richard Wilson; but it faded into the background relatively quickly, after several telling contributions from archival scholars and because there was no way of finally settling the issues one way or the other. Shapiro did not have to bother with it because his was not a cradle-to-grave biography, but both Bate and Duncan-Jones saw no reason for believing that Shakespeare had ever been in Lancashire. Neither also did René Weis, which is surprising on several counts. As will become evident later, of all the academic Shakespeare biographers who provide the main focus of this book, Weis is the least sceptical, the one most inclined to accept all those stories in what Chambers called 'the Shakespeare mythos'. Moreover, he has a special interest in Catholicism, painstakingly identifying a number of prominent Stratford residents whom he believes were recusants (as those Catholics who paid fines rather than attend church were called). According to him, these included the Shakespeares' next-door neighbours in Henley Street, the Badgers. 'There is no evidence', Weis characteristically writes, referring to the Jesuit Robert Parsons who accompanied Campion on his 1580 mission, 'of Campion and Parsons passing through the Badger house during this period, *but none that they did not.*'[8] The Jesuit who interests him most is Father John Gerard, who wrote an interesting autobiography describing his capture, torture and, amazingly enough, escape from the Tower of London.[9] Weis devotes a whole chapter to Gerard for no better reason than that he was a contemporary of Shakespeare and his story helps us to understand Shakespeare's times better. Why, then, he does not make more of Campion, whose career was equally dramatic and whose connection with Shakespeare is at least far more of a possibility, is a puzzle. It is a puzzle because the reasons which have been advanced for that connection are no worse or better than those used to support many of the stories about Shakespeare which Weis blithely accepts. The rigour which he appears to be exercising in rejecting the Lancashire hypothesis can have no value when that same quality is so often in abeyance elsewhere.

Bate, Duncan-Jones and Weis do not believe that the Houghtons' 'Shakeshafte' was Shakespeare, but Ackroyd accepts the suggestion in its totality and it helps him to tell not only an exciting, but also a more coherent story. One of the reasons for this is that the Houghtons and Heskeths lived not far from the greatest power in their land, the fourth Earl of Derby. He had a son called Fernando Strange, who was the patron of an important London theatre company to which several of the actors who went on to make up the Lord Chamberlain's Men at one time belonged. The Houghton will does not explicitly identify Shakeshafte as an actor but, on the assumption that he was, it becomes easy to speculate that the talents of this person (aka Shakespeare) were made known to Lord Strange, so that there was an easy entry into one of the leading theatrical companies once he went to London. For Ackroyd, therefore, there is very little mystery about the so-called 'lost years' because Shakespeare's stay in Lancashire provided all the necessary ground work for what, after the interlude of his marriage, would come later.

Ackroyd is significant for the total contrast he offers on the Lancashire question to most of the other biographers, but the most revealing case here is that of Stephen Greenblatt. He begins his relatively long section on these matters by indicating that, as far as Shakespeare in Lancashire is concerned, he is only dealing with a possibility:

> Will's life, if he actually sojourned in the north, would have been a peculiar compound of theatricality and danger. On the one hand, a life of open, exuberant display, where for the first time Will's talents – his personal charm, his musical skills, his power of improvisation, his capacity to play a role, and perhaps even his gifts as a writer – were blossoming in performances beyond the orbit of his family and friends . . .[10]

Already, the number of precise attributes which the fifteen- or sixteen-year-old Shakespeare is here described as displaying in Lancashire encourages the reader to forget that he may never have been there, and that same process becomes more evident as Greenblatt explains what he means by 'the other hand'. This is that, in the Houghton or Hesketh households, Will

> would have lived a life of secrets, where even the lowest servant knew things – a locked cabinet containing the chalice, books, vestments, and

other objects with which to celebrate Mass; mysterious strangers bearing ominous rumors of Mary, Queen of Scots, or of Spanish armies, mutterings of conspiracies – that could, if revealed, bring disaster upon the family.

The effect of the clutch of detail here is to overpower easily whatever force there might have been in the initial '*would have* lived a life of secrets'. This is a tense of the verb that, in any case, often implies certainty, as it seems to me it does when Greenblatt goes on to draw a conclusion from the dark side of Shakespeare's stay in Lancashire and say, 'The atmosphere of the entertainments in which Will would have performed was compounded of festivity and paranoia.'[11]

The dates in which Shakespeare was supposed to have been in Lancashire, Greenblatt notes, roughly coincide with Campion's mission to England so that he finds it 'altogether possible' that the two men met and therefore feels free to imagine the mixture of admiration and distaste Shakespeare must have felt in the Jesuit's presence. There would be the respect of a fervent young Catholic for one of the heroes of his religion but also, reading back from the evidence in the plays, resistance to the degrees of conviction and self-abnegation which, after Campion's death, would eventually lead to his being canonised. Shakespeare understood all his life, Greenblatt tells us, that 'saints ... were dangerous people. Or perhaps, rather, it would be better to say that Shakespeare did not understand saints, and that what he did not understand, he did not entirely like.' Nor is there is any indication in his writings, he continues, of 'deep admiration for the visible church'. In illustration of this last point, Greenblatt quotes the attack on the Pope which is put into the mouth of King John in Shakespeare's play of that name (3.i). He knows that this passage has often been cited as proof that Shakespeare had never been a Catholic so follows immediately with, 'This coarsely explicit piece of Protestant pope-baiting is by no means the sum of Shakespeare's mature attitude towards the Catholicism in which he had been immersed as a young man.' But the most important topic on which Shakespeare and Campion would have differed, Greenblatt says, is sex and he quotes in illustration Romeo's eroticised address to Juliet as a 'dear saint' in *Romeo and Juliet*'s first act (v). There are purposes in this and other passages of a similar kind which are, he feels, 'lightyears from Campion's, and the distance might already have been

## The female line and Catholicism

apparent even – or perhaps especially – in Lancashire in 1581'. Greenblatt then provides the historical details of Campion's arrest, torture, interrogations and gruesome death before delivering his principal subject back to Stratford and concluding, 'In the summer of 1582, as if to mark his decisive distance from Campion ... Will was making love to [Anne Hathaway].'[12] It takes a considerable effort on the part of readers to remind themselves that this lovemaking could not have marked a 'decisive distance from Campion' if Shakespeare and the 'fugitive Jesuit' had never met.

The account by Greenblatt of Shakespeare in Lancashire includes a number of phrases which indicate that no one can be sure he was ever there. 'If the adolescent knelt down before Campion,' he writes, 'he would have been looking at a distorted image of himself,' and then later, more explicitly, 'Shakespeare – assuming that he is the Shakeshafte of Houghton's will – stayed in Lancashire at least until August 1581.'[13] But he shifts often into writing as if there were no doubt that Shakespeare was Shakeshafte and this is an impression with which most of his readers are bound to come away. What he therefore offers, and what makes his pages on Shakespeare and Campion worth looking at in some detail, is a clear example of that plausible deniability referred to in my second chapter. The story of Campion is excellent copy, and Greenblatt makes fine use of it, but to anyone who wondered whether it ought to be included in a life of Shakespeare, he could point to those phrases which suggest that the attraction of the material has not made him forget his intellectual responsibilities. Questioned on the matter, he could disassociate himself from Ackroyd and rightly claim that he never entirely commits himself to the Lancashire hypothesis. He is therefore indulging in a particular kind of 'what if' life-writing which is not easy to define, but very common in Shakespeare biography. In his discussion of *Love's Labour's Lost*, Ackroyd identifies nearly all the characters with real-life originals. Thus Armado is Gabriel Harvey, Moth is Thomas Nashe, Holofernes John Florio and so on. 'The connections are there,' he concludes; 'whether they are real or fanciful, is another matter.'[14] Yet for biography as a branch of history, whether the connections are real or fanciful is the *only* matter, and that seems to me equally true of those Greenblatt makes between Shakespeare, Campion and Lancashire.

One obvious problem for anyone who believes that Shakespeare had staunchly Catholic parents, and was involved as an adolescent in the Catholic underground, is that, if he had that background and those experiences, they left no easily discernible trace. 'Not surprisingly,' Greenblatt writes, 'Shakespeare never referred openly to Campion,'[15] but neither did he make any overt reference to anything that would confirm the Lancashire hypothesis, although that does not, of course, mean that it is thereby refuted. In what is known of the details of his life (as opposed to his writings) there are no strong indications of a refusal to conform. An obscure clergyman made some notes in the late seventeenth century in which he claimed that Shakespeare 'dyed a papist'.[16] If he did, he kept it remarkably quiet and was buried in his local church in the orthodox fashion. All this a pity for biographers because, whereas pretexts can clearly be found for including the dramatic story of Campion's mission in a life of Shakespeare, they are much thinner on the ground when it comes to an equally enthralling 'Catholic' event which took place later in his lifetime, the Gunpowder Plot. It is true that because many of the plotters came from Warwickshire, Michael Wood can imagine the Shakespeare of 1605–6 as someone in possession of dangerous secrets. Anthony Holden strikes a similar note when, after noting that the theme of sleep is 'obsessive' in *Macbeth*, he asks whether it is 'entirely idle to wonder if Shakespeare himself was suffering sleepless nights' while writing the play. The sensible answer to this rhetorical question is surely yes, but Holden then continues, 'He had cause enough, as papist families of his long acquaintance went to the gallows in the wake of "Powder Plot".'[17] These are suggestive hints which no one has been prepared to follow recently, so that what one is left with is a childhood which is widely assumed to have been Catholic, especially because of his mother; a period in Lancashire which for some is certain, others likely, and others still, improbable; and then nothing at all to provide a convincing answer to the question which everyone interested in Shakespeare would like to have answered: namely, what his religious views were, and how, over the period of his lifetime, they changed or developed.

# 5

## Boyhood and youth

SHAKESPEARE COULD ONLY HAVE migrated to Lancashire in what we would now call his adolescence, but before that would have come the years of his boyhood. Just like the early relationship with the mother, these are often regarded in modern biography as 'formative'. 'Une vie, c'est une enfance mise à toutes les sauces', Jean-Paul Sartre once wrote, but more directly relevant in this context is Woodrow Wilson's claim that, 'A boy never gets over his boyhood, and never can change those subtle influences which have become a part of him, that were bred in him when he was a child.'[1] According to this statement, the parents or forebears of biographical subjects may provide them with their genetic inheritance but, during the years of their upbringing, there is another, more sociological or environmental legacy which is just as important (nurture as the complement to nature). What the 'subtle influences' were which became part of Shakespeare would therefore be something most authors of his life would obviously love to know.

The major assumption about Shakespeare's boyhood is that he attended the grammar school in his home town. His writings prove him to have been educated and there does not appear a reasonable alternative to his having acquired that education in the only public school Stratford boasted, especially when his tuition there would have been free. The very dim possibility that he was somehow educated at home is made even dimmer by the familiarity he displays with grammar-school procedures in the creation of characters such as Holofernes in *Love's Labour's Lost,* or Sir Hugh Evans in *The Merry Wives of Windsor.* There are many other signs in the plays that Shakespeare had been a grammar-school boy, yet the uncomfortable fact remains that no attendance records survive to make it a certainty. Shakespeare at Stratford grammar school therefore falls into that category of the probable with which responsible history is largely made. What helps to confirm its status there is that, whereas the recent biographers are divided on whether he was ever in Lancashire, they are unanimous in their belief that he attended the grammar school, only disagreeing on the question of quite when he left (an important matter when considering the possible influence of John Cottam).

To describe Shakespeare's grammar-school education as no more than a probability may appear to remove some underpinning from my criticism of his biographers for their speculations. If one of the more generally accepted facts about him is no more than *probable*, why complain of a lack of rigour in the investigation of other areas of his life? A way to meet this charge may be through the intermediary of Samuel Schoenbaum. Close to the start of *Shakespeare's Lives*, Schoenbaum talks of the pitfalls faced by biographers and then describes how they continually have to distinguish between three categories: 'the probable, the possible, and the preposterous'.[2] The phrasing is characteristically memorable but, in so far as it can be taken to indicate all the varieties of information from which biography is fashioned, it also seems to me misleading: an alliteration-led mistake.

The first weakness in Schoenbaum's list is that it ought surely to have begun with 'the verifiable', even if the use of that word runs the risk of falling foul of a good deal of relatively recent thinking associated with what was once described as the new history. Verifiable events or stages in Shakespeare's life would include his christening, his marriage, the birth of his children, his various purchases of land and property, his membership of the Lord Chamberlain's Men, his death and so on. Our knowledge of all these episodes is verifiable because it rests on documentary evidence. Documents can, of course, be forged; they can be misread; and they can be subject to clerical error. At one moment in the process leading up to Shakespeare's wedding, for example, he was recorded as about to marry a woman called Ann Whateley. This has been convincingly explained as a mistake, yet it illustrates how far the process of verification in biography is likely to be from the certainties attainable in most forms of science. But then no one in their right mind would think of the history of a life as a science, and certainly not an exact one.

The probable takes its place naturally below the verifiable, but the difficulties come with the second term on Schoenbaum's list. One way of evoking these is to recall the common proverbial saying that 'anything is possible'. This is not, of course, true, yet an astonishingly large number of phenomena can be categorised in this way. They only stop being possible when the opposite can be proved, a situation of which Shakespeare biographers are not slow to take advantage. This is why it was potentially misleading of Schoenbaum to create, below the possible, a third category of the preposterous. Some suggestions made about Shakespeare's life may strike many individuals as ludicrous but it is rare that they can be shown to be false; and there is sometimes no less to be said for them than conjectures which chime in better with what those individuals happen to think about Shakespeare already. This difficulty in distinguishing fairly between the possible and the preposterous makes it seem all the more important to have a clear dividing line between the possible and the category above. Yet there are, of course, no rules in this imaginary world of categories, and no strict dividing lines between one and the other. All that therefore can be offered are criteria and examples. As an example of the probable, Shakespeare's time at Stratford grammar school serves very well. If the standards which establish it as such were to be held in mind by all Shakespeare's biographers, who then decided that they would eschew the possible in favour of the probable, the books they wrote would be a good deal shorter.

There are not only no surviving attendance records for the Stratford grammar school of Shakespeare's time but also no documents which tell us what was taught there. This last lacuna is not true of all England's other grammar schools so that, on the assumption of a reasonably common practice, it becomes feasible to work out the books he would have studied, as well as the rhetorical exercises he would have been asked to perform. Jonathan Bate has skilfully traced the effects of these latter into the plays (or back from the plays), and also identified, more thoroughly than most, the places in the writing where he believes Shakespeare is remembering standard grammar-school texts.[3] The effect is to confirm that Shakespeare did indeed attend Stratford grammar school, although what his experience was there remains the mystery it always was. With the help of the plays, and surviving documentation from or about other schools, it may be possible to reconstruct the likely curriculum, but not what Shakespeare felt at the time about the books he read, how he responded to his teachers, what they felt about him and generally whether he was diligent, lazy, precocious, bored or anything of the other things schoolboys can be. In this matter of his early education, that is, there is no way to transform chronicle into biography. To do that one would have to have the recollections of those who taught him, the reminiscences of boys in his class, and his own autobiographical account. The general state of biographical knowledge of Shakespeare makes one less inclined to regret the absence of these records than thankful for those which make his mere presence in the school the probability which it is.

Placing Shakespeare in the grammar school at Stratford accounts for a good deal of his boyhood, in that lessons began at 6 o'clock (7 in the Winter), and went on until 5 for six days of the week (with half-days on Thursdays and Saturdays). There are a number of anecdotes about what he might have done in the time then left over, which belong in a different context, but the familiarity he displays in his writings with all the flora and fauna of the English countryside would suggest that his pursuits were very much those of a country boy: someone who had easy and immediate access to Nature, even though he lived in a town. One of these pursuits would appear to have been hunting, the sport or practice so often referred to in the plays. That Shakespeare was an eager and sometimes over-enthusiastic hunter is an idea associated with a story which might just as well be considered here, even though it is related more to his early manhood than his boyhood or youth. It has four main sources, all with different details, but a composite version would be that the young Shakespeare fell into bad company and went poaching deer at Charlecote, in the park of the local magnate, Sir Thomas Lucy. Caught and punished (perhaps whipped), he retaliated by writing some satirical verses on Lucy and, as a result, was forced to leave Stratford and make his way to London. Many years later, he paid Lucy back for his persecution by depicting him at the very beginning of *The Merry Wives of Windsor* as Justice Shallow, absurdly proud of his ancestry and of his coat of arms with its 'dozen white luces' (a luce being a pike, of which there were three in the Lucy family's coat of arms), but also determined to prosecute Falstaff because he has 'beaten my men, killed my deer and broke open my lodge'.

The first person to tell parts of this tale, sometime during the final two decades of the seventeenth century, was Richard Davies, the same obscure clergyman who claimed that Shakespeare 'dyed a papist'. Rowe gave a more circumstantial account in his 1709 biography and, much later in the eighteenth century, two scholars conveniently provided versions of the satirical verses which Shakespeare supposedly directed against Lucy and which Rowe had only been able to mention, not quote (what was *in*convenient was that their two versions were quite different).[4] The common source of all four writers appears to have been gossip or rumour circulating in Stratford, and elsewhere, long after Shakespeare was dead. An explanation of the durability of the story can be found in the difficulty of disproving it. Industrious burrowing in the nineteenth century resulted in the discovery that, at the time Shakespeare was a boy or young man, the Charlecote estate did not have a deer park; yet what it did have, the retort quickly came, was an area known as a 'free warren', where Shakespeare could have poached rabbits or other smaller game. Elizabethan legislation, it was also pointed out, would not have allowed a young person to be whipped for poaching; but it was easy for proponents of the Lucy connection to point out that not every great landowner proceeded strictly according to the law or to suggest that, in any case, whipping was one of those details of the story they were happy to let drop. The case was trickier in respect of those lines in *The Merry Wives* which were supposed to confirm the Lucy hypothesis. They are notoriously obscure but, even accepting that they were meant to make fun of the Lucys, it might seem strange that Shakespeare waited so long to retaliate and, for those who believe that he was chiefly responsible for the first part of *Henry VI* (written much closer to his presumed humiliation), even stranger that in this play one of the ancestors of the Charlecote Lucys is treated with respect. The use of a passage in the plays for confirmation of an event in his life is, moreover, often susceptible to a special kind of reversal. If the poaching story is hard to disprove, it is also not easy to show that the opening exchanges in *The Merry Wives* are not the root cause of the deer-stealing episode rather than one of its effects. As Schoenbaum neatly puts it,

> Could the legend possibly have originated, long after the dramatist's death, among Stratfordians who read *The Merry Wives of Windsor*, recollected a local jest about luces and louses, and interpreted the passage in accordance with their own resentment of a powerful local family?[5]

A familiar sign that Shakespeare's poaching from Lucy belongs very much to the possible rather than probable aspect of his life is the division it creates among his recent biographers, with

Duncan-Jones and Bate ignoring it completely. Weis is the most enthusiastic, asking why anyone should disbelieve Rowe and giving to the various accounts of the episode the status of 'independent corroborative witness'. As for the satirical verses Shakespeare is supposed to have written, no one, he says, has produced any 'hard evidence against their authenticity'.[6] In a demonstration of the dependence of one possible event in Shakespeare's life on another, so that the final effect is of a house of cards, Weis also insists on Lucy's standing in the Stratford community as a loyal government man, active in the pursuit of hard-line Catholics. This would have made him, the suggestion is, particularly keen to punish someone like Shakespeare and given Shakespeare unusually strong motives for retaliation.

Weis's defence is robust, but it begins in a weak way. Although the credibility of the poaching episode has, he writes, 'been repeatedly impugned, this is the only account with roots reaching back into the seventeenth century to offer any explanation for Shakespeare's abandonment of his wife and family'.[7] It is true that no one knows when, how and why Shakespeare left his wife and family in order to perform on the stage in London, but intellectual convenience is a poor and inadequate reason for adopting an explanation. That needs to be valid in its own right, irrespective of any ulterior purpose it might serve. In this case, persecution by Lucy conveniently not only provides a reason for Shakespeare quitting Stratford but also absolves him from leaving his wife and family in the lurch (what else could he do?). What this suggests is that Greenblatt must be wrong in his treatment of the poaching story when he claims that 'modern biographers are sceptical because they believe that Shakespeare was not that kind of person'.[8] The favourable uses to which the story can be put suggest rather that they have more legitimate reasons for their scepticism. Through it can, after all, be glimpsed a Shakespeare who, rather like Prince Hal, was wild in his youth (although not *too* wild), but who then sobered up: one who, having been obliged to leave the provinces and desert his wife (*force majeure*), then made good in London. Perhaps one of the most compelling aspects of the episode was that it showed a Shakespeare in conflict with a higher social class when he was later able, through his own efforts, to achieve a status comparable, or at least not too far removed from theirs. The poaching episode, that is, easily slots into the Dick Wittington aspect of Shakespeare's traditional life story.

The way Weis reveals the advantages of believing in the poaching makes one doubt his motives for accepting it and tends to undermine his general position. Something similar happens, although in a far more complicated fashion, in the pages which Greenblatt devotes to the matter. He begins in a familiar way, claiming that the four versions we have of the story are 'independent', and that though Sir Thomas Lucy may not have had a deer park, 'he did maintain a warren, an enclosed area where rabbits and other game, possibly including deer, could breed'. As for the whipping, it might not have been a legal punishment, but Lucy 'may have been inclined to teach the young offender a lesson, particularly if he suspected that the poacher and his parents might be recusants'. These are all the kinds of arguments which Weis uses, as indeed does Michael Wood, so that it is something of a surprise to find Greenblatt then writing, 'Throughout Shakespeare's career as a playwright, he was a brilliant poacher – deftly entering into territory marked out by others, taking for himself what he wanted, and walking away with his prize under the keeper's nose.' There are special reasons for this abrupt change of mode which I shall discuss later but here it is sufficient to note that whether or not the poaching story has any foundation in fact, has momentarily become immaterial. In the middle of the paragraph which opens with this remark we are told, 'What we know, and what those who originally circulated the legend knew, is that [Shakespeare] had a complex attitude towards authority, at once shy, genially submissive, and subtly challenging.' Leaving aside how we do, in fact, know these interesting things if the poaching is what the word 'legend' implies, or rather how Greenblatt knows them, this statement again seems to leave open whether or not we are meant to take the poaching episode seriously; it is therefore disconcerting to be told, at the end of this same paragraph, that the 'formative experience' which gave rise to Shakespeare's attitude 'may well have been a nasty encounter with one of the principal authorities in the district'.[9] This is disconcerting because it jerks readers back to the issue of the veridicality of the poaching episode which, they might reasonably have thought, had previously been abandoned. Shakespeare's poaching is clearly not verifiable, and there are no strong reasons for regarding it as preposterous, but the intellectual luxury of treating it as a possibility leads to the kind of confusions Greenblatt here demonstrates, and to temptations which responsible biographers ought surely to resist. No one can deny that, in order to write a satisfactory life of Shakespeare, one would need an account of the circumstances which led to his first leaving Stratford, but what is equally undeniable is that the ones available are only possible rather than probable.

# 6

# *Marriage*

Scarcely was Shakespeare's boyhood over before he was a married man. Marriage is a key event in many people's lives, but all we know about Shakespeare's is limited to a few external facts. We know, for example, that he was eighteen at the time of his wedding and that, if her tombstone is to be believed (the only surviving evidence), Anne Hathaway was all of eight years older. This was a disparity in age unusual for the period, but another detail which emerges from the data is less so. The marriage was facilitated by an application for a special licence. Applying for a special licence was quite a complicated procedure, involving (in this case) a good deal of expense and travel, but it allowed two people who wanted to get married to avoid the delays in the normal reading of the banns, especially in periods of the church year when it was not permitted to read those banns. The most obvious explanation for all parties wanting to accelerate the process in this way can be found in the christening of William and Anne's first child, six months after their wedding.

No one knows where the wedding of Shakespeare and Anne Hathaway took place – there is no record of it in the Stratford parish church. A peculiarity in one of the marriage licence documents which I have mentioned previously is that Anne is described as Anne *Whateley* from Temple Grafton. Since there was a Whateley whose suit was being dealt with in the Worcester consistory court on the same day that William and Anne's representatives had their application for a special licence confirmed, it is commonly assumed that whoever drew up the document made a straightforward error of transcription.[1] But Temple Grafton has seemed right to some because this might possibly have been the native village of Anne's mother. Those biographers keen to establish that Shakespeare had a Catholic upbringing have favoured Temple Grafton as a likely location for the wedding because they know, from a survey of Warwickshire clergy undertaken in 1586, that the priest of the church there was old, and regarded by puritanically inclined Protestants as 'unsound'.[2] It has therefore become possible to imagine a typically Catholic ceremony of the kind which Peter Ackroyd has evoked in considerable detail:

> The woman stood on the left side of the groom, in token of Eve's miraculous delivery from Adam's left rib; they held hands as a symbol of their betrothal. In the church porch the priest blessed the ring with holy water; the bridegroom then took the ring and placed it in turn on the thumb and the first three fingers of the bride's left hand with the words '*In nomine Patris, in nomine Filii, in nomine Spiritus Sancti, Amen*'. He left it on this fourth finger, since the vein in that finger was supposed to run directly to the heart.[3]

Ackroyd goes on to describe how the couple being married would wear linen cloths on their heads to protect them from demons as they knelt to partake in the nuptial mass, and how it was customary for the bride to 'carry a knife or dagger suspended from her girdle'. After the ceremony, he explains, there would be the wedding feast where 'the newly joined couple might then receive gifts of silver, or money, or food'. His account is full of interesting historical details and he ends it by saying directly of William and Anne, 'and so we leave them on this apparently auspicious day.'[4] The most obvious meaning for the adverb is that the Shakespeares' marriage did not turn out very well, but it might also be there to indicate that Ackroyd has described a typical marriage of the time between two people whose families had Catholic sympathies without there being the slightest actual proof that Shakespeare's was of this kind, wherever it was held.

A pregnant bride was troubling to many commentators in the nineteenth century; it hardly accorded with their notions of Shakespeare to have the National Bard indulging in pre-marital sex. This may explain the enthusiasm and industry with which Halliwell-Phillipps explored troth-plighting, the sixteenth-century custom whereby a couple pledged themselves to each other in front of witnesses. In the eyes of many of the time, this would allow them to sleep together before the more official wedding (as Edgar

Fripp later went so far as to say, 'the domestic contract was the binding ceremony, marriage in church was the concluding rite'[5]). If Shakespeare and Anne Hathaway had pledged themselves to each other in this way, then her pregnancy at the time of the church wedding would have raised no eyebrows. It is a question of sixteenth-century attitudes so that, as Halliwell-Phillipps put it, 'If the antecedents of Shakespeare's union with Miss Hathaway were regarded with equanimity by their own neighbours, relatives and friends' – a fact he considers 'all but indisputable' – then 'upon what grounds can a modern critic fairly impugn the impropriety of their conduct?'[6] This is a question which must have brought comfort to the many in the late nineteenth century who were unhappy with the thought of a lascivious eighteen-year-old Bard or an immodest Miss Hathaway, and it may even have provided solace in more modern times, although hardly to those who, knowing the bare facts of Shakespeare's marriage, have been surprised and puzzled by the vehemence with which Prospero tells Ferdinand at the beginning of *The Tempest*'s fourth act that he must not break Miranda's 'virgin-knot before / All sanctimonious ceremonies may / With full and holy writ be minister'd'. Yet if the adventitious reasons for supporting the troth-plighting thesis do not make it true, neither do they make it false, and it has received considerable support in modern times, notably from Germaine Greer in *Shakespeare's Wife*. As usual, there is nothing which would allow us to decide the issue one way or the other.

Troth-plighting can be invoked to deal with the fact that Anne Hathaway was pregnant when she married Shakespeare, but not that she was eight years older. A traditional way of interpreting the age difference is to cast her as a woman conscious that she was in danger of remaining on the shelf and determined therefore to take advantage of an inexperienced youth. This conclusion is arrived at by taking the known facts and interpreting them in the light of prejudices about older women who marry younger men. Its most usual support has been *Venus and Adonis*, Shakespeare's first narrative poem (and publication). In this astonishing display of linguistic dexterity, a lustful, experienced Venus quite literally throws herself, not so much at as on an adolescent virgin, heedless of his protest, 'Who plucks the bud before one leaf put forth?' Inspired by Ovid, the poem was a huge success, especially among the kind of elite readership perhaps not always prepared to take plays very seriously. There are more references to it in Chambers's list of contemporary allusions than to any other of Shakespeare's works, and it is largely responsible for the application to him of words like 'sweet' or 'honey-tongued' (although these hardly do justice to the combination of eroticism and comedy which make *Venus and Adonis* so distinctive). That it had an autobiographical element is always possible but, in such a stylised treatment of a well-known story from a recognizable source, what precisely that was cannot be known without those details of how and where it was composed which are entirely lacking.

Casting Anne as a desperate cradle-snatcher is part of a denigration of her which has helped to explain or excuse a couple of details relating to Shakespeare's married life. The first of these is that since he would have to have spent a majority of his time working in London (when he was not on tour), he and Anne must often have led separate lives. The second is that in his will he left her only his second-best bed (a famous matter that I shall be forced to come back to). These two facts combined might suggest that he was not a particularly attentive or affectionate husband, a proposition which can be countered with the idea that Anne Hathaway was, in any case, a wholly unsuitable partner for England's greatest writer. Trapping him into marriage at an early age, was she even literate? Stephen Greenblatt thinks it highly unlikely that she was and says that it is 'entirely possible that Shakespeare's wife never read a word he wrote'.[7]

Some might feel that Anne's illiteracy would have been an advantage when it came to the Sonnets. According to Shapiro, their publication in 1609 must have left Shakespeare with 'a bit of explaining to do the next time he went home to his wife in Stratford'.[8] This certainly seems possible if one thinks of the Sonnets as autobiographical, and yet sandwiched between those that refer to the narrator's passionate love for a young man and the disgust inspired in him by a dark-complexioned mistress, is a strangely simple poem made all the more unusual because its lines are octosyllabic, in contrast to the decasyllabic lines of all the other sonnets in the collection. 'Those lips that love's own hand did make / Breathed forth the sound that said "I hate"' is how sonnet 145 begins and it is only since 1970 that it has been widely accepted that it contains an allusion to Anne Hathaway. Duncan-Jones is one of the many who believe this, describing how the death of Anne's father had left her, 'a mature and spirited country girl', free to exploit her freedom and consort with local youth. In a 'combination of boredom with the sexual curiosity natural to his years', Shakespeare was led into what Duncan-Jones chooses to call a 'dalliance' with Anne and 'what was probably his first experience of sex'. That was hardly his fault because at that time he 'was probably changing from boy into man, and experiencing the uncontrollable surges of testosterone accompanying that stage of development'. He was 'sowing wild oats, with little or no thought to the lifelong problems he would reap'. In the 'first weeks of their dalliance' (which would be followed by a 'compelled marriage'), Shakespeare was 'grateful to Anne for her compliance, and persuaded himself that he loved her'.[9] It was around this time that he would have written sonnet 145, whose composition at this early date is indicated not only by its manner and form, but also by the hidden reference to Anne in its final couplet: '"I hate" from "hate" away she threw, / And saved my life, saying "not you".' Andrew Gurr was the first to suggest that '"hate" away' makes 'Hathaway', and Stephen Booth later reinforced that interpretation by finding 'Anne' in the 'And' of the final line.[10] This is a reading that is possible without being certain, but if Shakespeare did write this sonnet as part of his courtship of Anne and if it is, as some biographers like to fantasise, his first composition, then the possibility of her being illiterate might seem to diminish. Not perhaps very far, however, since Shakespeare could have read the poem to her; he could have written it, even though he knew she had no interest in poetry; or it could have nothing to do with her at all.

Germaine Greer is happy to accept that Shakespeare wrote sonnet 145 for Anne and, quoting from its third line ('To me, who languished for her sake'), she uses it to challenge the usual account of who seduced whom. 'It was not the woman who seduced the boy,' she writes, 'but he who "languished for her sake", to the point of death, it would seem, and only then did she succumb to his importunity, and so save his life.'[11] Her book is a remarkable enterprise in that, if we know very little about Shakespeare, we know even less about his wife; but she uses social history to contest the traditional portrait of Anne. Insisting that she could indeed read, Greer lays particular stress on the number of women in Elizabethan and Jacobean England who were involved in trade or business generally, and offers a lively if entirely hypothetical portrait of Anne, competently and successfully running the family's affairs in Stratford while her husband was away in London. In the process of doing this, she provides an interpretation of a detail in the Shakespeare record which has often been thought puzzling. In 1601 a shepherd who worked for the Hathaway family made a will in which he left to the Stratford poor 'forty shillings that is in the hand of Anne Shakespeare, wife unto Mr William Shakespeare'.[12] Greer argues that shepherds often used other people in the way we now use banks and that this item in the shepherd's will therefore provides a

> scintilla of evidence that Anne Shakespeare was economically active in her own right. Even if the only money she had access to was her husband's income [she continues], Anne may have been empowered to lend and spend it as she thought fit, which would give the lie to those people who want to believe that Shakespeare's wife did not enjoy her husband's trust or respect.[13]

The idea Greer wants to get away from is of Anne Shakespeare as a weak, despised dependant. Exaggerating a little the degree to which her subject has been (even in more recent times) the victim of misogyny, she uses her historical knowledge to build up a picture of Shakespeare's wife which flatly contradicts at a number of salient points the conventional view – the one which emerged when the meagre facts available were creatively interpreted in the light of ideas about women's role in society that have now become outdated. Greer interprets them in the light of her feminism, and with the support of a good deal of historical data; but that does not mean that the facts are any the less meagre or that there is anything in them to support the idea that Anne Shakespeare was a sixteenth- and seventeenth-century businesswoman. Towards the beginning of her book Greer writes:

> All biographies of Shakespeare are houses built of straw, but there is good straw and rotten straw, and some houses are better built than others. The evidence that is always construed to Anne Hathaway's disadvantage is capable of other, more fruitful interpretations, especially within the context of recent historiography.[14]

This concept of good and rotten straw is a strange one as far as houses are concerned since, as any passing wolf knows, it is never an ideal building material. In so far as the words stand for the very little we know about Anne Shakespeare, there are no objective criteria which would allow us to decide what was a good or rotten reading, not of the women of her time but of her *individual* experience.

The unanswerable biographical questions concern the nature and quality of Shakespeare's married life. If (as Greer thinks) his wife ran his affairs back in Stratford, then there are suggestions in the documents that it would have been with the help of two of his brothers. He had a third brother, Edmund, who, born in 1580, went to London to become an actor and was buried there in 1607 at an expense which has caused most biographers to speculate that Shakespeare must have paid for the funeral.[15] Gilbert was the one closest to him in age, being only two years younger. There are indications that he also spent some time in London as a haberdasher before returning to his home town, but none that Richard, born in 1574, ever left it. It is with Shakespeare's brother Richard that, according to Stephen Dedalus in his long account of the relations between Shakespeare's life and art in the Scylla and Charybdis section of *Ulysses*, Anne would have cuckolded her husband, an event which (for Stephen) would explain the remarkably intense representation of sexual jealousy in characters such as Othello or Leontes.

For Greenblatt, what Stephen has to say about Richard and Anne is part of 'one of the greatest meditations on Shakespeare's marriage'. This is a hard claim to understand when, however much Stephen's lecture may constitute a great part of a great book, its epistemic value is practically nil; but it may help to explain the chapter in Greenblatt's biography which is devoted to Shakespeare's marriage ('Wooing, Wedding, and Repenting'). Chiefly an analysis of married relations as they are represented in the plays, this includes the claim that, 'It is, perhaps, as much what Shakespeare did *not* write as what he did that seems to indicate something seriously wrong with his marriage,' a fine illustration of the argument from absence. Greenblatt observes that both Hotspur and Brutus are reluctant to take their wives into their confidence when they become involved in plots against the State and suggests that this shows how, to the question of what degree of intimacy husbands and wives can achieve, 'the answer Shakespeare repeatedly gives is very little'. He accuses Shakespeare of a 'reluctance or inability to represent marriage, as it were, from the inside', although he recognises that he is able to imagine the feelings of an unhappy wife: it was as if 'the misery of the neglected or abandoned spouse was something he knew personally and all too well'. Comedies traditionally conclude with marriages but Greenblatt believes that Shakespeare was unusually unconcerned to predict a prosperous future for those in his plays, and he feels that the sourness at the end of *Measure for Measure* or *All's Well That Ends Well* is not the result of carelessness but seems rather 'to be the expression of a deep scepticism about the long term prospects for happiness in marriage'. For him, Shakespeare was either unwilling or unable to 'imagine a married couple in a relationship of sustained intimacy' and he finds it significant that the only apparent exceptions to this rule are Gertrude and Claudius in *Hamlet*, and Macbeth and his wife. Surveying all this material, he says he finds it difficult '*not* to read [Shakespeare's] works in the context of his decision to live for most of his long marriage away from his wife' and he goes on, in relation to the bequests in Shakespeare's will, to talk of 'the failure of the marriage to give him what he wanted' and the 'strange ineradicable distaste for [Anne] he felt deep within him'.[16]

As I have no doubt indicated before, Shakespeare's plays are so varied and complex that one can almost always find in them what one is looking for. There are many possible alternative readings to Greenblatt's (Greer offers the beginnings of one), concentrating more on plays such as *The Merry Wives of Windsor*; and it might be objected that the criminality of Claudius, or the Macbeths, does not cancel out the understanding Shakespeare is able to display, in their respective plays, of married intimacy. But this is to be drawn into a quite pointless game. It was Tolstoy who began *Anna Karenina* by saying that 'All happy families resemble one another, each unhappy family is unhappy in its own way' and, however dubious that generalisation might be, it is clear that the dysfunctional offers more scope to a writer than its opposite. To relate Hotspur's refusal to involve his wife in his plot, or the marriage of Bertram and Helena at the end of *All's Well That Ends Well*, to Shakespeare's private life would require a depth of knowledge about his marriage which we have never had and will never possess. Stephen Dedalus can make daring, speculative links because he is a character in a novel and, in any case, eventually declares he does not believe in what he says. To make them in a biography seems to me a betrayal of the genre.

# 7

## *The theatre*

A STAPLE OF MANY BIOGRAPHIES is a demonstration of how the eminent subject first displayed signs of that eminence. The early sketches of Picasso, the childhood compositions of Mozart, the first writings of the Brontës, all of these are indications of the great achievements which were to come. There is a prototype for the description of anticipatory signals in St Luke's gospel. There, the parents of Jesus are described as losing their twelve-year-old child on a visit to Jerusalem and then finding him in the temple, where he had been astonishing the rabbis with the depth of his knowledge and understanding.

There is nothing in what is known of Shakespeare's background to suggest he would be interested in the theatre, and nothing therefore to connect his youth to his adult career. It would be of initial biographical interest, for example, to know how his enthusiasm for drama was first aroused. The records show that travelling theatre companies certainly visited Stratford when he was growing up there, and often at a time when his father was heavily involved in Corporation affairs. As part of the process whereby they were given permission to act, it was customary for such companies to provide a special performance for Corporation officials. In the year stretching from Michaelmas 1568, at a time when John Shakespeare was high bailiff, both the Queen's and the Earl of Worcester's Men visited Stratford. Did Shakespeare's father take his five-year-old son to the special performances these companies offered, so that it was then that he first caught the acting bug? Halliwell-Phillipps asked himself this question, if in rather different language from mine, and the reply he gave is particularly interesting from the point of view of biographical method:

> If . . . it can be shown that, in a neighbouring county about the same time, there was an inhabitant of a city who took his little boy, one born in the same year with Shakespeare, 1564, to a free dramatic entertainment exhibited as were those at Stratford-on-Avon, before the Corporation under precisely similar conditions, there then arises a reasonable probability that we should be justified in giving an affirmative reply to the enquiry.[1]

The surname of the little boy to whom Halliwell-Phillipps here refers was Willis and he came from Gloucester. In the account he wrote towards the end of his life, he describes how, when his father took him to the play, he 'made me stand between his legs as he sat upon one of the benches, where we saw and heard very well'.[2] This detail, applied to Shakespeare, finds its way into most of the recent biographies and Greenblatt uses it to evoke 'Will's own primal scene of theatricality'. The bailiff's son, he suggests, 'would have stood between his father's legs. For the first time in his life William Shakespeare watched a play.'[3] If the matter were not so trivial, and if it were not highly likely that the young Shakespeare did at some point, and in some fashion, see the players when they came to Stratford, it would be worth insisting more forcefully that the early experiences of a man who came from Gloucester could never be a reliable template for those of someone brought up in different circumstances forty miles away.

A source of theatrical inspiration for Shakespeare which is often cited, and which is additional to whatever he might have seen in Stratford, is the celebration held in Kenilworth in 1575. This was when the Earl of Leicester stage-managed costly and elaborate festivities for the visit of Queen Elizabeth. It is assumed that, in taking his eleven-year-old son there, John Shakespeare gave him a taste for spectacle. Part of that spectacle was a water pageant presented to Elizabeth when she was returning from the hunt. In the course of this she was serenaded by someone who represented Arion, that 'famous Musician, in tire and appointment strange, well seeming too his person, riding aloft upon his old friend the Dolphin, (that from head to tail was four & twenty foot long)'.[4] According to Greenblatt (and many others), Shakespeare's imagination 'drew on the scene at Kenilworth' when he was writing *A Midsummer Night's Dream* and particularly the lines in which Oberon remembers how,

> ... once I sat upon a promontory,
> And heard a mermaid on a dolphin's back
> Uttering such dulcet and harmonious breath
> That the rude sea grew civil at her song. (2.i)

The link seems very weak – a mermaid on a dolphin's back is a common image in mythological writing and illustration – but Greenblatt finds it enough to allow him to assert that 'the memory of Kenilworth served to evoke the power that song had to create hushed order and to excite an almost frenzied attention. This paradox – art as the source both of settled calm and of deep disturbance – was central to Shakespeare's entire career.'[5]

These two speculations about Shakespeare's introduction to the theatre, or to theatrical effect, are examples of passive experience rather than early manifestations of unusual ability. The only possible indication of the latter has been found in a tale Aubrey tells in his brief life:

> [Shakespeare's] father was a Butcher, & I have been told heretofore by some of the neighbours, that when he was a boy he exercised his father's Trade, but when he kill'd a Calfe he would doe it in a *high style*, & make a Speech. There was at this time another Butcher's son in this Towne, that was held not at all inferior to him for a naturall witt, his acquaintance and coetanean, but dyed young.[6]

For a long time this was dismissed as yet another example of Aubrey's untrustworthiness; after all, John Shakespeare was a glover not a butcher. More recently, however, a more complicated picture has been built up of his business activities. It is suspected, for example, that he sometimes dealt in wool, and it is assumed by many that he would have had a lot to do with preparing the leather from which his gloves were made. From there to butchering one or two of the animals which provided the leather might be considered a short step. But a marginally more reliable avenue to the rehabilitation of this anecdote was provided in 1971 by Douglas Hamer. He had found records concerning entertainment provided for the five-year-old Princess Mary in 1521 and, among them, a payment to a man for 'killing a calf before my lady's grace behind a cloth'. He was able to identify these last words as a reference to an old mumming play and then boldly continue:

> I suggest that a calf-killing play of this type lies behind Aubrey's statement, and that the boy Shakespeare wrote, or re-wrote, the verses, and that he himself, as a butcher's son, did the 'killing' in 'high style',

Shakespeare's earliest dramatic work in verse, and his first appearance as an actor.[7]

In the world of Shakespeare biography, every scrap, no matter how unappetising it may seem, is seized on ravenously. Assuming that calf-killing shows would feature at holiday time, Duncan-Jones finds it 'entirely believable that the mirth-loving Shakespeare family regularly contributed such a show to Christmas or Shrovetide festivities in Stratford, and that young William achieved fame among neighbours for his virtuoso enactment of it'.[8] In this context, 'entirely believable' is clearly equivalent to what in so many others is merely described as 'possible'.

In a book published just as this one was going to press, Duncan-Jones has endeavoured to bolster her case for Shakespeare's early fame as an actor by first of all claiming that the neighbours to whom Aubrey refers must have meant to say that it was not his father but his *god*father who was a butcher. Her main evidence for this appears to be that William was also the Christian name of a prominent Stratford butcher called Tyler (godchildren being usually named after their godparents), and that this Tyler had a son called Richard who featured in the first draft of Shakespeare's 1616 will. Young William, she speculates, may often have witnessed calves being killed in Tyler's slaughterhouse, or even – although this seems an unnecessary qualification for being able to *perform* the killing of a calf in a mumming play – been 'formally apprenticed' to him. She can find no further records of such a play or interlude to go with the one from 1521 that Hamer discovered, but by supposing that the calf killing might have been incorporated into a dramatisation of the Bible's ever-popular story of the prodigal son (so often referred to in Shakespeare's plays), or some stage version of the legendary Guy of Warwick's encounter with a troublesome beast known as the Dun Cow of Dunsmore Heath, she feels she can rescue Aubrey's remarks and conclude again that 'William and his brothers may have performed a "disguising" or mumming show that became celebrated in Stratford.' Readers who follow Duncan-Jones's argument closely are likely to be surprised at the lengths to which a biographer will go to deliver one of the traditional constituents of a life story. That constituent is, of course, what is present in the remarks Aubrey claims were made by the neighbours, although they (Duncan-Jones herself admits) must have been at least the *great-grandchildren* of anyone John Shakespeare knew in the 1570s and 1580s.[9]

*The theatre*

We have, in my view, no secure knowledge of how Shakespeare first became interested in the theatre, or of when he first displayed an aptitude for it; and yet by 1592, when he was twenty-eight, he was well established, as the attack by Greene (or Chettle) shows. He could only have reached that position via one or more theatre companies, but there is nothing to indicate which he had joined before a record of 1595 that shows him to be a member of the Lord Chamberlain's Men. I have already said that one reason for the popularity of the Lancashire hypothesis has been that it allows biographers to associate Shakespeare with the Earl of Derby's son, Lord Strange, and that there are records showing how several of the Lord Chamberlain's Men had previously been attached to Lord Strange. Yet there is nothing to make it certain that Shakespeare was ever one of them.

The most successful of the companies which flourished at the time when Shakespeare would have been making his way in the theatre world was the Queen's Men. Several of the plays in their repertory were clearly very well known to him, a good example being *The Famous Victories of Henry V*, which is a source for many scenes and characters in the two parts of *Henry IV* and *Henry V* itself. Since this is a company about which something is known, it would be convenient to be able to attach Shakespeare to it, even if there must have been more ways of becoming as familiar as he shows himself to have been with *The Famous Victories* than acting in it. The something that is known about the Queen's Men is, above all, that in June 1587 one of its members (William Knell) killed another in a brawl. This would have meant that when they played Stratford a few weeks later they were almost certainly a couple of actors short. 'As Shakespeare's own English history plays were to show,' Duncan-Jones writes, 'one man's sudden death is very often the occasion of another man's sudden promotion. *So it may perhaps have been* for Shakespeare himself in the summer of 1587.' She knows that an elite company like the Queen's Men was only likely to engage new actors who already had some training and suggests therefore that it was '*perhaps* . . . from among Leicester's Men' that Shakespeare was 'drafted in June or July 1587'.[10] In this way, she avoids offending against common sense while at the same time not entirely depriving her reader of the dramatic scenario in which the depleted Queen's Men trundle into Stratford and find in a local boy the answer to all their needs.

*If* Shakespeare was 'for a time among Leicester's Men',

Duncan-Jones continues, his service '*may have been* fairly brief'. However brief it was, it could well have qualified him to become a Queen's Man but that still leaves the question of how he made his first breakthrough. '*My conjecture is*', Duncan-Jones begins, and then goes on to describe the Sir Fulke Greville (father of the writer with the same name) who lived only a dozen miles to the west of Stratford. She supposes that he saw Shakespeare performing in the town, perhaps in his calf-killing role, took him into his service and later, since he was 'very closely allied to the Dudleys' (Leicester's family name), passed the young man on to the Earl. Thus

> as a member of Leicester's Men for some time between 1584 and 1586, Shakespeare *would have* quickly shown his versatility both in writing and performing. He *would have* been a natural choice to supply one of the gaps left by Knell's death in June 1587.

What is so effective here is again that 'would have' has the mere appearance of the conditional; but what is more interesting from the point of view of biographical method is how, when Duncan-Jones later reverts to the question of Shakespeare and the Queen's Men, any hint of that conditional (previously evident in all the words I have italicised) has disappeared. Only a little later, for example, she speculates about the work Shakespeare would have done for the Queen's Men 'while he was a full-time member of the company in the later 1580s'.[11] Her treatment of the issue is only one example among hundreds, in her work and those of the other biographers, of how what might have been is gradually converted into what was.

Shakespeare must have quickly graduated from being an actor to also writing plays (if he did not offer himself as an actor / author from the outset), but he appears to have continued acting until at least 1603, when he is listed as performing in Jonson's *Sejanus*. The obvious questions therefore concern the kind of actor he was and the roles he played. Almost a century after his death, Rowe indicated the difficulty there was in finding these things out:

> His Name is Printed, as the Custom was in those Times, amongst those of the other Players, before some old Plays [he writes], but without any particular Account of what sort of Parts he us'd to play; and tho' I have inquir'd, I could never meet with any further Account of him this way, than that the top of his Performance was the Ghost in his own *Hamlet*.[12]

## The theatre

For most of the information in his biography Rowe relied on the actor Thomas Betterton (c. 1635–1710), who had apparently been able to pick up no more useful green-room gossip than this on the question of Shakespeare's roles. The task was not likely to become easier with the passage of time. In notes which he made in the middle of the eighteenth century for an enlarged biography of Shakespeare which he might never have completed, the antiquarian William Oldys (1696–1761) has a story that he claimed to have been told by one of Shakespeare's brothers. This person said he had a faint memory of once having seen 'brother Will' act in one of his own comedies,

> wherein being to personate a decrepit old man, he wore a long beard, and appeared so weak and drooping and unable to walk, that he was forced to be supported and carried by another person to a table, at which he was seated among some company, who were eating, and one of them sung a song.[13]

The character described here has been convincingly identified as Adam in *As You Like It*; yet, given the quality of the report, it is astounding how easily the idea that Shakespeare played Adam has been accepted as part of what is known about him. It is particularly astounding because Oldys records that the brother to whom he refers 'lived to a good old age ... even some years, as I compute, after the restoration of Charles II'.[14] This is remarkable when the records clearly indicate that all Shakespeare's three brothers predeceased him.

That Hamlet's ghost and Adam were parts that Shakespeare himself played has passed into biographical lore, despite the exceptional frailty of the evidence. The only other information of real substance comes from one of the six people in Chambers's list of 'Contemporary Allusions' with something of possible biographical significance to say. This is John Davies of Hereford, called such in order to distinguish him from another John Davies who was also a writer. He referred to Shakespeare on three occasions in his poetry and always in a way which connects him with the stage. In the first of these references, which occurs in a poem published in 1603, Davies talks of both Burbage and Shakespeare as men in regard to whom 'fell Fortune cannot be excus'd / That hath for better uses you refus'd.' What he means is made clear in a couplet which comes a few lines later and where he writes: 'And though the stage doth stain pure gentle blood, / Yet generous you are in mind and mood.' In a poem published two years later, Davies makes much the same point, complaining in the process that Shakespeare and Burbage had not been rewarded (by Fortune) 'to their desserts'.[15] Both these references are complicated by the fact that we would not know who their subjects were if the initials RB and WS had not been added to the margins of the poems opposite specific lines; and that in many other of these lines Davies is not merely clouding the issue by discussing Shakespeare and Burbage together, but talking of actors in general. Yet in his *Scourge of Folly*, published around 1610, he devoted what was then known as an epigram solely 'To Our English Terence, Mr Will. Shake-speare'. The first four lines of this eight-line poem read:

> Some say (good Will) which I, in sport, do sing,
> Had'st thou not plaid some Kingly parts in sport,
> Thou had'st been a companion for a King;
> And, been a King among the meaner sort.[16]

Here then, to Adam and Hamlet's ghost, we have 'kingly parts', but it would have been helpful if the phrase had been more specific. There is, after all, a world of difference between Henry IV and (say) the King of France in *All's Well That Ends Well*. The possible range is very great, especially if one thinks that all Davies might have meant by 'kingly' is aristocratic. The question that needs to be considered also is whether he was generalising from one or two performances he happened to have seen, or had a decent, overall knowledge of Shakespeare's acting career.

Rowe, Oldys and Davies provide the most substantial indications of how Shakespeare performed on the stage, a desperate situation for anyone anxious to know the kind of actor he was. Yet recently, in his *1599*, James Shapiro has made an interesting possible addition to the data in an argument which concerns the epilogue to the second part of *Henry IV*. Nearly all the editors print this epilogue as if it were one speech, delivered on a single occasion, while at the same time recognising that it falls into two distinct parts. The first of these parts, which most editors follow the First Folio in printing second, was almost certainly spoken by the clown of the Lord Chamberlain's Men, William Kemp, since it begins, 'If my tongue cannot entreat you to acquit me, will you command me to use my legs,' a clear reference to the jig which often followed the performance of a play in the commercial theatre and for which Kemp, a celebrated dancer, was famous. This is the epilogue in which Kemp (if it was him) promised that 'our humble author' would later continue the story which had just ended and that the continuation would have 'Sir John in it', a pledge Shakespeare notoriously failed to fulfil in *Henry V*. The second part of the epilogue is very different in tone from the first and would have been delivered, Shapiro conjectures, at a Court performance of *2Henry IV*, where there would have been no concluding jig. He believes the lines would have been delivered by Shakespeare himself since at one moment the speaker says, 'If you look for a good speech now, you undo me, for what I have to say is of my own making.' The speech itself is deft and elegant, a distinct variation on the other epilogue's more homely version of the conventional appeal to the audience to be indulgent; and it ends with a *coup de théâtre* as the speaker kneels: 'and so I kneel down before you – but, indeed, to pray for the Queen'. According to Shapiro, the fact that the speaker was kneeling in submission to his audience in the Queen's presence would mean that the members of that audience would then be obliged to kneel also. Making that happen successfully would require considerable stage presence, but also an actor who was used to playing gentlemanly parts. That it was Shakespeare cannot be certain since 'of my own making' is a phrase that could easily have been spoken by someone else. But even if we had documents to show that he was the actor concerned, we would still not then know what impression Shakespeare made on an audience when he was not playing himself but other parts.[17]

# 8

# *Patronage, or who's who in the Sonnets*

A MINOR SIGN OF THE vital importance of patronage in Elizabethan and Jacobean England can be found in the names of the theatre companies: the Queen's Men, Lord Strange's Men, Pembroke's Men, and so forth. Only with an aristocratic patron at their head could actors feel protected from State authority and avoid the risk of being categorised as vagabonds. The proof of Shakespeare's association with the Lord Chamberlain's Men comes from that record of a payment in March 1595 which he, along with two other of its members, received for performances at Court in the previous December. He stayed with the same company for the rest of his career although, after the death of Elizabeth, they acquired an even more powerful patron and became the King's Men. It was in that capacity that they performed numerous times at Court in the early years of James's reign.

The fiction was that these performances were the be-all and end-all of their existence and that when, in the time between them, they also performed in the public theatres, they were merely practising for their next Court appearance. But they could hardly have believed that when they made so much more money in the thriving commercial sector than they did as Court dependants (well paid as their appearances there might be). Nearly every biographer of Shakespeare spends many pages telling how, in the late 1590s, Richard Burbage, the company's leading actor, was in dispute with the man who owned the land on which stood the building where the Chamberlain's Men usually performed ('The Theatre', as it was confusingly called). They go on to describe the way in which he and his brother Cuthbert solved the problem by dismantling this building in London's northern suburbs, carrying most of its components across the river to Southwark, and erecting there what became the hugely successful Globe. There are nearly always many more details in these accounts than are necessary for the story of Shakespeare's life, rather than a history of the theatre; but what they do offer is a likely explanation of how and why he continued to thrive during his years in London, and was able to make so many investments back in Stratford. As an actor in, and a writer for, the Lord Chamberlain's Men, and a leading figure, to judge from the appearance of his name together with those of only Burbage and Kemp in the 1595 record of payment, Shakespeare appears to have done very well out of the success of his company in the 1590s. But once the Globe was in operation, his share of the takings increased because he had been part of the syndicate which financed its construction. The land, property and tithes which he eventually owned in Stratford have been reasonably taken to suggest how profitable this involvement in the financial, as well as artistic, aspects of the theatre proved.

The popularity of theatre-going among almost all social classes was very high during Shakespeare's adult life, a fact not perhaps unrelated to his own exciting and often innovative contributions, and it therefore provided a good environment for making money. Yet for the investor it was very far from being risk-free. A major problem was that the theatres were frequently closed down, because of some social disturbance (an apprentice riot, for example), or more frequently because of periodic outbreaks of bubonic plague. In June 1592, for example, before the formation of the Lord Chamberlain's Men, there began a period of closure which was lengthened by a plague outbreak so that it lasted for almost two years. Because the restrictions normally applied only to London, one common resource for actors in these circumstances was to go on tour. There is no proof that Shakespeare ever toured with a theatre company, but it is altogether probable that he did so. On this occasion, however, there is a suggestive coincidence between the closure of the London theatres and an apparent attempt on his part to abandon play-writing for a while and pursue an alternative, or perhaps merely parallel, career as a poet.

If patronage was important in the life of an actor, it was much more so in that of a poet. Any poet without a private income, and with ambitions to live by his pen, needed to seek out someone rich and influential who liked his work and was therefore willing to clothe and feed him, or find him some secretarial post. One accepted first move in this search was to dedicate one of your works to a likely patron. When, in 1593, Shakespeare published his first long poem, *Venus and Adonis*, he dedicated it to the young Earl of Southampton. The major lack in any attempt to write a life of Shakespeare is the absence of any letters. The *Venus and Adonis* dedication is in the form of a letter (a dedicatory address), but one so ruled by the prevailing conventions that it is of little biographical use. Shakespeare treads the familiar path of self-deprecation. He is worried, he says, about the effect his 'unpolished lines' will have on Southampton, and about how the world might censure him for 'choosing so strong a prop to support so weak a burden'. If his lordship finds something in what he has written, he will take advantage of 'all idle hours' to offer him some 'graver labour'; but 'if the first heir of my invention prove deformed, I shall be sorry it had so noble a godfather, and never ear so barren a land, for fear it yield me still so bad a harvest.'[1] This is elegantly turned but to imagine these phrases allow us a glimpse into Shakespeare's genuine feelings about his own capacities (as a real letter might) would clearly be naïve.

It is not surprising to find Shakespeare targeting Southampton as a possible patron when several other poets of the time were doing exactly the same. Brought up as a ward of Lord Burghley following the early death of his father, the young Earl, who must have already manifested some interest in the arts, was in 1593 nearing his majority and free disposal of his income. There is no proof that Shakespeare's approach to him was successful, although *Venus and Adonis* itself was a runaway best-seller, going through more editions that any other long poem of the period. What nevertheless makes it very likely that Southampton did respond to a poem so many other people appeared to appreciate is the dedication to him of *The Rape of Lucrece*, Shakespeare's second long poem which he published roughly a year after the first. The tone of this is confident rather than hesitant. 'The love I dedicate to your Lordship is without end', it begins and Shakespeare then goes on to refer to the warrant he already has of Southampton's 'honourable disposition'. 'What I have done is yours,' he continues, 'what I have to do is yours, being part in all I have, devoted yours.'[2] All this certainly sounds as if Southampton had not ignored him, but there is nothing to tell us what form the Earl's acknowledgement had taken. If he gave

Shakespeare money, one would like to know how much it was; and if he took him into the household he was establishing chiefly in his country house down at Titchfield in Hampshire, it would be interesting to discover quite what that meant and for how long it was.

It was Rowe who, in 1709, reported that, according to William Davenant, Southampton had shown Shakespeare 'uncommon marks of favour and friendship' and on one occasion had given him £1,000 for some purchase he had in mind.[3] Although this provides an explanation for the investments Shakespeare was able to make in Stratford which is alternative or complementary to theatre revenues, most biographers since have been sceptical, balking at the sheer enormity of the sum cited and pointing out that this was a period during which Southampton was heavily in debt. But Duncan-Jones is convinced that money changed hands, although she thinks it is more likely to have been £100 than £1,000 (which Shakespeare would then have used for the purchase of his family's coat of arms); and René Weis accepts the claim in its original form, insisting at the same time, 'that Shakespeare knew Southampton well is a matter of record'.[4] It is difficult to know what record Weis is talking about here since, although the Earl had a turbulent public career which excited much comment, none of the documents associated with him makes any mention of Shakespeare. Symptomatic of the way scholars have tried to find some connection were the efforts of G. P. V. Akrigg, author of what is still the standard biography of Southampton. Responding to a claim that the name Gobbo appeared in the Titchfield parish register, Ackrigg transcribed that document from its beginnings in 1587 to the burial entry for Southampton in 1624, but found no Gobbos. 'The names misread as "Gobbo"', he somewhat gloomily reported, 'were Holte and Hobbes'.[5] Discovering a Gobbo in Titchfield would have at least *suggested* that this was where Shakespeare had found the name for one of the characters in *The Merchant of Venice*, and that he must therefore have spent time at Southampton's country house.

How convenient biographers find it to believe that Shakespeare was a part of Southampton's household can be illustrated from Bate's second account of all these matters in his *Soul of the Age*. 'There is a strong possibility', he writes there, 'that Shakespeare spent part of the plague year in some form of service in Southampton's household in Titchfield in Hampshire', and he then goes on immediately, in the next paragraph:

The association with Southampton had three key consequences. It transformed Shakespeare from jobbing playwright to courtly poet ... Politically, it brought him into the orbit of the Earl of Essex, to whom young Southampton was devoted ... And intellectually, it introduced him to the work of the Anglo-Italian man of letters, John Florio, Southampton's tutor, through whom he was exposed to Italianate culture and later, the essays of Michel de Montaigne, whose subtle, sympathetic mind was perfectly attuned to his own.[6]

These are rich rewards for placing Shakespeare firmly in Southampton's household but, since that is commonly understood to have been in Titchfield, and Bate initially describes Shakespeare's presence there as only a 'possibility' (and given the evidence available, whether the possibility is 'strong' or otherwise could only ever be a matter of opinion), this paragraph ought really to have begun, 'The association with Southampton would have had three key consequences', and continued accordingly. I have described previously how often in Shakespeare biography 'might have' becomes 'was', but usually there is an interval between the first, apparently tentative claim and later assertions. The example from Bate is useful because here the transformation appears to take place on the same page and from one sentence to the next.[7]

The only clear sign that Southampton and Shakespeare might have been associated in some way are the latter's two dedications. Apart from a performance of *Love's Labour's Lost* by the King's Men in 1605, which was arranged for James's consort and took place in Southampton's London residence,[8] there are no indications of any contact after *The Rape of Lucrece* and Shakespeare did not publish another volume of poetry until 1609, when his Sonnets appeared. A great deal had happened to Southampton in the intervening fifteen years. After refusing to marry Burghley's granddaughter, and incurring in the process a massive fine of £5,000, he made one of Elizabeth's maids of honour pregnant, married her and was consequently imprisoned for a while. In 1601 he took a prominent part in the Earl of Essex's abortive rebellion and, as a result, having narrowly escaped execution, found himself in prison again. Released and pardoned on the accession of James I, he was by 1609 once again an influential and powerful figure and a suitable person therefore to whom Shakespeare could have dedicated his poems. But of course, as everyone knows, the 1609 volume does not carry a dedication from the author but only one signed with the initials of the publisher, Thomas Thorpe, and addressed to a mysterious 'Mr. W. H.', the 'only begetter of these ensuing sonnets'.

Anxious to keep Southampton at the centre of affairs, several biographers have pointed out that his family name was Henry Wriothesley, which is 'W. H.' reversed, and then made the only apparently obvious assumption that the person to whom the poems were dedicated would also be the person to whom they were addressed. Others have claimed him as the addressee without bothering with the dedication at all, or suggested that, in talking of a 'begetter', Thorpe was referring to someone who had procured the sonnets for him rather than to the individual who might have inspired them. Plumping for Southampton in this way is useful because it sets parameters for the other problems of identity thrown up by the Sonnets. The best known of these concern the rival poet whose addresses the speaker in the poems appears to feel might be of better quality, and more heeded, than his own; and the dark-complexioned woman (the famous 'dark lady') who is, or was, the speaker's mistress, but has also perhaps slept with the addressee. Most biographers have felt free to speculate about who these two people were but none more brazenly than A. L. Rowse. In the preface to his revised edition of *Shakespeare the Man*, published in 1988, Rowse claims that the Sonnets were patently autobiographical and that the Mr W. H. of the dedication was clearly 'the publisher's man, *not* the young Lord within the Sonnets' because that young Lord was 'the obvious person, Shakespeare's patron, Southampton'. Since previous biographers had not noticed 'this obvious point', they had made 'a complete muddle of Shakespeare's life and work'. He himself, on the other hand, had been able to 'reduce the unnecessary confusion to order and make sense of both life and work', providing 'unanswerable certainty'. This was why the biography he was offering was definitive, 'all confusions cleared up and problems settled'. Later on, in the body of his book, Rowse describes how 'pitiable' he thought it that people had not realised how Shakespeare had written his sonnets 'in the course of his duty to the young lord upon being accepted as his poet', and insisted that the story they told was 'perfectly clear', although 'the key was lost for so long.' This key was the identity of the dark lady and Rowse felt he had eventually found it in Emilia Lanier, the daughter of Court musicians who were of Italian extraction (hence the swarthy complexion). He noted how he had always been convinced that, if the identity of the dark lady was one day discovered, she would prove to be a member of the Southampton set. 'This turns out to be true,' he writes triumphantly, '– a complete vindication of fact and argument uncovered by rigorous dating and proper chronological method instead of absurd conjectures *in vacuo*, devoid of any historical reality.'[9] What makes this exasperating is that if any conjectures were truly *in vacuo*, Rowse's certainly were. His colleagues in Oxford can hardly have been pleased to find that the name of All Souls appeared at the end of his preface since what he has to say, but above all the manner in which he chooses to say it, brings so little credit to their prestigious institution. Later Shakespeare biographers tend to refer to Rowse with gentle irony and veiled criticism, but it would provide better insurance against moving in his direction if they admitted more openly that the tone he adopts, and the claims he makes, could only be described as fatuous.

Since there are no documents to establish who is who in the Sonnets, the biographer has chiefly to rely on what is known as internal evidence. Yet the poems are remarkable for failing to indicate with any specificity the time and place of the dramas they appear to recount or allude to, and the identity of the people concerned. The speaker in them mainly addresses a man younger than himself but there are no clues to the latter's name, which is ironic given that at one point he says, 'Your name from hence immortal life shall have' (81). There are hints that the younger man, or boy sometimes, has a higher social status than the poet, although none that he is *necessarily* aristocratic. At one point the poet says that he and the other man have known each other for three years. Unfortunately, as all the commentators now point out, three years is a familiar time span in the highly conventionalised world of Elizabethan and Jacobean sonnet-writing; but in any case it is not very helpful to biographers to be told that, at a certain moment, a relationship has lasted three years when there are no indications of when it began.

Chronology in the action of the Sonnets is important because it might throw light on chronology of composition. Recent stylometric analyses suggest that the poems were written at very different periods in Shakespeare's career. But that opens up the distinct possibility that the addressee of them all may not have been the same person and that it is only the order in which they appear which gives that impression. This order is in itself problematic, in that the strange dedication which prefaces the 1609 publication might well suggest that it was not authorised by Shakespeare, and that the sequence in which the poems appear is therefore not necessarily his. From those poems as they stand, it is possible to extract a rough-and-ready narrative involving a young man who is urged to marry and a poet who then declares his love for this same young man, establishing with him a relationship which endures many vicissitudes. After sonnet 126 the focus changes, as the poet now chiefly addresses the dark lady. When, therefore, in some of these later sonnets the poet complains that his own mistress has slept with the young man, it is natural to assume that this is the same mistress and young man as those who feature in sonnet 41, where a similar complaint is made. But that is only because the order in which the Sonnets appear invites us to read them as a more or less coherent story. Whether or not that order was in fact determined by Shakespeare himself, the idea that it corresponds to a similar series of events in his own life, and that he lived through a similar narrative, is clearly impossible to verify.

One simple proof of this last claim is the failure of biographers and scholars to reach any consensus on the identity of the young man, rival poet or dark lady after three hundred years of intense enquiry. It is true that, as far as the addressee of the Sonnets is concerned, Shakespeare's two dedications have made Southampton a popular candidate, but there has long been a strong party in favour of the Earl of Pembroke (who got the nod in Duncan-Jones's 1997 edition of the poems). Because his name was William Herbert he can be fitted easily into Thorpe's dedication without any reversal of the letters, although many have questioned why, if Pembroke is 'W. H.', he could have been referred to as 'Mr.'. Colin Burrow has illustrated the strikingly sycophantic manner in which Thorpe addressed Pembroke on other occasions and suggested that he is unlikely to have dedicated the Sonnets to him unless he had unaccountably 'forgotten how to grovel'.[10] His comment raises another issue associated with having two earls as the chief contenders for the young man of the Sonnets. No one can read the poems without being struck with their extraordinary intimacy of tone; and it is not only that the poet lavishes endearments on the young man but also that he is on occasion willing to criticise him severely, comparing his faults at one point to 'loathsome canker... in sweetest bud' (35). If it could ever be shown beyond doubt that in them Shakespeare was addressing either Southampton or Pembroke (or both), then the common idea we have of relations between commoners and great noblemen in the Elizabethan or Jacobean period might have to be seriously revised.

For those who want to believe in a single addressee for the first 126 sonnets, Southampton and Pembroke are the major figures, but there is more variety when it comes to the dark lady and the rival poet. Marlowe, Jonson and Chapman have all been proposed for the latter role, while dark ladies abound. In *The Genius of Shakespeare*, Bate insisted that 'the case for Southampton as the original patron / youth to whom the Sonnets were addressed looks irrefutable'; but for him the dark lady was not Rowse's Emilia Lanier but rather the sister of Samuel Daniel (author of a sonnet sequence published in 1592 and therefore a candidate for the 'rival poet'). Previous biographers had been keen on one of Elizabeth's maids of honour, Mary Fitton, as the dark lady, but a spanner had been thrown in their works when a portrait was discovered which showed her to be brown-haired and light-skinned. Bate avoided these kinds of difficulty by pointing out that in Elizabethan times 'darkness' should not necessarily be taken literally but is rather an indicator of social status, and that 'one thing we do know about Miss Daniel is that she was a low-born Somerset lass.' At the time Shakespeare could have known her, this woman was the wife of John Florio, and therefore a member of that household of Southampton's which Bate had already decided was the right place to look for the dark lady. She was also the mother of four children, two of whom, Edward and Elizabeth, were born in 1588 and 1589 respectively. Thus, Bate comments, 'The simile in sonnet 143 whereby "Will" compares himself to his mistress's "neglected child" would gain added poignancy if Mrs. Florio really were neglecting young Edward and Elizabeth as she lay in bed with Will.'[11]

Not many people have agreed with Bate in his identifications, but then it would seem that he no longer agrees with them himself. In his second treatment of the matter in *Soul of the Age*, there is no more talk of Mrs Florio and he is no longer so certain that all the sonnets were addressed to Southampton. Yet he does have a fresh candidate for a rival poet in John Davies of Hereford. Bate can show that this minor literary figure could well have been in what he believes is the right place at the right time, and that the references to Shakespeare in Davies's poems indicate that the two were acquainted, but his clinching argument comes from the Sonnets themselves. This is interestingly characteristic, in that it illustrates the choice biographers always have of taking very many of the phrases Shakespeare uses in a more literal rather than metaphorical sense. In the sonnets which refer to the rival, Bate notes, there is strong focus on the other poet's 'pen'. This last word is usually read as a reference to what the rival was able to compose with his 'worthier' or 'well-refin'd pen'; but once it is realised that Davies was far better known for his outstanding *penmanship* than for his compositions (he was a famous teacher of writing in the more literal, physical sense), then in Bate's view it becomes likely that he was at least one of Shakespeare's rivals for the addressee's attention.[12]

What is particularly interesting about Bate is that in both his books he is as convincing as anyone about why it is impossible to read the Sonnets biographically. In the first, he sets out many of the problems of doing so but then confesses that, although he began work on the Sonnets with 'a determination to adhere to an agnostic position on the question of their autobiographical elements', the poems have finally 'wrought their magic' on him (magic in this case meaning the power they supposedly have to tempt readers into a search for real-life equivalents).[13] In the second, he offers a much more comprehensive and definitive account of the obstacles to biographical reading, but then comes up with John Davies of Hereford. It is as if the Sonnets do indeed have a power which is not so much magical as bewitching. Yet Bate's position is not so very different from that of nearly all the other Shakespeare biographers. Stephen Greenblatt, for example, presents himself as a responsible sceptic and writes, 'If even to identify the young man of the first seventeen sonnets as Southampton is rash, to attempt to name these other figures [the rival poet and the dark lady] is beyond rashness.' Without the context, it will not be clear that the person who has committed the rashness of identifying the addressee of the first seventeen sonnets as Southampton is Greenblatt himself, and that he then goes on to assume that Southampton is the young man who features in the succeeding poems. More generally, he cannot resist claiming that the Sonnets show how Shakespeare 'could not find what he craved, emotionally and sexually, within marriage', and that their composition constituted 'acts of erasure' as far as his wife and family were concerned.[14] Like all the other biographers (that is), Greenblatt cannot stop himself taking at least a few steps into what Colin Burrow has memorably called that 'dank pit in which speculation wallows and founders'.[15] Burrow uses this striking phrase in relation to attempts to decode the initials 'W. H.', but although it has special relevance to the problem of who's who in the Sonnets, its application in the field of Shakespeare biography could reasonably be described as very general.

# 9

# *Shakespeare and the love of men*

THERE MAY BE NO way of identifying the participants in the various dramas implied in the Sonnets, yet the poems are nevertheless unique in Shakespeare's work in being written in the first person. This makes it hard for modern readers not to feel that they recognise in them the presence of what the Romantic poets taught us to regard as the autobiographical 'I', and not to believe that the attitudes they convey must therefore be the author's own. In this perspective, what the poems appear to offer are fragments of an emotional biography more direct than anything which can be found in the plays, and thus the closest possible answer to the puzzle of 'what Shakespeare was really like'. It would seem from the Sonnets, for example, that he was someone who began to worry about growing old at what, for us now, would be a relatively early stage in his life:

> That time of year thou mayst in me behold,
> When yellow leaves, or none, or few do hang
> Upon those boughs which shake against the cold
> Bare ruined choirs where late the sweet birds sang. (73)

The last of these famous lines has often been taken as a sign of Shakespeare's Catholic sympathies, his dismay at the dissolution of the monasteries; but the quatrain as a whole is the beginning of a moving lament in which the poet describes himself as in the twilight of his life, apprehensive of death, and expiring on the ashes of his youth. Although it could be that what is expressed is Shakespeare's own feeling at the time, it is important that sonnet

73 is part of a story in which the poet is continually contrasted with a beloved male younger than himself. It heightens the drama of the situation to emphasise the contrast between the two but, in any case, Shakespeare has made us familiar, through characters such as Orsino in *Twelfth Night*, with the extent to which lovers are liable to strike attitudes. There may be no indication of a deliberately struck attitude in sonnet 73 but in number 62 the poet describes himself as looking in the mirror and seeing a face, 'Beaten and chopped with tanned antiquity'. This is a wonderful phrase, although not one which helps us to discriminate between how Shakespeare really looked at this time, how he felt he looked, or how he judged it would be appropriate for a lover to describe himself who wanted dramatically (even melodramatically) to emphasise the difference between himself and the young man to whom he is devoted.

One notion which nearly all the biographers, and especially the more recent ones, have taken from the Sonnets is that Shakespeare was dissatisfied with his life in the theatre. The origins of this belief can be found first in sonnet 110, where the poet admits that he has 'gone here and there', making himself 'a motley to the view'; and then in the following poem, where he regrets that 'Fortune' has not offered him a better living 'than public means, which public manners breed' because, as a result of these, his name has received 'a brand' and his nature been 'subdued / To what it works in, like the dyer's hand'. It ought to be clear that the references to the theatre here are not exactly explicit – if 'making a motley to the view' can be translated as 'making a Fool of oneself', that is one part we can be reasonably certain Shakespeare did *not* play in the theatre since it was reserved for well-known specialist performers such as Will Kemp and Robert Armin. One person who has come to the biographers' aid here is the previously neglected John Davies of Hereford (flavour of the decade in this area of Shakespeare studies). I have already quoted the lines in Davies which have suggested to them that Shakespeare must have played 'kingly parts', and his regret that such distinguished men as Shakespeare and Burbage had been marked out by 'fell Fortune' for acting because, 'though the stage doth stain pure gentle blood / Yet generous ye are in mind and moode' – 'generous' being a word very much like 'gentlemanly' in this context.[1] Their relevance here is that they have been read as a confirmation of how, when the speaker in sonnet 111 complains of the fortune which has condemned him to 'public means, which public manners breed', he must be referring to the theatre, and have consequently been used to bolster the currently fashionable view of Shakespeare as a seeker after status and gentility. But that Davies was what we might now call a snob does not prove that Shakespeare was one also and, even if the usual reading of sonnet 111 is correct (which it could certainly be), it would still be impossible to determine whether the attitude it expresses is Shakespeare's own and not quite as much a part of a drama he is constructing as 'Beaten and chopped with tanned antiquity' might well be also.

Deriving biographical information from the Sonnets means deciding that Shakespeare can be taken in them as speaking directly for himself. It then largely involves assigning specific meanings to general remarks, or deciding that what may seem metaphorical is a literal statement of fact. A famous instance of this last process (which may on many occasions work the other way round) occurs in sonnet 37, where the poet says, 'So I, made lame by Fortune's dearest spite'. From the very beginning of scholarly interest in the Sonnets, there has been a tendency to conclude from this line that Shakespeare must have limped. How early it began can be shown from Malone who, in his 1790 edition of the poems, noted that in this same sonnet the poet goes on to suggest that once he can 'engraft' his love on to the blessings enjoyed by the young man, he will no longer be 'lame, poor, nor despised'. We know Shakespeare was neither poor nor despised, Malone argued, so why should we believe he expected to be taken literally when he said he was lame? The same commentator pointed also to the third line of sonnet 89 ('Speak of my lameness, and I straight will halt'), observing, 'If Shakespeare was in truth lame, he had it not in his power to *halt occasionally*.'[2] But these arguments did not cut much ice in a nineteenth century very largely determined to see in these references Shakespeare's confession that he was indeed, as Walter Scott put it, 'a halting fellow'.[3] That reading is now out of fashion but René Weis has made a determined effort to bring it back, suggesting that, for Elizabethan specialists, 'the idea of a halting or even club-footed Shakespeare is too much to contemplate.' Unafraid to contemplate it himself, he argues vigorously for taking the line in sonnet 37 at face value, and supports his reading by tracing the theme of disability into the plays. It may well be because of Shakespeare's own congenital deformity, he suggests, that he can portray so powerfully Richard III's satisfaction when he successfully woos Anne ('Was Shakespeare equally jubilant when he overcame his Anne's resistance to his advances?'). Extending his analysis further, Weis asks what the 'vicious mole of nature' to which Hamlet refers – the one wherein men are not guilty 'since nature cannot choose his origin' – can possibly be if not a reference to its author's own physical difficulties. He notes that the well-known speech in which these phrases occur comes shortly before the entry of the Ghost (one of the parts which, by tradition, Shakespeare is thought to have played), so that,

> it may be that one of the most celebrated passages of this iconic work of English literature is autobiographical, with Shakespeare again reverting to the predicament which had exercised him so profoundly in his sonnets. The ghost may limp, and the 'mole of nature' may be just that, a club-foot or spinal condition.[4]

Hamlet's 'vicious mole of nature' could seem to many an obvious reference back to Danish drunkenness, and it may seem important that he makes it before he has any idea what the Ghost looks like, but Weis is relying on an audience applying the phrase they have recently heard to Shakespeare as he limps on to the stage. The other part Shakespeare is reputed to have played is Adam in *As You Like It*, so that Weis is able to observe that this character talks of how his 'old limbs lie lame', while Orlando describes him at one moment as 'an poor old man, / Who after me hath many a weary step / Limped in pure love'.[5] Most recent biographers might be inclined to regard commentary of this kind as speculation wildly out of control, but the procedure on which it is based is very similar to the one they themselves often adopt. The manner in which Bate reads the 'pen' of the rival poet falls into the same general category as Weis's decision to take 'made lame by Fortune's dearest spite' literally. None of the biographical conclusions which result can be regarded as reliable without evidence from another quarter.

From the engraving in the First Folio, and perhaps the bust of Shakespeare in Stratford's parish church, it would appear that he lost his hair relatively early, but whether he was concerned about premature balding, or indeed dissatisfied with the theatre, are not matters which could be safely inferred from the Sonnets. It would be no more legitimate to think they were than it is for Peter Ackroyd to claim that we know Shakespeare must have had a 'sure sense of his worth' because 'one of the themes of his sonnets . . . lies in the full expectation that his verse would be read in succeeding ages.'[6] It is true that Shakespeare does declare that expectation on several occasions but to say that one's verse will outlive marble, or 'the guilded monuments / Of Princes', is such a familiar topos of the time that it would be dangerous to infer from it anything relating to his self-confidence. Yet one feeling, or set of attitudes, almost constantly present, is hard to ignore. Shakespeare's Sonnets are very unusual for the period in that most of them appear to be addressed to a man (many of the earlier ones can work just as well as poems written to a woman, but the order in which they appear make a male addressee for the first 126 seem highly likely). What is more, the beauty of the young man in question is constantly emphasised, and the terms used to address him are often exceptionally warm and loving. The natural tendency of a modern reader is to assume that Shakespeare must have been gay or at least – since there are clear expressions in the later sonnets of heterosexual desire and we know that he was married with children – bisexual. This is important because, in modern biography, the sexual orientation and behaviour of the subject has become a vital consideration. Sex is now judged to play such a crucial role in our lives that to ignore it becomes a dereliction of duty, especially since Freud attempted to demonstrate that aspects of personality with which it would appear to have no relation could be traced back to our early observation of sexual activity in adults, sexualised feelings towards our parents, or infantile sexual drives. The huge success, many years ago now, of George Painter's life of Proust or Michael Holroyd's *Lytton Strachey* created an expectation that biographers should deal with their subject's sex lives in similarly absorbing detail, that they should give us chapter and verse. What this means, as far as Shakespeare is concerned, is not merely that we should be told that, in modern parlance, he had 'homosexual tendencies', but also how, where and when he slept with the addressee of the Sonnets.

This is clearly not going to happen yet some recent Shakespeare biographers have attempted to move at least some way towards meeting public expectation in this matter by concentrating their fire on Southampton. A surviving miniature of him by Hilliard from 1594 suggests a somewhat androgynous youth and Duncan-Jones has cited an observation made on Southampton by a soldier who served with or under him in the army which the Earl of Essex had taken to Ireland shortly before his abortive rebellion. He was called William Reynolds and reported how a certain Captain Piers Edmonds ate and drank at Southampton's table during the campaign and 'lay in his tent'. 'The Earl of Southampton', he claimed, 'would clip and hug him in his arms and play wantonly with him.'[7] The first problem here is that a Renaissance portrait showing only the hair and face, like the one by Hilliard, is hardly a reliable indicator of sexual behaviour; the second that Duncan-Jones is herself willing to characterise Reynolds as a 'crazy soldier' who repeatedly denounced the 'sodomitical sins' of city dwellers.[8] His report also comes after the Essex rebellion, when Southampton had become an enemy of the State, and it was routine in the period to denounce such people as sodomites (especially if they happened to be Catholics). The young Earl may, of course, have had what is now known as a homosexual phase but that he cannot afterwards have remained exclusively homosexual is suggested by the trouble he brought on himself by procuring a wife among Elizabeth's maids of honour. Yet whether he was or was not gay, and at this distance in time it is clearly very hard to tell, has little or no bearing on Shakespeare's own sexual practices, and neither can it help to settle the question of whether Southampton was the man to whom most of the sonnets were predominantly or exclusively addressed. It is a paradox of Duncan-Jones's position that she does not think he was, much as she wants to make capital out of Reynolds and suggest that Shakespeare and the young Earl enjoyed a physical relationship.

> It might be thought [she writes on this last topic] that the social difference between the young nobleman and the yeoman playwright was far too wide to permit of physical intimacy. Yet later examples, such as those of Oscar Wilde and E. M. Forster, suggest that wide social difference can in itself act as an aphrodisiac.[9]

The problems of comparing Shakespeare's habits with those of Wilde or Forster will be obvious enough, especially when they are compounded with those of determining whether Shakespeare was, in fact, a practising homosexual, or a homosexual at all. The word is a relatively recent one and hard to apply to a culture like the Elizabethan or Jacobean, where men openly expressed their love for one another and such expressions might easily be accompanied by hugging and kissing. The way in which Shakespeare depicts the love of Antonio for Bassanio in *The Merchant of Venice* hardly suggests that he felt, or expected his audience to feel, that there was anything transgressive in this older man's intense devotion, or that it implied past or future contact of an explicitly sexual nature. Since sodomy was a capital crime in the period, it could be argued that this is not surprising in such a public arena as the theatre but that the Sonnets (which Shakespeare may well not have wanted to publish) are a different, more private matter. Yet this brings the question back once again to the nature of the Sonnets themselves. In a book entitled *Homosexuality in Renaissance England*, Alan Bray looked closely at Richard Barnfield, the author of the only other surviving sonnet sequence to be addressed to a male in Shakespeare's time. Noting that entries made in Barnfield's commonplace book were 'both robustly pornographic and entirely heterosexual', Bray insisted that it would be wrong to make too much of the very distinct homoerotic elements in Barnfield's published work and warned against 'the assumption – which should never be made with Elizabethan or Jacobean poetry without independent support – that they are the product of personal experience'.[10] More recently, Colin Burrow has said of the Sonnets that ' "Shakespeare's homosexuality" is a readerly fiction generated by a desire to read narrative coherence into a loosely associated group of poems.'[11]

There is a danger here in citing Bray and Burrow of appearing to want to defend Shakespeare against what can easily sound like a *charge* of homosexuality. This is a position into which some of his biographers like to manœuvre their critics so that they can then accuse them of being mealy-mouthed, wedded to conventional ideas and latter-day Bardolaters. There is a reluctance, Weis claims, to accept the idea of a Shakespeare who was disabled and Greenblatt says that there is a similar reluctance to think of him as a poacher. Some would say there is also a reluctance to acknowledge that he was homosexual, that this is a notion some find too disagreeable to contemplate. Because the subject is still a somewhat sensitive one, it is hard to find the right tone in which to insist forcefully that this is certainly not so here. Apart from his known association with women, or one of them at least, Shakespeare may well have had sexual relations with boys or with men. That is certainly one of the many possibilities of his life experience, yet whether he did or not cannot be known without that 'independent support' to which Bray refers and which, as in so many other instances, is sadly lacking. 'Whereof one cannot speak, thereof one must keep silent,' Wittgenstein famously says, and that is certainly a rule which seems appropriate when dealing with such an intimate and difficult to investigate matter as sexual orientation and behaviour.

# 10

## *Shakespeare and the love of women*

Anxiety to defend Shakespeare against any suggestion of homosexuality left many commentators in the nineteenth century between a rock and a hard place. Not wanting to find anything which might disturb them in the first 126 sonnets, they tended to concentrate instead on the remainder, only to be forced to conclude – since they were reading biographically – that Shakespeare must have been an adulterer. Yet rather a National Bard who cheated on his wife than one who was gay, and there were ways of obscuring the idea of adultery by talking Shakespeare up as red-blooded, someone whose writings exhibited (as Rowse puts it) 'the natural bawdy of the highly sexed normal heterosexual'.[1] This tactic may help to explain the popularity then, and indeed since, of the well-known Manningham anecdote. John Manningham was a law student at the Middle Temple and in 1602 recorded the following in his diary or commonplace book:

> Upon a tyme when Burbidge played Richard III, there was a Citizen grewe soe farr in liking with him, that before shee went from the play shee appointed him to come that night unto hir by the name of Richard III. Shakespeare, overhearing their conclusion, went before, was intertained, and at his game ere Burbidge came. Then message being brought that Richard III was at the dore, Shakespeare caused returne to be made that William the Conquerour was before Richard III. Shakespeare's name William. (Mr. Touse.)[2]

Manningham noted down this story along with three others (all of them more or less comic), and he indicated his source in each case. The man who told him about Shakespeare and Burbage was probably William Towse – the name has proved hard to read – who was not an actor but another member of the Middle Temple.

One reason why this story has found such favour can be found in its date; almost all the others originate at least fifty years after Shakespeare's death and are for that reason immediately suspect, but this is from his own time. A second is that its truth has been felt by some to have been confirmed. Anyone reading what Manningham says might well wonder why it is that, if the citizen's wife was expecting Burbage, Shakespeare was so readily entertained. This problem was addressed when what is recognisably the same anecdote appeared more than 150 years later in Thomas Wilkes's *General View of the Stage* (1759). Wilkes provides more detail than Manningham and at one point fills the latter's narrative gap by saying,

> The lady was very much surprised at Shakespeare's presuming to act Mr Burbage's part; but as he (who wrote *Romeo and Juliet*), we may be certain, did not want wit and eloquence to apologize for the intrusion, she was soon pacified, and they were mutually happy till Burbage came to the door.[3]

It has been thought important that Manningham's diary was not discovered until the nineteenth century and that Wilkes is therefore very unlikely to have copied the anecdote from him. This opens the possibility of two different sources for the same story and has prompted Bate to say (in his first book) that its two versions provide 'independent corroboration of the incident's underlying truth'.[4] It is this supposedly 'independent corroboration' which has combined with its date to make the Manningham anecdote so popular.

Yet, of course, the existence of two different versions of the story of Shakespeare, Burbage and the citizen's wife in no way confirms its truth. One way of seeing that is to think of all the comic stories which used to circulate a few years ago about George W. Bush. If, in a hundred years, two different versions of one of these survived from different sources, they would hardly be reliable indicators of how he had behaved in certain circumstances, or proof that he was quite that dim. The story Manningham recorded is a *joke*, which is highly relevant to the question of its reliability (factual accuracy not being the most striking feature of the comic imagination); and it is the least trustworthy kind of joke in that it is elaborated around, and quite possibly originates with, an all-important punch-line. No one can expect the truth from someone trying to ensure that a punch-line works and there are, in any case, improbabilities in the story which are only partly resolved by Wilkes.

Considerable though these improbabilities may be, they are not of a kind to deter Duncan-Jones, who assumes that what is involved in Manningham's anecdote is an off-stage version of those 'bed tricks' in Elizabethan and Jacobean drama which would strain credulity were not the element of convention in them not so recognisable. What she feels able to deduce from the story is that 'there was a strong physical similarity' between Shakespeare and Burbage: 'the substitution could not have been attempted', she writes, 'unless the two men were of similar height, build, colouring and, perhaps above all, voice.' The further conclusion she draws is that Shakespeare must have been an excellent actor since 'on this occasion he successfully impersonated Burbage, and a Burbage who had come freshly from one of his most powerful (and sexy) performances.'[5] This is a staggeringly speculative biographical haul on two matters which have always intrigued Shakespeare's admirers: what he looked like and how gifted he was on the stage. But it is only made possible by Duncan-Jones's decision to ignore the version of the story provided by Wilkes since he suggests that the lady was surprised to find Shakespeare 'presuming to act Mr Burbage's part' and had to be talked round. The question of how legitimately Duncan-Jones achieves her results is perhaps less important here, however, than the use she makes of the Manningham anecdote to support a view she has of Shakespeare's character, and her feeling that he lacked respect 'either for women or for female intelligence'. Reverting to the story when she is pondering aloud why Shakespeare should have had dealings with both the writer George Wilkins and Sir William Dethick, the Garter King of Arms and another man who had 'a nasty habit of making physical attacks on women', she notes that what Manningham describes 'gives Shakespeare himself a reputation as quite a "lad" – not, perhaps, violent towards women, but more than happy to view a woman opportunistically as "fair game"', and she then complains (to whom or about whom is not entirely clear) that 'there was no question of considering the sensitivities of a woman who fancied Burbage but ended up in bed with Shakespeare.'[6] The character of prominent figures from the past is no doubt a legitimate object of enquiry, but if it is going to be blackened, one hopes that it will usually be on better grounds than Duncan-Jones provides here.

Bate, Duncan-Jones and Weis all make extensive use of the

Manningham anecdote but Greenblatt ignores it, as does Bate in his second book. The interesting case is Shapiro, who introduces it as an illustration that, however 'gentle' Shakespeare might perhaps have been, he was not necessarily a pliant man in his relations with other members of the Lord Chamberlain's Men. The text from Manningham is quoted in full and introduced with the explanation that he had 'jotted it down in March 1602 (though the apocryphal story may already have been in circulation for a few years)'.[7] The adjective is easy to miss on first reading but, once noticed, is bound to prompt a reader to ask why on earth Shapiro has not only included the story in his narrative, but also taken it as evidence of an aspect of Shakespeare's character, if he does not believe it to be true. One answer might be that many biographers like to have their cake and eat it, but also that slipping 'apocryphal' into a parenthetical phrase is a clear illustration of that search after plausible deniability I mentioned in my second chapter.

An example of some of the linguistic devices alluded to in that chapter which is particularly flagrant, and therefore easy to illustrate, can be found in one biographer's dealings with another popular story which supports the idea of a Shakespeare who was a red-blooded heterosexual, with the same kind of virile qualities as those evinced in the poaching episode. This is the one told by Aubrey who, writing in the late seventeenth century about the Restoration dramatist Sir William Davenant, claimed that Shakespeare knew Davenant's parents and would always stay at the inn they kept at Oxford on his annual trips back to Stratford from London.

> Sir William [he went on] would sometimes, when he was pleasant over a glasse of wine with his most intimate friends e.g. Sam: Butler, (author of *Hudibras*) etc., say, that it seemed to him that he writt with the very spirit that Shakespeare [did], and seemed contented enough to be thought his Son: he would tell them a story as above, [in which his mother had a very light report, whereby she was called a whore].[8]

In the seventeenth century, writers who admired Jonson were known as 'the sons of Ben' so that it might be thought that Davenant, an enthusiastic promoter of Shakespeare's work, was here using the same kind of language. But Aubrey's final sentence denies this and Spence reported having heard Pope say that 'the notion of Sir William Davenant being more than a poetical child only of Shakespeare, was common in town; & Sir William himself seemed fond of having it taken for truth.'[9] Around 1742, Spence also reported a story which involved the young Davenant being called back from school because Shakespeare had arrived to stay with his parents. On his way home the boy met the head of one of the colleges, who asked him why he was in such a hurry. It was because, the boy replied, his godfather Shakespeare was in town, whereupon the don reproached him with, 'Fie, child . . . have you not learnt that you should not use the name of God in vain?'[10] Like the Manningham anecdote, this is recognisably – *just* recognisably – a joke and like that story it also exists in two versions. As early as 1709, the antiquarian Thomas Hearne recorded the gist in his diary, describing the story as something 'reported by Tradition in Oxford'.[11] One has to feel that this 'tradition' is one which Davenant had started with his half-playful allusions to his parentage, although its antecedents must be older than that suggests since this same joke about a godfather appears in a jest book published in 1629, but with quite different participants.[12]

A great deal of labour has been expended on an effort to discover the facts of the Davenant case and whether, in the first instance, his parents and Shakespeare were indeed close friends: they appeared to have lived in London until 1601 before moving to Oxford, where the tavern they kept did not provide accommodation so that, if Shakespeare did stay with them, it could only have been as a guest. In his biography, Anthony Holden ignores the insuperable difficulties of proving a close connection and simply repeats Aubrey's assertion that Shakespeare 'would always break his two-day ride' between Stratford and London by staying at the same tavern in Oxford where 'John and Jeanette Davenant were long-standing friends'. He concedes that Davenant *fils* was an engaging rogue, and that his boast of being Shakespeare's son may therefore have been wishful thinking, but he then moves to dispel the doubts he has raised by noting that 'four centuries of detective work have failed to disprove' the relationship. I have already pointed out how common this move is but here what is interesting are devices which are as much linguistic as logical. These are clearly in evidence when, in reference to the Davenant affair, Holden writes that, according to Plutarch, Cleopatra was thirty-eight at the time of her 'tempestuous fling' with Mark Antony, 'exactly the same age as Jeanette Davenant while Shakespeare was writing *Antony and Cleopatra*'. Unfortunately for symmetry, Shakespeare himself was forty-three, 'some ten years younger than Antony'. Still, 'was it pure coincidence, if he was bedding the wife of the Oxford tavern-keeper, that he now chose to conjure – through the besotted eyes of an older man – the most alluring, highly-sexed woman ever to emerge even from his capacious and libidinous imagination?'. This is the familiar rhetorical question but more significant is the way the word 'if' has been so encapsulated into a general speculation about the relation of literature to life that it loses its conditional force. Something similar occurs when, a little later in his book, Holden is discussing Shakespeare's situation in 1608. 'Over the last four years,' he writes, '[Shakespeare] had put himself under tremendous strain: if his private life had remained adventurous, if indeed he had suffered the stress of an eventful extra-marital affair, he had also produced three of his mightiest tragedies.' Although the presence of two 'ifs' in this sentence suggests that Holden is keeping open the possibility that all he has had to say about Shakespeare and Jeanette Davenant is conjectural, the reader is clearly being persuaded into assuming it is not because the meaning which has in fact been given to those 'ifs' is 'even though'.[13]

Holden's book was published in 1999. In the following decade, the academic biographers showed more caution than he does in dealing with the Davenant material, although René Weis is a predictable exception. William Davenant was born in 1606, which means he must have been conceived the year before, the possible date of composition for one of Shakespeare's greatest plays. 'It may be', Weis writes, 'that Jane Davenant's information about her pregnancy triggered *King Lear*' (given the importance in it of Gloucester's adultery). The tense or mood of the verb here might suggest that the reader can still regard Shakespeare's affair with Mrs Davenant (called here Jane) as no more than a possibility; but Weis goes on to speculate that the relationship between Lear and Goneril in the play could well reflect that between Shakespeare and his elder daughter, Susanna, saying then of the latter: 'If she had found out about his affair with Jane Davenant, that would be explanation enough of difficulties between father and daughter.'[14] Here, in order to make room for a conjecture about Shakespeare's family relations, his extramarital affair has to become a certainty. Something roughly analogous can be seen in Stephen Greenblatt's biography. He is careful, in relaying the information from Aubrey, not to give the impression of endorsing it but he then notes that, if Davenant's 'heavy hints' about his paternity had any truth in them, 'Shakespeare would have been in Oxford at various times in the late spring and summer of 1605.' This is important for Greenblatt because, when the royal family visited Oxford in August of that year, they were greeted with a theatrical performance which he feels had a significant influence on the composition of *Macbeth*. As part of the ceremonies, three boys dressed as sibyls spoke of King James's family tree, stressing the importance in it of Banquo and predicting a prosperous future. This was, Greenblatt says, 'a welcoming event ... that seems to have particularly interested Shakespeare' and whether he 'stood in the crowd watching it or heard it from one of the bystanders – [it] seems to have stuck in the playwright's imagination'.[15] Although the reference to bystanders provides Greenblatt with the usual get-out clause, the general impression readers are left with is that they have had implicitly confirmed Shakespeare's presence in Oxford in the Summer of 1605, and therefore the Davenant story.

If material of the Davenant variety was not included in biographies of Shakespeare, plastered or not with health warnings, they would all look much more like Bill Bryson's lively and intelligent *Shakespeare: The World as Stage* (2007), which largely steers clear of trouble and as a result weighs in at only a quarter or third of its academic competitors. But the story has a special attraction because of its relevance to the question of Shakespeare's sexual nature which is felt to be raised by the Sonnets. Byron and D. H. Lawrence are two other writers who have been thought to be bisexual but when one thinks of the difficulty of establishing details of their sexual behaviour with any certainty, despite the wealth of material available, it is hardly likely that we will ever learn anything in this regard about a man who died almost four hundred years ago. This can be celebrated, as far as the Sonnets are concerned, by those who value them precisely for their enigmatic nature. But there are rich and rewarding ambiguities and others which are merely frustrating, so that it is hard to disagree with Lawrence when, in a short biographical introduction to a collection of his own poems, he writes: 'If we knew a little more of Shakespeare's self and circumstance how much more complete the Sonnets would be to us, how their strange, torn edges would be softened and merged into a whole body.'[16] That this will never happen as far as the poems' sexual content is concerned, is perhaps not quite the disaster it might seem for biography. There is a case for thinking that sex is not always and consistently as central to every individual's life as we are encouraged to believe, and that there are other impulses which play an equally important role – the desire people have for status and to be thought well of by others, for example. That is a driving motive which people who work in universities understand very well so that it is perhaps not too surprising that, in the recent flurry of biographies of Shakespeare written by academics, his striving after gentility has been a major theme. The trouble is that the evidence for that aspect of his character is no more convincing that it is for him as the lover of Southampton or the father of William Davenant.

# 11

## *Friends*

FRIENDS OF THE CENTRAL figure can often play a vital role in life-writing. It is from their records that biographers gather useful information about their subject's habits or behaviour, while who or what the friends were sometimes provides an important clue to that subject's character. A life of Virginia Woolf which did not take account of the phenomenon known as Bloomsbury would be inconceivable, and it would be an inadequate biography of Dr Johnson which failed to pay at least some attention to his relations with the other members of his famous club. There may well be literary figures who were completely friendless, deeply misanthropic, but it is hard to think who they are. Byron is someone who was thought to have chosen a life of deliberate isolation but that reputation was a consequence of what he wrote rather than the way the lived. In his private life he was a sociable individual, forming a warm and close friendship with a man he first met at Cambridge (John Cam Hobhouse) and then, later, with his fellow poet Shelley. That Shakespeare had no close friends seems highly improbable so that what one would like to discover is who they were and how his relations with them began, developed and (in some cases, perhaps) deteriorated. Anyone who has read this far will not be surprised to learn both that this is an impossible task and that there is a long tradition of Shakespeare's biographers bending over backwards not to make it seem so.

One individual whom almost all the biographers are convinced was Shakespeare's friend is Richard Field. When Katherine Duncan-Jones refers to Shakespeare's 'old friend, the printer and publisher

Richard Field', or Jonathan Bate talks of the 'undoubted friendship' of Shakespeare with Field, they are treading where hundreds have trod before.[1] The circumstantial evidence for their assumption can seem quite strong. In the first place, Field was also from Stratford, only migrating to London at the age of seventeen in order to be apprenticed to a printer. That he could do this implies that he was educated and where else would he have received the requisite education than at the same grammar school which there is such a strong presumption Shakespeare also attended (hence Bate's description of Field as an 'old school-friend' of Shakespeare and Duncan-Jones's reference to him as 'Shakespeare's Stratford school-fellow'[2])? The father of Field was a tanner, a trade closely allied with glove-making, and when he died John Shakespeare was appointed one of the assessors of the goods he left behind. This suggests that the two men knew each other, as they almost inevitably would in a small provincial town with a relatively restricted class of artisans.

Here, then, is the groundwork for a friendship between Shakespeare and Field but, for those wanting to believe in it, there is what seems like much more. During his early years in London, Field lived the Elizabethan apprentice's dream. The printer for whom he mostly worked was a Huguenot refugee called Thomas Vautrollier and, when he died, Field married either his widow or his daughter (the scholars are not sure which) and took over the business. He was thus very much his own man when, in 1593, he undertook the printing of Shakespeare's immensely popular *Venus and Adonis* and then, about a year later, its successor, *The Rape of Lucrece*. This indicates what must have been at least a professional relation between the two men from Stratford and an important advantage to biographers of making it more is that doing so solves what has always been one of their major problems. It is clear from Shakespeare's plays that he must have been familiar with a number of books which would have been too expensive for him to buy. How he acquired access to them is a puzzle which can be enlisted in support of the idea that he had a long relationship with the Earl of Southampton but which has otherwise given rise to some outlandish theories: that as a boy he was taken to be educated in a local aristocrat's household, for instance, or even that he only pretended to write the plays while the real author was someone like the Earl of Oxford, who was better educated and had the means to buy as many costly books as he pleased. Shakespeare's supposed friendship with

Field obviates the need for such extravagances since a book such as North's Plutarch, or the 1589 Latin edition of Ovid's *Metamorphoses*, came in fact from his printing shop. That his business specialised in books at the expensive end of the market has made it easy for biographers to imagine that when Shakespeare needed to consult or work with a book the purchase of which was well beyond his means, he simply went round to see Field. Duncan-Jones puts the familiar case when she talks of the 'possibility, or even likelihood that Shakespeare regularly used Field's printing house in Blackfriars, near Ludgate, as a working library, and even did his writing there'.[3] As a general claim about where and how Shakespeare worked, this runs into the difficulty of the wide variety of sources he used, by no means all of which can be associated with Field. Stephen Greenblatt points out, for example, that *The Mirror for Magistrates* and Holinshed's *Chronicles*, two crucial sources for Shakespeare's early historical writing, 'were not published by Field or his former master Vautrollier'; but he then goes on to add, making the best of a bad job, 'it is quite possible that Shakespeare's friend may have owned copies or put him in touch with those who did.'[4] The idea that Field was a close enough friend of Shakespeare to allow him to drop into a busy printing shop whenever he liked, make free with the books that happened to be there or discover from him where they could be found, brings such intellectual, problem-solving rewards that biographers find it hard to abandon. Shakespeare and Field must have been good friends, they often appear to be saying, because, if they were not, how else could one explain Shakespeare's access to expensive books? They seem to prefer the risk of creating the impression that they believe in the friendship chiefly because it suits them to do so, to the acknowledgement that the surviving information prevents anyone from making clear how Shakespeare came by many of his sources.

Shakespeare and Field were probably at school together and they must have had commercial dealings when they were both in London (individuals from the same town who came to the capital certainly tended to help each other out and stick together); but there is no conclusive evidence of *friendship* and there are several minor details which ought to make one hesitate before speculating about it so confidently. The most significant of these is perhaps the affair of the Blackfriars theatre. This was a building bought by James Burbage (father of Richard) in 1596 for the considerable sum of £600, and he then spent a lot more money fitting it out as a suitable indoor venue for the Lord Chamberlain's Men. But when he wanted to begin using it, there were strong and effective objections from a number of influential local residents which prevented him from doing so. One of the residents who signed the petition against the opening of the theatre was Richard Field. This could certainly be construed as an unfriendly act against Shakespeare, whose interests were so strongly tied to those of the Burbages, but it would perhaps be a mistake to draw that conclusion since it would imply there is enough available evidence regarding relations between Shakespeare and Field to make any debate either for or against the idea of their friendship meaningful. Not wanting to give up the idea that the two Stratford men were friends, but perhaps uneasily conscious of how little justification there is for it, biographers have sought a clinching argument, and they have found it in one of the first plays to be staged at the Blackfriars playhouse when, in 1608, Shakespeare's company was finally able to move there, long after any recorded relationship between him and Field.

'Uniquely among Shakespeare's Warwickshire friends', writes Duncan-Jones, 'Field achieved a friendly allusion in one of the plays,' and she then describes the moment in *Cymbeline* when Innogen, disguised as a page, comes across a headless corpse.[5] Because this corpse is dressed in the clothes of her exiled husband Posthumous, Innogen assumes that it must be his, whereas it is in fact the body of the doltish Cloton, whom her evil step-mother had wanted her to marry. After she has spent some time bewailing her apparent loss, an officer of the invading Roman army enters and asks the 'page' with whom he is confronted for the name of his dead master. Not wishing to say anything which might reveal her own identity, Innogen tells him that it is 'Richard du Champ'. Several of the recent annotated editions, and almost all the biographers, take this to be what Duncan-Jones calls a 'friendly allusion' to Richard Field, some of them citing in support the way in which, in Spanish editions of Protestant propaganda which he printed, Field would refer to himself on the title pages as 'Ricardo del Campo'. Campo does, of course, mean a field, but it hardly helps those who find this significant that, in the books in French for which Field was responsible, his name retains its English form.

Shakespeare and Field, writes James Shapiro, 'were close enough friends for Shakespeare to casually insert Field's name into *Cymbeline*', hinting at the weakness of his position with his adverb.[6] The sudden appearance of a French name in a play about Romans and Britons which takes place well before the Norman Conquest is certainly strange, but then anachronism is hardly an unfamiliar phenomenon in Shakespeare. It could nevertheless be that when he was looking for the name of a French knight, his former printer was at the forefront of his mind; but it could be also that he chose 'du Champ' because, as French names go, it is very much in the Smith / Jones category. The main problem does not, however, lie in this area but in interpreting 'du Champ' as an act or proof of friendship. Even if Richard du Champ is a reference to Richard Field, a possibility which must always remain doubtful and could never be confirmed, its purpose is far from clear. Duncan-Jones points out that, in trying to deceive the Roman officer, Innogen says the headless corpse is that of 'my master / A very valiant Briton, and a good'; yet the audience has been made vividly aware that it is in fact the body of the mentally challenged Cloton, who had thought it would be a good idea to rape Innogen wearing her husband's clothes. Associating an individual one knew with the corpse could therefore only be deeply equivocal, a gesture that might be either friendly, hostile or ironic, or then again, purely accidental, according to the time of day. René Weis, never fearful that he might over-egg the pudding, has tried to reinforce the Field identification by pointing out that, when Innogen is asked for her own name by the Roman officer, she says it is 'Fidele'. This, he observes, is a version of the French *fidèle* (and Field was married to a Frenchwoman), but also 'very close to an anagram of Field'.[7] Most readers are likely to find this kind of reasoning spectacularly unconvincing, but it is hardly less so than that which has tried to make 'du Champ' a tribute to Shakespeare's 'old friend' Richard Field.

In Shakespeare's time, the word 'friend' had (like so many other of the words he uses) nuances which we have largely lost. When, for example, Macbeth laments that his crimes mean he cannot look forward to such benefits of old age as 'honour, love, obedience, troops of friends', the last word indicates something nearer to what we might call followers or supporters. Yet friendship in the modern sense was fully understood and Elizabethans must have been as aware as we are that it exists in many different forms. Those established at school often depend on contemporaneity, so that it might (or might not) be significant that Field was at least two-and-a-half years older than Shakespeare. These school friendships are like all those with people from one's local area in that, as they develop, they tend to rely more on accidental proximity and shared experience than on common intellectual interests. Shakespeare's will suggests that he certainly had local friends, the Hamnet Sadler, for example, after whom he appears to have named his own son and to whom he left the traditional two marks, or 26 shillings and sixpence, to buy a mourning ring. Several other Stratford residents also received the same amount for rings, although the nature of Shakespeare's relations with them, the extent (that is) to which these were or were not largely professional, is not clear. The individuals who were not local and to whom in 1616 he also left money for mourning rings are Burbage, Heminges and Condell, the three surviving members of the original Lord Chamberlain's Men. They were former business associates and representatives of the life he had led in London. It was another of these associates, the actor Augustine Phillips, who, when he died in 1605, had left Shakespeare thirty shillings in his will. Bequests of this kind may have involved some degree of social obligation or convention but, in Shakespeare's case, they are perhaps the strongest evidence we have that he did have friends he valued in both Stratford and London. Field has been attractive to biographers because he has seemed to bridge the gap between the two groups, so that it is a blow to them that, although in 1616 he was alive and well, his own name appears nowhere in Shakespeare's will.

What one would really like to know is not so much the fellow actors but the fellow *writers* Shakespeare knew in London, and whether there were any of them with whom he could discuss his craft. Biographers who seek to answer this question, and discover which of the playwrights of the day might have been his friends, are naturally drawn to the two candidates about whom there is most information. Marlowe is then not much use to them because he was killed towards the very beginning of Shakespeare's career and, despite René Weis's claim that 'it would have been odd indeed had [Marlowe and Shakespeare] not been close as friends and rivals,'[8] there is no evidence that the two men knew each other well. But Ben Jonson is a different matter. Eight years younger than Shakespeare, it was not until 1598 that the Lord Chamberlain's Men put on Jonson's *Every Man In His Humour*. According to Nicholas Rowe, writing in 1709, the members of the Lord Chamberlain's Men who first had this play presented to them were unenthusiastic and it was Shakespeare himself who realised its merits and persuaded his colleagues to accept it. Edmund Malone famously said of Rowe's biography that it contained only eleven facts, eight of which were wrong and one of which was doubtful,[9] so this otherwise unsupported story of Shakespeare's intervention ought perhaps to be taken with a pinch of salt. Yet since we know that the Chamberlain's Men not only staged *Every Man In His Humour* but that Shakespeare was later listed by Jonson as having acted in it, there is a strong presumption that the two men were well acquainted. How well acquainted is then the obvious but impossible question.

According to a tradition which developed from the middle of the seventeenth century, the answer is very well. In a book published in 1662 entitled a *History of the Worthies of England*, Thomas Fuller talks of the many 'wit combats' which took place between Shakespeare and Jonson in which the younger man was like a Spanish galleon, heavily freighted with learning, while the older, who carried less baggage, resembled a nippy English man of war (and everyone remembered who had won that battle).[10] The man who arrived to be the vicar of Stratford in 1662 reported local gossip which referred to a 'merry meeting' which had taken place between Jonson, Michael Drayton (fellow writer and Warwickshire man) and Shakespeare, just before the latter died.[11] The location for this was supposed to be Stratford itself but, as the legend of 'merry meetings' developed, they were usually assumed to have taken place in London at the Mermaid Inn. In the dramatisations of Shakespeare's life which became particularly numerous in the nineteenth century, it is nearly always in the Mermaid that the two men are shown exchanging pleasantries, quaffing good English ale, and pritheeing each other to their hearts' content. Anthony Burgess keeps up the tradition these texts established when, in his biography of Shakespeare, he says that 'Ben and Will, over a fish dinner at the Mermaid, ... argued much about their art.'[12] The choice of establishment is not entirely fanciful. In a poem addressed to Jonson which dates from around 1613, and is assumed to be by Francis Beaumont, the author writes, 'What things we have seen / Done at the Mermaid! Heard words that have been / So nimble, and so full of subtle flame';[13] and when Shakespeare finally bought a London property in 1613, one of the people who assisted him in the transaction appears to have been the landlord of the Mermaid. But of course whether Shakespeare and Jonson ate and drank together there is unknown, as is the nature of any conversations they may then have had.

On this last point, dubious assistance is available from Nicholas L'Estrange, who died in 1655 leaving a manuscript collection of 'Merry Passages and Jests'. One of these concerns Jonson and

Shakespeare and is worth quoting in full, not because it has any particular credibility but because it further illustrates an important point about the use of evidence in biography already made in the previous chapter:

> Shakespeare was Godfather to one of Ben Jonsons children, and after the christning being in a deepe study, Jonson came to cheere him up, and askt him why he was so Melancholy? no faith *Ben* (says he) not I, but I have been considering a great while what should be the fittest gift for me to bestow upon my God-child, and I have resolv'd at last; I pry'the what, says he? I faith *Ben:* I'll e'en give him a douzen good Lattin Spoones, and thou shalt translate them.[14]

The problem here is not so much that there is no evidence of Shakespeare ever having been a godfather to one of Jonson's children, nor that the joke recorded seems rather feeble (some of the jokes in the early plays are pretty feeble also). It lies rather in the very fact of its *being a joke*, one which is based on the similarity in sound between Latin as a language and the latten which was a copper alloy, much like brass, widely used in Elizabethan times. That the joke has been adapted to the people involved, playing as it does on that superiority in classical learning which Jonson had publicly implied he held over Shakespeare, does nothing to guarantee its historical authenticity. All the objections against using the Manningham diary entry as evidence apply with equal force here. Most recent biographers of Shakespeare have steered clear of the Latin / latten anecdote, although Jonathan Bate has claimed that, 'regardless of its factual basis', the story 'has the authentically *representative* truth of anecdote. It shows us a Shakespeare who thinks quickly and who likes to tease.'[15] Certainly, for people who believe they already know that Shakespeare thought quickly and liked to tease, the unverified and unverifiable spoons story might be representative and provide confirmation, although, as far as the first part of that belief is concerned, it shows him thinking slowly rather than quickly; but for anyone curious to know what kind of relationship Shakespeare and Jonson enjoyed, it strikes me as having no biographical value. Confidence in it can hardly be increased by the knowledge that, in another manuscript collection roughly contemporary to that of L'Estrange, the joke about the spoons also occurs, although in that case it is Shakespeare's child who is being christened and Jonson who is given the all-important punch-line, what Schoenbaum ironically refers to as 'the devastating stroke of wit'.[16]

## Friends

Some form of relationship the two dramatists nevertheless did have. We know that because Shakespeare's company put on Jonson's plays but, more obviously, from the fact that it was Jonson who wrote the long, commemorative poem which appears at the beginning of the First Folio: 'To the memory of my beloved, The Author Mr. William Shakespeare: And what he hath left us'. The appearance of 'beloved' here might appear to settle any argument as to whether Jonson and Shakespeare were intimate, yet the word was much more easily employed in the early seventeenth century than it is now and does not necessarily and inevitably imply close friendship. What 'beloved' might reasonably lead one to expect, on the other hand, are some incidental personal details about the individual to whom it is applied, whereas, in fact, Jonson's poem is all about Shakespeare's writing and says very little about the man. Almost the only biographical information it conveys is that Shakespeare had little Latin and less Greek, the point of this remark being that he nevertheless wrote works which compare favourably with anything 'insolent Greece, or haughty Rome' produced. When Jonson calls him the *sweet* Swan of Avon he is referring to the reputation Shakespeare had in his younger days for writing particularly mellifluous verse, and even his reference to him as 'gentle' (in the poem but also in the verses opposite the title page with its portrait – 'This figure which thou here see'st put, / It was for gentle Shakespeare cut') may be as much an allusion to social status as character. His use of 'beloved' in his title might suggest that writing the poem was a labour of love, which it could well have been; but it was also clearly a commission in which the restraint tradition imposes on anyone writing about the dead is coupled with a need to say things which would advertise and sell a book. The result is a stream of unqualified and rather general expressions of admiration for Shakespeare's writing which, were the subject any other author, one would be tempted to call extravagant: the antithesis of the measured judgement which the other Johnson was to produce in his *Preface to Shakespeare*.

Jonson's tone about Shakespeare is rather different when the circumstances are more informal. After his own death, a number of his loose papers containing ideas for further work, as well as all sorts of random reflections, were hastily brought together and published under the title *Timber: or, Discoveries*. Among them were to be found the following remarks about Shakespeare:

> I remember, the Players have often mentioned it as an honour to Shakespeare, that in his writing, (whatsoever he penned) he never blotted out line. My answer hath been, 'Would he had blotted a thousand!' Which they thought a malevolent speech. I had not told posterity this, but for their ignorance, who chose that circumstance to commend their friend by, wherein he most faulted. And to justify mine own candour, (for I loved the man, and do honour his memory (on this side idolatry) as much as any.) He was, (indeed) honest, and of an open, and free nature: had an excellent Phantasy; brave notions, and gentle expressions: wherein he flowed with that facility, that sometime it was necessary he should be stopped. '*Sufflaminandus erat*'; as Augustus said of Haterius. His wit was in his own power; would the rule of it had been so too! Many times he fell into those things, could not escape laughter: As when he said in the person of Caesar, one speaking to him: *Caesar thou dost me wrong*. He replied: *Caesar did never wrong, but with just cause* and such like: which were ridiculous. But he redeemed his vices, with his virtues. There was ever more in him to be praised, than to be pardoned.[17]

What is most immediately striking about this passage is that it partially contradicts what Jonson had said in his poem. There he had insisted that Shakespeare not only was naturally gifted but had worked hard to improve his gifts, 'For a good poet's made, as well as born. / And such wert thou.' Here he complains that Shakespeare did not always work hard enough. The passage confirms that he admired Shakespeare immensely, so that there is no reason to think of the *bulk* of his poem as hypocritical; but it suggests that he was exasperated by the general tendency his own poem had exemplified to think of Shakespeare as a writer who could do no wrong. He could sometimes, Jonson insists here, write silly and illogical lines, although the example he chooses appears trivial and does not, in any case, appear in the First Folio (where the only surviving text of *Julius Caesar* is to be found).

All this is interesting but the main reason for quoting the *Timber* passage in full is that it contains a rare item of genuine biographical information. Like a diamond buried in a heap of glass beads, this is not often given the prominence it deserves because, in their efforts to overcome the impassable barriers to a life of Shakespeare, biographers tend to lump it together with the worthless material they would like us to believe is equally informative. It is true that the diamond is tiny but when Jonson says that he loved Shakespeare who was honest ('the most laudatory term in Jonson's lexicon of praise', according to Schoenbaum[18]), and of an open and free nature, we should be inclined to believe him because he makes this declaration in a private context and without any obvious expectation of being published. It helps also that the remark is casual, wholly subsidiary to the main point he wants to make about Shakespeare's writing. 'Loved' is, of course, open to the same problems of changing usage as 'beloved' in the title of Jonson's poem, but its appearance in this informal context shows that there is no need to regard the words in that title as dictated by convention, and that he must have liked Shakespeare a good deal. If it does not also show he must have been Shakespeare's friend, it is both because one man can 'love' another at a distance and, to postulate friendship, one would need some surviving sign of a reciprocal feeling on Shakespeare's part.

In the relationships of great writers, intimacy is often difficult because of elements of competitive envy on one or both sides. Jonson's criticism of the line from *Julius Caesar* is consistent with a scornful remark about Shakespeare's history plays in the Prologue to *Every Man In His Humour*, and an equally disparaging allusion to *Titus Andronicus* in the 'Induction' to *Bartholomew Fair*. These two references, together with Jonson's remarks in *Timber*, and another in his *Conversations with William Drummond* about Shakespeare lacking art, can be and indeed were often taken to support Rowe's contention that, while Shakespeare may have helped Jonson to have one of his plays performed, the latter did not show an 'equal return of Gentleness and Sincerity' but instead was always enviously sniping at a man whom he regarded chiefly in the light of a competitor.[19] Yet if there was some envy and resentment in his feelings for his older and probably more successful contemporary, that clearly would not prove that he did not love him, or that the two men did not get on. Quite what form the relationship took, however, is one of the many questions which have not been resolved and which, without that mythical cache of private documents which has now been mouldering away in someone's attic for almost four hundred years, never will be.

# 12

## *London life*

ALTHOUGH WE HAVE NO idea when it was, there must have been a moment in Shakespeare's life when he entered London for the first time. This is why an often elaborate feature of all the biographies is a description of the capital as it might have been in the late sixteenth century. Perhaps because he was a novelist, as well as a biographer, Anthony Burgess is self-consciously aware of how inevitable this description has become, beginning the fifth chapter of his life of Shakespeare with: 'This is the moment for the traditional florid cadenza to mark Will's first glimpse of London. Very well, then.'[1] All the biographers supply cadenzas that are more or less florid, stressing London's recent rapid expansion, its vibrant commercialism or its bad sanitation. It is not surprising that Peter Ackroyd, who is also a novelist and has a particular interest in the history of London, should perform this task as well as any.

> A traveller entering the city for the first time [he begins] could not help but be profoundly moved or disturbed by the experience. It assaulted all the senses with its stridency and vigour. It was a vortex of energy. It was voracious. The traveller was surrounded by street-traders or by merchants beseeching him to buy; he was hustled and jostled. It was a city of continuous noise – of argument, of conflict, of street-selling, of salutations such as 'God ye good morrow' and 'God ye good den' – and more often than not it smelled terribly of dung and offal and human labour.[2]

Ackroyd's account then continues for several paragraphs in the same vein.

Detailed descriptions of London in the late sixteenth century help to establish how different life in the city was from what it is now, but there is then always the problem of locating Shakespeare within them. It is an unwritten rule of biographical writing that, to understand the subject, one needs also to understand his or her environment, but so little is known about Shakespeare that, in his case, it is often difficult to see where the two intersect. One feature of Elizabethan life which is sometimes used to explicate a few of the more uncomfortable moments in his plays (the gulling of Malvolio, for example) is the cruelty of its judicial punishments. In illustration of these, most of the biographers point out that, on London Bridge, the heads of traitors were regularly displayed. Greenblatt is typical of his colleagues in the manner in which he then tries to associate this phenomenon with Shakespeare, suggesting that

> when he first walked across the bridge, or very soon after, Shakespeare must have realized that among the heads were those of John Somerville and the man who bore his mother's own name and may have been his distant kinsman, Edward Arden.

and then claiming that the lesson he learnt from the sight was, 'keep control of yourself; do not fall into the hands of your enemies; be smart, tough, and realistic; master strategies of concealment and evasion; keep your head on your shoulders.'[3] The heads on the bridge which had already been separated from their shoulders, Greenblatt is able to note, attracted the attention of foreigners, one visitor in 1592 counting thirty-four and another in 1598 much the same number; but whether Shakespeare ever paid much attention to them is unknown, as is also whether there was any meaningful family connection between his mother and Edward Arden.

As I have said before, making Shakespeare a 'master of concealment and evasion' is one way of dealing with our ignorance of his life, and a good example of the argument from absence. For many years, it must have been felt that he had demonstrated this mastery in concealing where exactly in London he had lived, a detail of some importance for those wanting to bring environment and subject into close association. There are tax records to indicate that, at some date before 1596, he was living in St Helen's parish in Bishopgate; but that no later than 1598, and perhaps as early as the winter of 1596 to 1597, he had moved across the river to Southwark. The assumption is that this move more or less coincided (the dates do not quite fit) with the construction on the Thames's south bank of the Globe from the dismantled elements of 'The Theatre'. That is to say that the significance of an address for Shakespeare in Southwark would seem to be that he liked to live close to his work; but that was not the conclusion which could be drawn when, in 1909, a quite specific address for him in London was finally found in what I have already referred to as the Belott / Mountjoy papers. Stephen Belott was an apprentice who, in 1604, fulfilled the Jacobean dream of marrying the boss's daughter; but things did not turn out as well as he might have hoped. In 1612 he took his father-in-law, Christopher Mountjoy, to the Court of Requests (a rough equivalent of our small claims court) on the grounds that the £60 he had been promised at the time of his marriage in 1604 had never been paid, and that there were also £200 which Mountjoy had said he would leave him in his will but which did not seem likely to materialise either. One of those called to give evidence was a gentleman from Stratford called William Shakespeare who, it turned out, had not only been a lodger in the Mountjoys' house around the period of Belott's marriage but had also, at the specific request of Mrs Mountjoy, been involved in the negotiations which preceded it, even to the possible extent of having witnessed their troth-plighting. Here, then, was not only an exact address but also an exceedingly rare example, in the signed deposition which he contributed to the case, of Shakespeare speaking *in propria persona.*

The discovery of the Wallaces was sensational and highly significant; there has been nothing comparable since. Yet even they were disappointed. They were looking, above all, for what one of them called 'personal expression',[4] but there are features of the way Shakespeare's deposition was recorded which militated against that. In cases like the one involving Belott and Mountjoy, the procedure was to draw up a series of questions, or 'interrogatories', which were put in the same form to each witness. In Shakespeare's replies to these, there is so much repetition of expressions in the questions that very few of his words can properly be described as his own. The result is that, although the deposition may be a rare and possibly unique record of his voice, the context, and the barbarous legal jargon, mean that we fail to come away feeling that we have really heard it. As Charles Nicholl has put it, because what Shakespeare said in giving his evidence had to be 'shaped to the formulae of court depositions', his answers 'cannot be reconstructed as to their particular tone'.[5]

Most commentators agree that when Shakespeare does manage

to say something in his deposition, it is remarkably uninformative. On all the crucial questions which interested the court, such as Mountjoy's initial attitude to his apprentice and the sums he had promised him on his death or when he married his daughter, he is either vague or non-committal. Another witness in the case testified that he had gone to see Shakespeare before it began and been told by him that Christopher Mountjoy had promised to give his daughter a dowry of about £50. The documents make clear that, when he came to give his evidence, Shakespeare declared that he could not remember what the sum had been. Nicholl glosses this discrepancy by quoting the last words of Parolles in *All's Well That Ends Well*, 'I will not speak what I know',[6] but one can think of many other explanations for it: that the other witness was not telling the truth, for example, or that on reconsideration Shakespeare decided he really could not remember. It is, of course, possible that Shakespeare deliberately chose not to commit himself and to withhold what he knew, but the difficulty here for his would-be biographers is the usual one of a lack of any corroborative detail. In the deposition as a whole, perhaps the only phrases which strike the eye are in Shakespeare's claim that Mrs Mountjoy 'did sollicitt and entreat this depondent to move and perswade the said complainant to effect the said marriadge'.[7] The doubling of the verbs here might be interpreted as an indication that Mrs Mountjoy put special pressure on Shakespeare, or that Stephen Belott was a particularly reluctant bridegroom, were it not that this linguistic practice was second nature in Jacobean times, as much, perhaps, for legal clerks as for great dramatists (the deposition was signed by Shakespeare but is not, of course, in his hand).

Squeeze as they might, the biographers have been able to extract very little from Shakespeare's deposition in the Belott / Mountjoy case; and yet the documents remain very interesting. The specific London address they yield was a house on the eastern corner of Silver and Monkwell Streets in Cripplegate Ward which served Christopher Mountjoy as both his residence and business premises. What they offer which is more important, however, is at least a suggestion of the kind of people with whom Shakespeare regularly mixed. Both the Mountjoys were Huguenot refugees, a fact which might seem a body blow to all those anxious to establish that Shakespeare was a secret Catholic, were it not that the reasoning to which their anxiety characteristically leads makes it easy to present him as deliberately choosing to lodge with French

Huguenots because it provided more effective cover. They were also, like his own family, in trade, being what was known at the time as tiremakers. This meant that they manufactured the wire contraptions, sometimes studded with diamonds, which Elizabethan and Jacobean ladies of fashion wore on their heads, that they were involved in the kind of highly skilled specialist activity often in the hands of immigrant workers. The Mountjoys worked for the Court but it is possible also that they supplied their goods to the theatre since heavy spending on costume was routine for Elizabethan and Jacobean companies.

There is a lot to be learned about the Mountjoys from the case brought against them by their disgruntled former apprentice and son-in-law, although perhaps even more from the diary, or more accurately casebook, kept by Simon Forman, a popular astrologer and quack doctor of the period. This remarkable document is particularly interesting for Shakespeareans because Forman was a theatre-goer and gives eye-witness reports of three of Shakespeare's plays; but its significance here lies in both the Mountjoys having been among his patients or customers. Towards the end of 1597, Mrs Mountjoy consulted him twice, once because she had lost a purse and expected Forman to give her indications of how to find it; and then because she wondered whether she might be pregnant. From other indications in the casebook, it appears that this was a worry to her because she was having an affair with a dealer in cloth called Henry Wood, who lived nearby. The hint this gave that Mrs Mountjoy might have been promiscuous has occasionally been used by biographers at the more popular end of the market to suggest she had an affair with Shakespeare also. Anthony Holden, for example, takes advantage of the fact that *Othello* is quite possibly one of the plays composed while Shakespeare was the Mountjoys' lodger to ask, 'Who might have caused him such powerful emotions at this particular time, feeding the frenzy behind Othello's "goats and monkeys"? Who, for one, but the indirect cause of his future legal woes, Mary Mountjoy senior?' (Mrs Mountjoy's daughter was also called Mary.) Holden's insertion of 'for one' here protects him from the absurdity of claiming that Mrs Mountjoy was the sole inspiration for Othello's jealous rages; but he exaggerates when he describes Shakespeare's appearance as a witness in a civil law suit in 1612 as a 'legal woe'. His main resource is not, however, exaggeration but that familiar standby of many Shakespeare biographers, the rhetorical question.

> Was Mary senior flighty enough to seduce her lodger ... and then to torment him with her attentions to Wood or indeed her husband? Had she and Shakespeare secretly been lovers for five years or more before he moved in, the name of Mountjoy in *Henry V* being his coded thanks for her flirtatious help with the play's adventures in French?[8]

Perhaps it does not much matter here that the chronology is potentially confusing, and that if Shakespeare had indeed been Mrs Mountjoy's secret lover for five years she would not have had to 'seduce' him when he became her lodger. Perhaps also it would be fruitless to point out that 'Mountjoy' was a name or title he would have found in the records, or that there was someone of that title prominent at Court. All that clearly counts for Holden is being able to plant in the reader's mind the idea that something certainly went on between the landlady and her lodger. The rhetorical questions do that but Michael Wood achieves a similar effect by different means. 'Shakespeare was perhaps close to Mrs. Mountjoy,' he writes, 'though to suggest he might have been responsible for her pregnancy in 1597 is perhaps to over-stretch the evidence.'[9] The reference here to 'over-stretching' the evidence is strange when no objective observer of the matter could ever conclude that there was any; but the trick is to imply that, though Shakespeare may not having been sleeping with Mrs Mountjoy as early as 1597, he must have done so later.

The number of people that Shakespeare can clearly be shown to have known is so few that, when one is discovered, his biographers display an irresistible tendency to claim that he must have had significant relations with him or her. It is a question of joining up the dots, when there are no available grounds for doing so, or, in the case of Mrs Mountjoy, guilt by association (assuming that the Forman casebook *does* provide us solid evidence that she was adulterous). Only a few indulge in this method as far as she is concerned, but there are more takers when it comes to George Wilkins, another person who was called to testify in the Belott / Mountjoy dispute. He ran the lodging house or inn to which Belott and his young wife retreated shortly after their wedding, taking with them whatever 'household stuff' they had been given on that occasion (the precise value of this stuff was a major bone of contention). But he was also a writer. Around 1606, a play of his entitled *The Miseries of Enforced Marriage* was performed by Shakespeare's company and he was also the co-author of *Pericles* (he appears to have written the first two acts while Shakespeare took care of the rest).[10] These literary successes were short-lived, or so it would seem from the fact there is no trace of new work after 1608 and plenty of evidence that, between 1610 and 1618, he was primarily an inn-keeper. The evidence in question comes from the records of the Middlesex sessions and shows that Wilkins was repeatedly prosecuted in these years. The nature of the charges, three of which involve beating up women, strongly suggests that the inn he kept also functioned as a brothel and this is confirmed by its address, which was on the corner of Turnmill Street, a location notorious at the time for its thieves and prostitutes.[11]

Shakespeare must certainly have known who Wilkins was, independently of the connection they both had with the Mountjoys. Yet the responsibility he shared with him for *Pericles* does not mean that they were necessarily intimate. Co-authorship was a complicated activity in the period which may sometimes have involved collaboration, but an equally likely scenario is that Shakespeare was given *Pericles* to complete because Wilkins had failed to do so, or because what he had provided was deemed unsatisfactory. In this latter case especially, there would be no reason for the two writers involved to feel warm towards each other. Katherine Duncan-Jones, however, has no doubt there was 'a close association' between them and accuses previous biographers of Bardolatry in their refusal to acknowledge it. 'But what would "gentle Shakespeare" possibly have been doing in the company of such a man?', she ironically enquires. In a section of her book entitled 'Shakespeare in bad company: George Wilkins', she suggests that the Mountjoys would not have provided meals for their lodgers and that therefore it was most likely that Shakespeare and Belott 'often dined and supped in Turnmill Street, where Shakespeare customarily stopped on his way back from the Globe Theatre'. The very clear indication is that this was where Wilkins kept his inn, although the records suggest that in 1605, when Shakespeare and Belott would be dining together, he had not yet moved there.[12] She goes on to quote two misogynistic jokes from a collection of *Jests to make you Merry* which Wilkins put together with Dekker in 1607 and says that they give 'some of the flavour of Shakespeare's hours of relaxation'; and she points out that the second half of *Pericles* contains a scene in a brothel. Later she speculates that Shakespeare's 'visits to Turnmill Street may have left him with a legacy of chronic and humiliating sickness'. In her view, it was Wilkins he went to see there so that 'the period of Shakespeare's association with Wilkins was a distress-

## London life

ing deviation from his commanding role as the King's Men's leading playwright'.[13] As she builds up her picture of Wilkins leading Shakespeare into bad company, it takes some effort to remind oneself that there is no evidence that the two men *did* know each other well, even though Wilkins was an acquaintance of the Mountjoys, wrote a play in which Shakespeare probably appeared and was the co-author of *Pericles*. These are three dots it would take information rather than speculation to join up and, whereas the latter is abundant, the former is in desperately short supply. The brothel scenes in *Pericles*, and more especially those in the tavern in the *Henry IV* plays, do suggest that Shakespeare knew a good deal about the London underworld, but where and, above all, how he acquired his knowledge is a closed book.

There are two counts on which the Belott / Mountjoy papers are disappointing. Shakespeare's own deposition conveys nothing of biographical interest while at the same time, although there are in the papers many intriguing suggestions of a particular *milieu*, quite how he was associated with the various individuals which comprised it remains unknown. Both problems are made clear in *The Lodger: Shakespeare on Silver Street*, the book which Charles Nicholl has recently devoted to these matters. This begins with the claim that, in the hundred years since it was discovered, Shakespeare's deposition in the Belott / Mountjoy case has been 'oddly neglected as a biographical source'.[14] I doubt very much that this is true, although it may well be that Nicholl is the first person to make the case the rationale for a whole book. What he writes is packed with fascinating detail about Jacobean England but there are fundamental problems about the whole enterprise which can be illustrated from its second part, the section entitled 'Silver Street'. This begins with a chapter called, 'The house on the corner', in which Nicholl establishes that nothing whatsoever now survives of the Mountjoys' residence and then imagines how it might have been. The next chapter is called 'The Neighbourhood' and is a description of all the Jacobean trades and professions in the Silver Street area. Following that there is a chapter on 'Househould stuffe' that begins with an account of archaeological digs around Silver Street which have unfortunately revealed nothing of any direct relevance to Shakespeare and ends with the list of those household goods, the 'stuff' Mountjoy gave his daughter when she married. In the final chapter of the section ('The chamber'), Nicholl imagines how Shakespeare's room in the Silver Street house might have been furnished and, by suggesting what books it might have contained, is able to write a few pages on his likely reading. All this is very well researched and interesting to read but it tells us nothing new about the Mountjoys' lodger, once again making background compensate for the inevitable absence of foreground. At the beginning of his book, Nicholl declares that,

> To find out more about the Mountjoys and their world has seemed to me worthwhile in itself, but is primarily a means to find out more about their lodger, the famous but so often obscure Mr Shakespeare, with whom they were in casual daily contact.[15]

If Nicholl really meant what he said here, his book would be a failure since Shakespeare is no less an obscure figure by the end of it than he was at the beginning. 'And now for the first time', writes Michael Wood in reference to the Belott / Mountjoy papers, 'we have detailed knowledge of [Shakespeare's] private life.'[16] One of the effects of *The Lodger: Shakespeare on Silver Street* is to demonstrate just how limited that knowledge still remains.

# 13

## Politics

It is hard to read Shakespeare's plays without feeling that he had a strong interest in politics. Although they almost never have contemporary settings, parallels with the politics of his day have been found everywhere in them. Yet a commonplace of Shakespeare criticism is the impossibility of discovering from the plays where precisely he stood on the key issues. The difficulty is the same as trying to find out from them what his religious views were, although saying that is perhaps unnecessary, given the interdependence of religious and political affairs in the late sixteenth and early seventeenth centuries. One burning issue in the 1580s and 1590s, for example, was who should succeed the childless Elizabeth, especially as she herself refused to name a successor. Questions of succession are always important in a monarchy but for the largely Protestant establishment around Elizabeth they became doubly so as they looked back with dismay at what had happened when Edward VI had been succeeded by his half-sister Mary. Shakespeare no doubt had his own thoughts on the question, but there is no way of telling from his writings what they were.

Another political issue which was also simultaneously religious concerned Elizabeth's foreign policy. Towards the end of her reign there was a war party at her Court, led by the Earl of Essex, who, in urging a stronger, more aggressive attitude to Spain, was also positioning himself as a militant Protestant. For his opponents among Elizabeth's advisors, one problem with war was that it cost so much and necessarily led to placing a tax burden on her subjects which was potentially destabilising. There was a clash of cultures here between an old aristocracy committed to warlike, chivalric values and those whose interests were more financial or mercantile. Signs of this clash are certainly reflected in Shakespeare's plays but nowhere does he clearly espouse one cause or the other.

Biographers of Shakespeare are addicted to the politics of his day because it gives them something interesting to talk about. Perhaps the most celebrated event of Elizabeth's reign with a significant political dimension was the defeat of the Spanish Armada in 1588. This is inconveniently early as far as any knowledge of Shakespeare's life is concerned, but many of the biographies manage to incorporate some of its details. Jonathan Bate, for example, having in his second book approached Shakespeare's life and career via Jaques's famous speech about the seven ages of man in *As You Like It* (2.vii), slides over the awkwardness that Shakespeare was never himself (as far as we know) 'a soldier . . . / Seeking the bubble reputation / Even in the cannon's mouth' by beginning his fourth section with an account of Elizabeth's speech to her troops during the Armada crisis.[1] Others have used details from the episode to indicate the mood of national optimism in which Shakespeare began his career, or as an example of how ambivalent a crypto-Catholic might feel at witnessing the humiliation of Spanish power. What he did in fact feel, and where he was when the attempted invasion took place, is unknown but Leslie Hotson felt he had found a direct reference to the Armada when he concluded that the fifth line of sonnet 107 – 'The mortal moon has her eclipse endured' – was a description of the crescent form in which the Spanish galleons attacked.[2] Very few commentators now accept this reading. Links both more plausible and more substantial can be made to a political episode which was less crucial than events surrounding the Armada but had nevertheless great national significance: the eventual fall and execution of the Earl of Essex. One of the warmest supporters of Essex may well have been the Earl of Southampton, but to establish that Shakespeare was therefore drawn into the Essex political camp, one would have to begin by knowing in what sense, and to what extent, Southampton really did become Shakespeare's patron and the kind of contacts they had with each other after the publication of *The Rape of Lucrece* in 1594.

Southampton is only one of three major ways in which Shakespeare is linked to Essex. The second is through some lines spoken by the Chorus at the beginning of Act 5 of *Henry V*. These compare

Henry's return to London after Agincourt to that of a 'conquering Caesar' entering Rome, and they then go on:

> As, by a lower but as loving likelihood,
> Were now the General of our gracious Empress,
> As in good time he may, from Ireland coming,
> Bringing rebellion broached on his sword,
> How many would the peaceful city quit
> To welcome him!

This clearly refers to Elizabeth having recently sent an army headed by Essex to quash an Irish rebellion which was always in danger of being made even more threatening than it already was by help from Spain. The words Shakespeare uses suggest some doubt as to the possibility of Essex succeeding in this task and are certainly not warmly partisan, but they are the chief pretext James Shapiro uses to devote many pages of *1599* to the progress of the Irish campaign. The details he provides have an intrinsic interest and are often intriguing, as are the ways in which he draws a contrast between the unsuccessful attempts Essex made in Ireland to reassert chivalric values and the first founding meeting of the East India Company. This took place in September 1599 in 'Founders' Hall, on Lothbury Street, south of Moorgate', and Shapiro links Shakespeare to it only by the information that he 'wasn't among those gathered in Founders' Hall that September day'.[3] The link to Essex's Irish campaign through the lines in *Henry V* is really no more convincing and is a clear example of what 'a year in the life of William Shakespeare' really means. In a review of *1599* Jonathan Bate called it 'one of the few genuinely original biographies of Shakespeare'.[4] Concentrating on a single year certainly gives the book an air of originality but, in its substitution of historical for unobtainable biographical material, its methods are very familiar.

The Chorus in *Henry V* was right to be tentative about the circumstances in which Essex would return from Ireland. His campaign there not only went very badly but he exceeded the authority Elizabeth felt she had given him by beginning negotiations for a truce with the leading Irish rebel. His instructions had been to stay in Ireland as long as she required him there but, anxious that his position was being undermined by enemies at Court, Essex made an unauthorised and unannounced return to London, taking everyone by surprise and – in a startling breach of decorum – bursting into the Queen's dressing room in order to plead his cause. The consequence was a form of house arrest and the beginnings of an enquiry into how far his recent conduct in Ireland and elsewhere could be regarded as treasonable. That he eventually responded with a feeble attempt at organising a palace coup, ostensibly designed to save Elizabeth from her evil advisors, is a story told in all the Shakespeare biographies, most recently by Jonathan Bate, who adds a good deal of fascinating detail. The pretext for telling it is the third and most potentially substantial of possible links between Essex and Shakespeare. Two or three days before the Essex rising (as it usually called), several members of his entourage went to the Globe and commissioned a special performance of *Richard II* for Saturday 7 February 1601. The members of the Lord Chamberlain's Men with whom Essex's followers negotiated later claimed that they were reluctant to put on this play about the deposition and murder of a monarch at such short notice because it was old and unlikely to draw in the crowds; but they were given forty shillings as either an incentive, or insurance against any possible financial loss. René Weis speculates that their acquiescence was 'possibly also as a result of behind-the-scenes lobbying from Southampton', Shakespeare's 'one-time boon companion'; and Duncan-Jones is in little doubt that it was 'Shakespeare's long standing connection with Essex's close friend and confederate Southampton that constituted the first and most compromising link between the players and the two malcontent Earls'.[5] But in all the material Bate has carefully examined there is no sign of either Shakespeare or Southampton having been involved in the negotiations to put on the play, or of Southampton attending the performance.

Shakespeare's biographers have traditionally interpreted the performance of *Richard II* on 7 February 1601 as part of a planned and deliberate softening-up process for the Essex rising which took place on the following day. In that way their subject, or at least something he wrote, is moved to the centre of the political stage. But Bate and others have shown that when Essex unexpectedly left the security of Essex House and, with a number of what Macbeth would call his 'friends', went to the City in order to test the degree of his support there, it was because he had received the day before a summons to appear before the Privy Council and suspected, with some justification, that he was about to be arrested. Yet if Shakespeare's play was wholly incidental to these events, it is still reasonable to ask quite how compromising its performance might have been to him personally. The question is complicated by a book by Sir John

Hayward published in 1599 and entitled *The first part of the life and reign of Henry IV*. This dealt with the same matters as *Richard II*, began with a fulsome dedication to Essex, and was certainly regarded by the authorities as inflammatory. It is to this publication Elizabeth might have been referring when, in a much later document (the trustworthiness of which Bate has called into doubt), she is reported as saying, 'I am Richard II. Know ye not that?', words which Greenblatt cites in his biography as if he knows for certain they were her direct response to the commissioned performance of Shakespeare's play.[6] It is none the less clear enough that the authorities were not best pleased that it was performed since they afterwards called to them for interrogation Augustine Phillips, the member of Shakespeare's company who seems to have acted as its general manager. Perhaps they did not, in the end, regard the episode as especially important; perhaps they understand how easily men who made their living from acting could be subjected to *force majeure*; and perhaps they were sophisticated enough to appreciate the difference between the intentions which might lie behind a work of art and those later attributed to it. But whatever the reasons, the answers Phillips gave to their questions must have satisfied them completely since the Lord Chamberlain's Men were very soon back playing at Court, and on the eve (as it happened) of Essex's execution. Duncan-Jones conjectures that Phillips answered on behalf of his company because he had been 'pushed forward to save the skins of the more senior and surely more culpable Burbage and Shakespeare'; and Bate thinks that because the Essex revolt lengthened the time which Sir John Hayward was already spending in the Tower, he 'effectively took the rap on Shakespeare's behalf'.[7] Yet there is no foundation for either of these wild guesses and, in the abundant documentation spawned by the Essex affair, not a hint of Shakespeare's attitudes or what role (if any) he played in it. What this means is that the enthusiasm for *Richard II* of certain members of the Essex group no more establishes his link with it than the lines from *Henry V*, or the dedication of two of his early poems to Southampton.

After the Earl of Essex was duly executed, Southampton's death sentence was commuted to what was expected to be an indefinite term of imprisonment. His release in 1603 was because that was the year in which Elizabeth died. The death of the Queen prompted many tributes, in one of which Henry Chettle reproached Shakespeare for not having paid his respects. 'Shepheard', he wrote, tastelessly alluding to *The Rape of Lucrece,* 'remember our Elizabeth, / And sing her Rape, done by that Tarquin, Death.'[8] As far as we know, Shakespeare still failed to oblige and, in another illustration of the argument from absence, his omission has been regarded by Duncan-Jones as significant. What it indicates in her view is the low regard in which Shakespeare held women and it is in this context that she goes on to cite the Manningham anecdote as an illustration of how little respect he had 'either for women or for female intelligence'.[9] Other biographers have been more inclined to take the absence of an elegy as simply one more sign that Shakespeare was an Essex or Southampton man, who would have been pleased to see the back of Elizabeth and who went on to enjoy a close relationship with James I. This is a view which might seem to be supported by the rapidity with which the Lord Chamberlain's Men became the King's Men on James's accession; yet Leeds Barroll has very effectively shown why it would be wrong to interpret their change of name in this way, while at the same time demonstrating how little justification there is for assuming that James had any special interest in drama, or in Shakespeare.[10] That James and Shakespeare were somehow close is a belief which can be dated back to 1709, when one commentator described how James was 'pleased with his own Hand to write an amicable letter to Mr. Shakespeare' while, about twenty years later, another claimed that the king had 'honourd Shakespeare with an Epistolary correspondence'.[11] The person described in both cases as having once claimed to possess the letter from James is William Davenant. Given Davenant's track record in these matters, that it ever existed is about as likely as the familiar story that Shakespeare wrote *The Merry Wives of Windsor* because Elizabeth had said she wanted to see Falstaff in love. As we look back to Elizabethan and Jacobean times with our present scale of values, Shakespeare seems as important a figure in them as any other, and it is therefore pleasing to sustain the traditional belief that there were reasonably close relations between him and the two monarchs. Yet until Davenant's letter turns up, or someone discovers a reference by Elizabeth to *The Merry Wives,* all that we know about the period suggests how unlikely such relations must be.

There is no indication of how Elizabeth and James felt about Shakespeare, nor indeed, in spite of what is possibly praise of Elizabeth in *A Midsummer Night's Dream* or the implied flattery of James in *Macbeth,* he about them. That he failed to commemorate Elizabeth's death with a poem can hardly be construed as a political stance and the plays which deal with political matters have no simple messages. The followers of Essex could only have transformed *Richard II* into a play sympathetic to their interests by ignoring its complexities. It had clearly not been written with them in mind, so that the only way they could have had for making it topical in 1601 was to impose upon on it their own agenda. Yet just how far Shakespeare's plays are ever topical is a difficult question. At the beginning of *1599* James Shapiro exhibits his old historicist credentials when he says that 'it's no more possible to talk about Shakespeare's plays independently of his age than it is to grasp what his society went through without the benefit of Shakespeare's insights,' and he claims, somewhat improbably, that 'only recently has the tide begun to turn against the view of Shakespeare as a poet who transcends his age.'[12] This ideological position must be part of the reason why he feels able to convey so much information about 'the age' and it is challenging that, in the process of doing so, he tries to show how *Julius Caesar* is a much more topical play than one might have thought. He notes, for example, that shortly before it was performed (although not perhaps composed?), there had been an attempt to kill Elizabeth and suggests that this is what would have made its concern with political assassination seem particularly relevant. But he directs most of his attention to the opening scenes and what could be interpreted in them as an attempt by the tribunes to prevent the populace from turning a national holiday (the Feast of Lupercal) into a political event. He explains that, as the Reformation had proceeded, holy days had become a contentious issue, with their number sternly reduced; and that some Catholics reasonably complained that, whereas their own icons were destroyed, Elizabeth's image was sometimes treated as one. This is interesting material which could perhaps inflect some individuals' future experience of *Julius Caesar*. Data which are external to a work of art can certainly change its aspect, in either a major or (as perhaps in this case) a minor way; and yet it can also lie inert, or give to certain features of that work a salience which is unjustified and distorting. Whatever the case here, what is certain is that Shakespeare no more reveals his own hand on the question of holidays as he does on any of the other political issues *Julius Caesar* raises. Quite how topical the play felt in 1599 will always be impossible to judge but, although it dealt with the elimination of a leader who was threatening to becoming too autocratic, it seems reasonably certain that there is nothing in it from which a malcontent of the Essex variety could have *legitimately* drawn succour.

The general problem which the Essex affair raised concerned the role which those of a traditional military culture ought to play in civil society. It was one Shakespeare would deal with most directly and brilliantly in *Coriolanus*, several years after Essex was dead and no longer in the minds of his audience. This is a play where it is generally felt that Shakespeare is at his most political, but it is no surprise that it is also notorious for having been appropriated at different times by both the extreme right and extreme left, with equal fervour. If there were any Jacobeans who saw in it a retrospective reference to Essex, there must have been just as many among them who found it condemnatory as complimentary. This open-endedness of those of Shakespeare's plays which deal with political issues could be regarded as yet another indication of how 'discreet' he was. If the paucity of surviving documentation about his private life can be invoked to suggest that he was a man who liked to keep his head down, then the built-in ambivalence of his more political writing can be used to indicate that it was in his character always to see both sides of the question. But here some very rudimentary information about 'the age' does become significant. Shakespeare may have been a man of a naturally cautious and regressive temperament, or he may have been someone too profoundly aware of how the political world functioned not to remain above it. This may have been how he was but it is difficult to be sure when we know that the plays he wrote were subject to censorship and could not have been performed without government approval. When we read Elizabethan and Jacobean plays it often seems striking how relatively benign censorship was (the authorities appeared to have been much more concerned with books); but it did exist and any strong, clear message in one of them which annoyed the government would either never have seen the light of day, or have landed the author in serious trouble. If it is impossible to work out where Shakespeare stood on the major issues which preoccupied his contemporaries, that may be because it was in his character not to commit himself; but it may also be because he could only write what he knew would be approved and was therefore obliged to keep whatever strong opinions he had to himself.

# 14

# *Money*

IN 1926 D. H. Lawrence received from a friend a copy of a biography of Voltaire by Stephen G. Tallentyre, the pseudonym of the English writer Beatrice Hall. He said he found the book interesting but complained that it did not explain how Voltaire

> had made, had acquired for himself, by the time he was my age, an *income* of £3,000 – equivalent at least to an income of twelve thousand pounds, today. How had he done it? – it means a capital of two hundred thousand pounds. Where had it come from? Ask yourself? But that man Tallentyre is a cunning underhand biographer, who knows that women eat nothing but candy.[1]

The story of how Voltaire, while still a relatively young man, laid the foundation of his fortune by participating in a syndicate which cornered the market in lottery tickets is certainly one which no responsible biographer should omit, in the first place because it is a good story, but secondly because financial independence is an important biographical aspect of someone as controversial and risk-taking as he was: 'I think that it was not by chance that Voltaire became more outspoken as soon as his lines of retreat were secured,' writes Theodore Besterman, after having described how his subject became rich.[2] What it is then interesting to discover is Voltaire's *attitude* to money: how much it preoccupied him and the role it played in his internal soliloquies. I have said previously that the search for status can often be as powerful a motive force in individual lives as sex, but to some people money can matter as much as either. In a mischievous response to what must already have been early signs of Bardolatry, Pope wrote, in one of his imitations of Horace:

> Shakespear (whom you and ev'ry Play-house bill
> Style the divine, the matchless, what you will)
> For gain, not glory, wing'd his roving flight,
> And grew Immortal in his own despight.[3]

This is one interpretation of Shakespeare's relationship to money by which many of his biographers would later feel challenged.

When it comes to trying to think about Shakespeare and money, the initial feeling must be that here at last is a topic on which there is at least *some* information. A majority of the documents which survive concern either his acquisition of land and property, or his financial transactions. Apart from the record of how, in 1597, he bought New Place, for example, we know that in 1602 he paid £320 for about 120 acres of farming land near Stratford; that five months later he acquired a cottage adjacent to New Place; and that in 1605 he bought a half-interest in a lease of tithes. This lease had thirty-one years to run, the yield on the tithes was in the region of £60 a year, and the investment cost Shakespeare £440. The Wallaces discovered papers which showed that, in 1613, he finally bought a property in London (the Blackfriars Gatehouse) via a highly complicated legal arrangement which involved an initial down payment of £80. It is impossible to calculate precise modern equivalents of all these sums but in 1999 Anthony Holden cited a professor of economics who offered 'multiply by 500' as a useful rule of thumb.[4] Those who have wondered how he was able to accumulate so much capital have sometimes gone back to the story of Southampton's gift of £1,000, but the more usual explanation has been found in his connections with the theatre. By electing to invest in the building of the Globe, Shakespeare had become a much bigger 'sharer' in the profits of the Lord Chamberlain's Men than he had previously been as an actor and writer; and when the company incurred considerable costs by finally taking over the indoor theatre in Blackfriars, he again chose to be a part-sharer in the enterprise. The signs are that these two ventures made him a lot of money and explain why he could buy so much land and property.

What Shakespeare bought suggests that he became relatively prosperous but not how preoccupied he was with his prosperity. Clearer signs of his attitude to money have been found in a number of records which are not of purchases but relate nevertheless to financial matters. The only surviving letter written to Shakespeare, for example, is what has usually been interpreted as a request for a loan. Dated 25 October 1598 and addressed to 'my loving good friend and countryman Mr Wm. Shakespeare', it was written by Richard Quiney, the son and partner of a prominent Stratford businessman, Adrian Quiney, who had been bailiff or mayor of Stratford on three occasions.[5] Richard had himself been bailiff in 1592, as he would be again in 1601; and in 1616 his son Thomas would marry Shakespeare's younger daughter, Judith. Richard had come to London as the representative of the Stratford Corporation to petition the Privy Council for a reduction in the town's taxes and, perhaps because he was kept hanging around too long, appears to have run out of funds. The survival of his letter suggests that it might never have been sent and its wording is ambiguous enough to have convinced some that Quiney was not asking Shakespeare directly for a loan but rather his help in securing one. In that case, it could not be cited as evidence that Shakespeare was prosperous, someone who could lay his hands on £30 at the drop of a hat, but it might still support the idea that he was in the money-lending business. Yet in the Elizabethan period, members of the business community can so often be found lending money to each other, acting as guarantors or reclaiming bad debts, that it would take more than the puzzling Quiney letter to justify calling Shakespeare a 'money-lender' in the sense which his own Shylock has helped to give that term.

Two other records, only uncovered in the nineteenth century, might appear to offer promise of slightly more reliable information. Around 1604 Shakespeare sued in the local Stratford court a man called Philip Rogers for the recovery of thirty-five shillings – he had sold him twenty bushels of malt which Rogers presumably had not paid for, and then lent him two shillings. Between 1608 and 1609 he pursued, in the same local courts, someone called John Addenbrooke for the recovery of £6. Very little is known of Addenbrooke but Rogers was an apothecary and a Stratford neighbour. The sale of malt is interesting because in 1598, after several bad harvests and anxiety over grain shortages, Shakespeare was cited in a general survey by the authorities as storing in New Place the equivalent of eighty bushels of malt (only about a dozen men in the town held more). Eighty bushels seems a lot for domestic brewing purposes and might therefore suggest that Shakespeare ought to be regarded as a 'hoarder' – one of those people the government was worried about because in hard times they held back supply from the market in order to inflate the price. This is certainly James Shapiro's assumption when, in a critical review of those who have claimed, and continue to claim, that Shakespeare's plays were written by someone else, he says that 'Shakespeare's grain-hoarding and money-lending' have become 'biographical commonplaces'. Later in the same book he notes that, with Malone's discovery of the Quiney letter, a case was already building that 'Shakespeare cared more about cash than art,' a view he appears to endorse and one very similar to the point Pope was keen to make with his 'gain not glory'.[6]

As Pope's lines indicate, the idea of Shakespeare as money-grubbing is in awkward contrast with the notion of him as 'divine', someone almost super-human in his abilities and therefore in his character. The discomfort this contrast creates is illustrated by J. T. Looney, the man who in 1926 first made the extraordinary suggestion that Shakespeare's plays were really written by Edward de Vere, the seventeenth Earl of Oxford, with the actor from Stratford acting as a front. In his account of the movement this claim launched, Shapiro explains how Looney could not believe that someone who persecuted others for 'the recovery of petty sums', as Shakespeare appears to have done, could possibly have written *The Merchant of Venice*, or how a man responsible for plays of that quality could have 'retired to Stratford to devote himself to houses, land, orchards, money and malt, leaving no traces of a single intellectual or literary interest'. No writer of his stature, Shapiro interprets Looney as saying, 'could have cared that much about money'.[7] Since 1926 commentators have become more inclined to accept that it is possible to combine the writing of profound and moving works with a sharp business sense, and that there is no law which says poets have to be unworldly. Indeed, as Shapiro himself reminds us, the idea of a Shakespeare who indulged in hoarding and money-lending has become 'commonplace'. But what actual justification for it is there? Since so little is known about Addenbrooke, there is no way of knowing why he should have been hounded over such a comparatively long period for the £6 he owed. Rogers and the malt raise another issue which has been dealt with at length by Germaine Greer. She points out that 'the making of malt and brewing of ale was Stratford's chief industry,' and notes how many women were involved in it. Her conclusion is that 'the malt was Anne's business' and that she did well enough at this, and in other commercial activities, for her contribution to the family coffers to be larger than her husband's.[8] This would suggest that disputes in the local courts, although carried out in her husband's name and perhaps requiring his occasional presence, would be largely her affair, with some possible aid from her brothers-in-law. It would then be Anne who was the hoarder, for anyone (that is) brave enough to feel they can answer the highly complicated question of how one might define 'hoarding' in the late sixteenth century. The general case Greer makes sounds plausible enough but there are no documents to support it and it is for that reason no more certain than that Shakespeare was the skinflint some recent biographers have suggested he was. All that Shapiro's reference to 'biographical commonplaces' therefore illustrates is the way in which one unsubstantiated speculation is periodically replaced by another. Biographically speaking, in the notion of gain rather than glory, or money rather than art, the first term is parasitic on the second. In the vacuum created by the absence of data, that is, those who want to stress the mercenary aspect of Shakespeare's nature need the idealised figure as a host to feed off.

Perhaps the clearest example of the way this process works can be found in the writings of Ernst Honigmann. A distinguished scholar who has had more to do than anyone with promoting the 'Shakespeare in Lancashire' hypothesis, Honigmann has also written a number of essays in which he contests what he calls at one point 'our image of Shakespeare as kindly, a universally popular man'.[9] What he principally objects to is Jonson's notion of 'gentle' Shakespeare, pointing out that 'open, unequivocal tributes' to the said gentleness only appeared in print after Shakespeare's death, and that 'how a man impressed others in his life-time is not necessarily indicated by memorial verses written some years after his death.'[10] His ambition was to survey the evidence for an ' "ungentle" Shakespeare' and he did so effectively enough to have influenced the direction of Duncan-Jones's biography and perhaps determined its title (*Ungentle Shakespeare*). One of his chief points of reference is the Greene or Chettle attack since, as I said earlier, that would appear to indicate that there was at least one person in Elizabethan England who did not care for Shakespeare. Quite unconvincingly in my view, he interprets certain words used in that attack as an indication Shakespeare must at some point have refused to lend Greene money (a notion Greenblatt adopts enthusiastically). The way in which Quiney approached Shakespeare about securing a loan, the pursuit of Rogers and Addenbrooke in the courts, and the storing of the malt are all for him signs of a Shakespeare 'hard hearted in his business dealings'. 'A sweet and gentle Shakespeare is, in part', he writes, 'the fabrication of bardolatry; a very different man, sharp and business-like, speaks to us from some of the principal life-records.'[11] Of those life-records, the one which he appears to feel yields him most ammunition is the will. For Honigmann, many of its features are indicative of meanness and, as one example among several, he notes that Shakespeare appears to have left nothing to his servants. 'A gentleman usually remembered his servants in his will,' he writes, strongly implying that Shakespeare cannot have been one.[12]

What is involved here is yet another illustration of the argument from absence, but also the difficult question of the appeal to norms. Most decent people of the period left something for their servants and therefore Shakespeare cannot have been decent, is Honigmann's logic, even though we have no idea how many servants Shakespeare had, or what kind of arrangements might have been made for them, irrespective of the will. Appealing to norms can be complicated, as Greenblatt illustrates when he cites one of the usual explanations (or excuses) for the attempt to recover a total of about £8 from Addenbrooke and Rogers, and then rejects it. 'Shakespeare was hardly alone in pursuing such small sums', he writes; 'he lived in a litigious age, and the courts were flooded with suits of this kind', before then adding, '*But no one forced him to go through the process.*'[13] Here we are told what was normal and then reminded that no individual was obliged to follow the trend; yet the degree of constraint normality exerted in the past can be difficult to estimate. From our present point of view, for example, the provisions Shakespeare made in his will can appear very unfair since he left the vast bulk of his estate to his elder daughter, Susanna (partly perhaps in confirmation of her marriage settlement), and thereafter to any *male* descendant she might have; while to his younger daughter, Judith, he gave only an initial £150 with another £150 to follow after three years. No recent biographer of Shakespeare has denounced this division as an example of cruel favouritism since they all accept that, in his time, almost any other Jacobean gentleman would have made similar efforts to keep together the wealth he had accumulated. There is no talk in this instance of Shakespeare not being obliged to 'go through the process' and his treatment of his daughters therefore redounding to his discredit.

## Money

The question seems to be how far estimates of the character of biographical subjects need to be seen in the context of their time; but to the problem of deciding what, in any particular instance, is a satisfactory answer, there is added what is often the considerable further difficulty in establishing quite what that context was. When Honigmann deals with Judith's legacy, for example, his chief concern is with her husband. Judith married Thomas Quiney in February 1616 and in the following month he was forced to appear in the local church and confess to having had 'carnal copulation' with an unmarried woman who had recently died in childbirth.[14] Most commentators conjecture that it was these events which prompted Shakespeare to revise the three-page will which had been made in January, and certainly the new first page with which he completely replaced the old in March, only altering the other two, contains the complicated provisions concerning Judith's two proposed payments of £150. Honigmann is confident that those which regulate how the second £150 should be paid after three years are framed so as to prevent the recently disgraced Quiney from gaining access to his wife's money. One of the reasons which helps him to feel assured in his treatment of the issue is that he had edited, with Susan Brock, over 130 wills of men and women associated with the theatre between 1588 and 1642. It is on his knowledge of these that he is able to call when examining the provisions for Judith Shakespeare's second £150 and the question of whether these were deliberately designed to keep her new husband's hands off the money. In arguing that they were, Honigmann cites the widow of Shakespeare's colleague, Henry Condell, who says in her will, of a certain bequest, 'yet so I do intend the same as that my son-in-law Mr. Herbert Finch shall never have possession of the same'; and also the theatrical entrepreneur, Jacob Meade, who insisted in his that a sum of money should be retained by his executors for his daughter's use 'so long as it shall please almighty God that she shall live with her husband Michael Pyttes, whom I will shall have nothing to do or meddle therewith'. These phrases certainly suggest strong animus against sons-in-law yet, according to Honigmann, Thomas Quiney was 'put in his place even more humiliatingly'. That was because 'he was not mentioned by name, his very existence was not acknowledged, even though the most carefully hedged clauses of the will were clearly devised in response to his unwelcome arrival in the bosom of the family.'[15] But there is no warrant for saying that the provisions were 'clearly devised' to insult Quiney, and no certainty that the arrangements following Judith's marriage in February would have been any different had it not been revealed that he was a bad egg.

One problem Honigmann has is that he was not the first scholar to have thought of contextualising Shakespeare's will. More than fifty years before, for example, in an unusually detailed and exhaustive study, B. Roland Lewis claimed to have based his enquiries on 'a critical examination of several thousand wills, from that of Alfred the Great (†901) to that of Sir Walter Raleigh (†1618)', as well as 'firsthand acquaintance with the legal treatises of the day, particularly those bearing on testamentary documents, and with the activities of Probate and Prerogative Courts'. The widow Condell did not escape his broad sweep and he felt that, in comparison with what she said about her son-in-law, there was 'certainly in Shakespeare's will . . . not the least hint of a dislike for Thomas Quiney'.[16] Here, then, are two specialists who have read many wills from the period and come, on this point, to quite different conclusions. A more straightforward illustration of the problem of establishing norms, however, is associated with the £10 which Shakespeare left to the poor. Although the chief effect of Honigmann's examination of the will is to portray a man who was 'totally self-centred and shockingly tight-fisted', he calls that sum 'generous'. For Duncan-Jones, on the other hand, who adopts his point of view in so many other respects, it was 'minimal'. Clearly they cannot agree as to what it was normal for a Jacobean gentleman to leave to the poor.[17]

The great danger in raising these issues is again that of giving an impression of wanting to *defend* Shakespeare. He might well have been someone who, like Volpone, enjoyed assessing his wealth every morning and who, as Greenblatt claims in relation to those unpaid tax records which indicate the areas where Shakespeare might have lived when he first came to London, hated to let 'even small sums of money slip through his fingers'.[18] But then again, he might not. Our knowledge of his attitude to money is hardly much advanced by the episode which, for many years, was a chief focus of attention whenever the issue was raised. In 1614 there were proposals to enclose some of the land in Stratford from which he drew his tithe income. The Corporation of Stratford was hostile to this move and instructed its steward, Thomas Greene, to lead a campaign against it. Identifying himself in his diary as a 'cousin' of Shakespeare (with what justification no one knows), Greene tried to enlist the playwright's support. His own position was, however, complicated by the fact that he held tithes also and had managed to have himself included in an agreement which Shakespeare had made with the supporters of enclosure, indemnifying him against any financial loss he might incur, should the scheme go ahead. Characteristic of how puzzling this whole affair can be is an entry inserted retrospectively in Greene's diary which reads: 'Sept. W Shakespeare telling J Greene that J was not able to bear the enclosing of Welcombe.' 'J Greene' is usually taken as a reference to Thomas's brother John, while the second 'J' has – Jacobean handwriting being what it is – sometimes been read as 'I' (Thomas) or 'he' (Shakespeare). It was in part the impenetrable ambiguity of these words which prompted Chambers to say, after a careful review of all the evidence, 'Once more, Shakespeare's sentiments elude us.'[19] One entry which is, however, reasonably clear in Greene's diary is his report that, whatever Shakespeare's attitude to the enclosure proposal might have been, he did not believe it would succeed. After several years of often bitter and sometimes violent wrangling, that proved to be the case, although Shakespeare did not live long enough to see his prediction come true. The signing of a separate agreement certainly gives the strong impression of someone who knew how to look after his own interests, but without knowing more about the ins and outs of the affair, it is impossible to come to a responsible judgement of his behaviour, either in the context of his own time or as it might strike us now after many years of instruction from historians on the severe hardship enclosure tended to produce. And even if we were able to make that judgement, it would only relate to one moment of Shakespeare's life and not to the way he behaved in financial affairs during the course of it; Byron was an impulsively generous spendthrift in his youth but later became careful with money or even, in the view of some, mean. What the treatment of Shakespeare's attitude to money by his biographers tends to confirm is a conclusion which can often be drawn from their work. This is that while the mood among them periodically changes, the inadequate facts stubbornly remain the same.

# 15

## *Retirement and death*

A COMMON FEATURE OF MANY Shakespeare biographies is a detailed description of the two routes into Elizabethan London from Stratford, one through Banbury and the other via Oxford. Aubrey's gossip about the Davenants has often given the preference to the Oxford route, and it has been customary to accept also his assertion that Shakespeare made the trip to and from his home town 'once a yeare'.[1] Recently, however, it has been suggested that he must have spent much more time in Stratford than had previously been thought, especially in his Jacobean period. One reason for thinking this is that, as Jonathan Bate puts it, 'during the first six and a half years of James's English reign, the public theatres were closed for over four years, open for under two.'[2] Since the evidence for Shakespeare's acting is so sparse, the idea has grown that, in his later years, he became exclusively a writer and that he did his writing in Stratford, where he had accumulated a small library and was safer from the plague which was periodically ravaging the capital.

Although he is one of the principal proponents of this new current of thought, Bate is at the same time hostile to the traditional notion of Shakespeare having 'retired'. In contrast to the majority of his fellow dramatists, Greenblatt writes, Shakespeare 'made enough money to buy one of the best houses in the hometown to which he retired in his early fifties, a self-made man'. This conjures up the familiar picture relied on in so many plays and novels which deal with the end of Shakespeare's life, the one where the great man is found relaxing in his orchard after a lifetime of astonishing literary achievement. For very many years the moment in his work used to support this picture was Prospero's breaking of his magician's staff and his abjuration of his 'rough magic' in *The Tempest* (5.i).

> If these words reflect what Shakespeare felt in contemplating retirement [Greenblatt comments], then they mark a sense of both personal loss and of personal evolution. In *King Lear* retirement had seemed an unmitigated catastrophe; in *The Tempest* it seems a viable and proper action.[3]

The presence here of the biographers' 'if' must be partly in recognition of facts which Greenblatt's predecessors either did not know or tended to ignore: that Shakespeare did not give up writing after *The Tempest* but co-authored at least three more plays. One of these was *Henry VIII* (written with John Fletcher), during the first recorded performance of which, in June 1613, the Globe caught fire and burnt down. Although several members of the King's Men then came together to finance the theatre's re-building, Shakespeare does not appear to have been one of them, a fact which is usually taken as marking the end of his financial involvement in his company. What degree of involvement, of this and other kinds, he had had previously, and might have continued to have, is impossible to say. For Bate, the purchase of the Blackfriars Gatehouse was not what it is usually taken to be – simply another investment – but rather a sign of a continuing London connection; and he points out that when Thomas Greene spoke to Shakespeare about the enclosure issue in November 1614, it was in London. In a chapter he calls 'The Myth of Shakespeare's Retirement', he resolves any possible conflict between his suggestion that some of Shakespeare's greatest plays may have been written in Stratford and his hostility to the traditional retirement scenario by saying, 'Shakespeare may never have fully retired, but he may well have semi-retired much earlier than we suppose'[4] – a reasonable conjecture but one which there is unfortunately insufficient evidence to verify.

In so far as Shakespeare did at some point retire in some fashion (and he certainly appears to have died in Stratford), the inevitable question which arises is how far his retreat from an active life in London was forced on him by ill-health. Illness is of major significance in biography. Lives of Baudelaire without his syphilis, Proust without his asthma or D. H. Lawrence without his tuberculosis are hard to imagine. Whether the subject suffered from some debilitating condition for a long time before death, and what he or she finally died of, are matters which it is vitally important a biographer should know. But accurate diagnosis is always hard, and becomes increasingly difficult the further back in time one goes. It is widely agreed that Byron died because his doctors insisted on bleeding him excessively and thus fatally damaged his already weakened system. But quite what the mysterious 'fever' was which had weakened that system in the first place, remains unknown.

If diagnosis has become impossible for someone who died in 1824, there would seem to be no point in attempting to recover the medical history of a man who was buried over two hundred years earlier. Yet as I have already shown, insuperable difficulty is meat and drink to the Shakespeare biographer. There are in total six surviving instances of Shakespeare's signature and the one on his will is noticeably less firm and clear than the others. It has in the past been taken as a sign that, at the end of his life, he was suffering from some nervous disorder, perhaps some damage to his central nervous system. Syphilis is one of the diseases which does such damage and that Shakespeare died of venereal disease is an idea which has found a good deal of favour recently. Noting that this is what some recent writers have suggested, Peter Ackroyd uses a familiar trick of the biographers when he says that, 'Nothing in Shakespeare's life and character would exclude the possibility.'[5] Yet it is because we know so little about the life and character referred to that syphilis is only one of a hundred other life-threatening illnesses which cannot be excluded. Germaine Greer is also sympathetic to the syphilis hypothesis, suggesting that Shakespeare's failure to remember how much Mountjoy had promised Belott for his daughter's dowry was a consequence, not of the disease itself, but of the substances which, in the seventeenth century, were used to treat it. 'Syphilis', she goes on, 'provides a possible answer to two more questions: why Shakespeare's career ended so early and why he died so young.'[6] Perhaps it does, although Bate has argued that his career tailed off rather than ended early and whether, by Jacobean standards, fifty-two or three was a particularly early age to die is a moot point. The life expectancy statistics hardly suggest it was.

Apart from the signature, the only items of evidence which the majority of biographers who are keen to suggest Shakespeare died of syphilis can usually cite are the references to venereal disease in the writings. It is true that there are plenty of these, especially in plays like *Measure for Measure* or *Troilus and Cressida*; and also that his final two sonnets allude to the burning sensation which accompanies some forms of venereal infection, as well as to the hot-bath treatments for syphilis current in Shakespeare's day. But the assumption that the diseases authors write about must be ones they themselves have suffered is patently wrong and would lead, to take only one example among very many, to the false belief that when Thomas Mann wrote *The Magic Mountain*, he must himself have been tubercular. Among those biographers who believe Shakespeare died of syphilis, Duncan-Jones is perhaps the one who most feels she has further evidence which can support what is to be garnered from the writings. There is first of all the association with George Wilkins, whom she is convinced kept a brothel the frequentation of which may have left Shakespeare with 'a legacy of chronic and humiliating sickness';[7] and then there is John Hall, the husband of his elder daughter, Susanna. Hall was a doctor well known in the Stratford area, who kept notes on his patients. Anthony Burgess was one of the first to imply that the very absence of references to Shakespeare in these notes strengthens the case for syphilis because it suggests that 'decency prevailed over clinical candour.' Duncan-Jones makes the same point, suggesting that 'the absence or excision of Hall's notes may well be a consequence of his father-in-law's syphilis.' 'As a doctor who ministered to the aristocracy and the landed gentry,' she goes on, 'Hall may have been habitually careful to avoid explicit mention of this shaming condition, even when he observed it.'[8] Of course, Duncan-Jones does not positively state that Hall observed Shakespeare's syphilitic condition but there is considerable skill in making the reader feel that he did and in suggesting that the blank which scholars have drawn, when they have investigated Hall, is positive rather than negative. Like Honigmann's commentary on the exclusion of Thomas Quiney's name from Shakespeare's will, here is yet another example of the argument from absence.[9]

The general presumption is that, whatever he was suffering from, Shakespeare was already very ill at the beginning of 1616. If that is true, then the 'merry meeting' which, according to legend, he had with Jonson and Drayton, just before he died, cannot have been as merry as all that. It is to the first three months of this year that the two versions of the will probably belong. The provisions which concern his younger daughter, Judith, have been mentioned previously, and so have those which allow us to identify various of his friends. The will also shows what he was prepared to do for his sister Joan and that, at the time it was drawn up, the Blackfriars Gatehouse was being rented out to a man called Robinson. But the main information it conveys is Shakespeare's concern to transfer as much of his estate as was reasonably possible to his elder daughter and son-in-law, who were also made his executors. Notoriously enough, his wife only figures in a bequest which was squeezed between two previously written lines on the will's final page: 'Item: I give unto my wife my second best bed with the furniture.' If I have delayed until now trying to deal with the difficulties this sentence raises it is because they are endless and, if past experience is a reliable guide, are always likely to remain so.

Malone was one of the first to complain that the bequest indicated how little Shakespeare cared for his wife, claiming that he had 'cut her off not indeed with a shilling, but with an old bed'.[10] Later commentators pointed out that beds were highly valued commodities in Jacobean England which often figure in wills, and some went on to suggest that the second best bed in Shakespeare's household might have been the one he and his wife slept in (the best being reserved for guests), and it might therefore have had considerable sentimental as well as commercial value. As for Anne having been 'cut off', it was subsequently claimed that she would have been automatically entitled to a third interest in her husband's estate as long as she lived, although there has been some dispute about how uniformly this 'dower right' was applied in the country as a whole. Certainly, those who choose to argue that the complex legal arrangements which were made for the purchase of the Blackfriars Gatehouse were deliberately designed to prevent Anne from claiming her dower right on that property are simultaneously conceding that she was entitled to it on all the others.[11] There are none of the usual endearments to accompany the reference to Shakespeare's wife in the will, but then none in the document as a whole. Those who have looked at other wills drawn up by Shakespeare's lawyer, Francis Collins, and in particular his own, have suggested that this was typical of the way he operated; yet several of the biographers feel confident they can detect in the wording Shakespeare's own voice. Duncan-Jones, for example, refers to its 'sour and mistrustful tone', attributing that tone to the dying man rather than his lawyer.[12] Anxious as he is to squeeze all he can from Shakespeare's deposition in the Belott / Mountjoy case, Charles Nicholl has to admit that the sentences in it 'cannot be constructed as to their particular tone' because everything is shaped to the formulae of court depositions. One would have thought that the will was also shaped to well-worn formulae, beginning as it does with a declaration of Christian faith from a current will-making handbook, and the conventional but, in this instance, very possibly false assertion that the testator is 'in perfect health and memory'. The subsequent provisions are, for the most part, couched in such standard legalese that trying to extract from them a particular voice would seem rather more than ambitious. In making that effort, Duncan-Jones chooses not to bring into meaningful relation her thoughts on the will with those concerning syphilis. Germaine Greer, on the other hand, while finding Shakespeare's statement of his last wishes 'shabby, mean-spirited', and not being inclined to forgive him for the second-best bed, none the less feels that his 'astigmatic will could be explained by the effect of mercury and / or arsenic on his brain'.[13] This is interesting in that a chief reason why biographers are so keen to discover what their subjects died of is so that they can then consider how that ought to effect descriptions of their behaviour. Was tuberculosis a factor in the writing of *Lady Chatterley's Lover*, for example, or how much should syphilis be taken into account when reading Nietzsche's last works? But in these cases we know for certain what Lawrence and Nietzsche suffered from, and the words which can be examined in the light of these illnesses are also quite definitely their own.

In June 1616 John Hall may have gone to London in order to prove his father-in-law's will and taken with him an inventory of the dead man's possessions. It would have been a great help to our understanding of the circumstances of Shakespeare's death if that document were still in existence. Yet it is, above all, the lack of any general context which makes the will far more enigmatic than astigmatic. Private arrangements made apart from the will were common in his day, but there is no way of telling whether, in Shakespeare's case, there were any. According to his monument in Stratford parish church, he died on 23 April (there is a record of his funeral on the 25th), at an age which is usually taken to be fifty-two but may have been fifty-three, depending on his date of birth. He was then buried in the church's chancel. This is a privilege which was accorded to tithe-holders, although not only to them, and it is one which leads one to say that if he did die 'a Papist', as was later suggested, it must have been as a very secret one. On his tombstone were later to be seen the following lines:

> Good friend for Jesus sake forbeare
> To dig the dust encloased here.
> Blest be the man that spares these stones,
> And cursed be he that moves my bones.[14]

Halliwell-Phillipps claimed that the tombstone we presently see is a replacement for the one which had been there about ninety years before he published his own book; yet at the end of the seventeenth century, a visitor to Stratford reported having seen this same epitaph and also transmitted a local rumour that it was Shakespeare himself who had composed it.[15]

The obvious meaning to attribute to the lines above is that Shakespeare's bones should not be disinterred and taken, as was the custom, to the nearby charnel house. Several other interpretations have, however, been offered, including the one by Frank Harris. Harris is an interesting Shakespeare biographer in that he begins his book by deducing his subject's character from the writings and then searches around for historical material to support his deduction (a method that nearly all his successors would denounce and yet which they often find themselves employing). His view is that Shakespeare wrote the epitaph in order to prevent his grave being re-opened to accommodate his hated wife.[16] An intriguing literary figure and an often entertaining writer, Harris is hardly the most trustworthy of commentators, but the lead he provides here has been followed by Greenblatt. When Shakespeare thought of the after-life, he suggests, 'the last thing he wanted was to be mingled with the woman he married'; and he adds that, rather than worrying that his bones would eventually end in the charnel house, 'he may have feared still more that one day his grave would be opened to let in the body of Anne Shakespeare.'[17] Germaine Greer feels that in his interpretation of the lines of the epitaph Greenblatt has made a 'nonsense' of them. 'What is stipulated', she insists, 'is not that the grave not be opened ... but that the bones not be disturbed.' In her view, the likely author of the lines was John Hall,

> who would have known only too well that, if Shakespeare's bones were ever to be exhumed for reburial in a more conspicuous place, posterity would see lesions on them and know beyond the possibility of doubt that the man of the millennium died of terminal syphilis.[18]

The hapless biography reader is thus faced with two possibilities. Either Shakespeare was afflicted by the kind of cadaveric anxiety which troubles his own Claudio in *Measure for Measure* (3.i) and was tormented by the thought of his senseless remains being mingled with those of his wife; or his son-in-law, already aware that his wife's father was 'the man of the millennium', deliberately strove to shield future generations from the discovery that Shakespeare died of a shameful disease. In the circumstances, it is perhaps as well that support for one hypothesis is as inadequate as it is for the other.

# 16

## *Post-mortem*

Anne Shakespeare outlived her husband by over seven years, dying in August 1623 at an age which her tombstone (next to his in the church chancel) gives as sixty-seven. Greer speculates that she might have had enough money to have subsidised the appearance of the First Folio in that same year. With half of the thirty-six plays the book contained previously unpublished (and therefore otherwise lost), this invaluable publication opens with not only Jonson's tribute, but also three other, shorter poems in praise of Shakespeare by Hugh Holland, Leonard Digges and someone who signs himself 'I. M.'. All three deal with the works rather than the man and seem like seventeenth-century equivalents of those gobbets of praise from recognisable figures which now customarily appear on the back of new books. The poem by Digges, who had Stratford connections, is nevertheless interesting in that, in the course of it, he insists that Shakespeare's name will live on even when Time has destroyed his 'Stratford moniment'.[1] This is a clear indication that the monument in question had been erected before the appearance of the other, more familiar iconic image of Shakespeare which readers of the First Folio saw as they opened its first few pages.

The half-length, life-size bust of Shakespeare which is the monument Digges refers to, is fixed against one of the walls in Stratford parish church. Set back in a niche and flanked by miniature Corinthian pillars, it depicts its subject writing and with his mouth slightly open so that, as Schoenbaum puts it, it seems as if Shakespeare is either 'declaiming his newly minted verses' or gawping 'in the throes of creation'.[2] It was probably the work of Gheerhart Janssen the younger, a sculptor of Dutch descent who operated out of Southwark. Over the years, it has been much altered. In the first instance it was painted but Malone mistakenly assumed that the paint was a later addition and had it treated with a stone-coloured wash. When his error was discovered, it was painted again. A reason for his mistake may have been his knowledge that, in 1747, the bust had undergone major repairs because it had 'through length of years and other accidents become much impaired and decayed'.[3] By comparison, the engraving in the First Folio could only suffer minor damage, from its repeated use in subsequent editions. It was the work of either the Flemish engraver Martin Droeshout or his uncle of the same name, and is almost certainly copied from a portrait. That there were such things is evident from what are known as the 'Parnassus plays', three satirical vehicles written by and for Cambridge students and performed in St John's college on various occasions between 1598 and 1603. At one moment during the second of these – the first part of *The Return from Parnassus* – a foolish and boastful character called Gullio cries out, 'Oh sweet Mr Shakespeare, I'll have his picture in my study at court.'[4] But if Droeshout was indeed working from a picture like the one Gullio mentions, one is tempted to say it cannot have been very good, although this is a hazardous statement, given the patent technical deficiencies of the engraving. It does not take much expertise, for example, to notice how the over-sized head is grotesquely separated from the puny shoulders, rather like, as Schoenbaum memorably puts it, 'the decapitated Baptist being served up to Salome' on a lace collar.[5] The man Droeshout depicted is bald, and so too is the figure in the Stratford church, but otherwise it is not easy to recognise the two images as representations of the same person, even at different stages of his life. If one put aside the notion that Droeshout was simply a bad artist, for example, one would have to say that in his final years Shakespeare developed shoulders he had never had before and that also the hydrocephalus which, on the strength of the massive forehead in the engraving, some commentators have attributed to him, had been miraculously cured.

A preliminary question for biographers is to know how far they can rely on these two images for an accurate impression of Shakespeare's facial features. Some scholars have argued that although the engraving may not have been from life, the bust would have been sculpted from a death mask,[6] but that is not certain and it must in any case have been much changed since it was first put in place. Both representations have traditionally been regarded as authentic because they were commissioned by people who had known Shakespeare and could therefore testify to their accuracy. Yet we have no way of knowing how pleased or disappointed these people were by what they eventually saw and, as far as the bust is concerned, those who paid for the commission were hardly likely to have it sent back, however misleading they may have felt the image to be. The engraving has the advantage of having been endorsed by Jonson in the verses which stand opposite it in the First Folio. These begin in a way which is somewhat equivocal:

> This Figure, which thou here seest put,
> It was for gentle Shakespeare cut,
> Wherein the Graver had a strife
> with Nature, to out-doo the life:

This suggests disappointment – the engraver has had a struggle not perhaps so much to outdo life as compete with her – but Jonson then goes on,

> O, could he but have drawne his wit
> As well in brasse, as he hath hit
> His face; the Print would then surpasse
> All, that was ever writ in brasse.
> But, since he cannot, Reader, looke
> Not on his Picture, but his Booke.[7]

The implication here is certainly that Droeshout has hit off Shakespeare's face well in his 'brasse' plate (this adjective being interchangeable with the word 'copper' at the time); but Jonson could hardly have said the opposite in the situation he was in and his general message is that no one is going to learn anything about the Shakespeare he knew by looking at the engraving.

None of those who paid for either the bust or the engraving may, of course, have ever been disappointed at all, but many since have felt their spirits sink. Droeshout's mild-looking, youngish man has appeared to some more like a lawyer's clerk than the world's greatest dramatist, while one observer famously claimed that the Stratford bust made Shakespeare seem like 'a self-satisfied pork butcher'.[8] Reactions such as these may help to explain the popularity of other images which do not have anywhere near the same claims to authenticity, but which are more attractive. There is, for example, the so-called Chandos portrait, in which the dark-skinned figure has bushy dark hair and sports an ear-ring (Shakespeare made up for the part of Shylock, has been one explanation for those who have felt that this picture makes its subject look Jewish). The Grafton portrait also has its admirers, especially since it was supposedly painted in 1588 and would thus depict Shakespeare when he was only twenty-four, 'a young blade, diffident, sensitive, intelligent, witty, ambitious; a provincial poet making his way in the world', as Michael Wood puts it.[9] Or there is the Davenant bust, now in the Garrick club, which shows an alert, sharp-featured and distinctly good-looking man with flowing locks. These are by no means the only contenders for a true likeness and the struggle to establish one or other of them as on the same footing as the bust or the engraving can be fierce, as was shown by the controversy which blew up in 2010 over the authenticity of a picture which is known as the Cobbe portrait (after the family which own it), and which is currently on display in the buildings of the Shakespeare Birthplace Trust.[10]

Those who own portraits which have some claim to authenticity have obvious reasons for wanting to establish it, but their efforts would not reach the news media to the surprising extent they do, were there not a general passion in society to know not only what Shakespeare was like, but also what he looked like. Most of us participate in a variety of this passion when we pick up a new literary biography and instinctively turn first to the portrait or photograph of the subject. It is as if we had never taken the force of the warning Shakespeare sounds when, in *Macbeth,* he has Duncan say that 'there's no art / To find the mind's construction in the face' (1.iv). Yet often those who make this move do so less in a spirit of discovery than out of a need to find a resting place for a number of impressions already created in them by the work of the subject. How dangerous this can be is finely illustrated by Proust in one of the best-known episodes of *À la recherche du temps perdu.* Marcel has long been an admirer of Bergotte, a writer he imagines as a 'godlike elder' and a 'Bard with snowy locks'. When he is unexpectedly introduced to him at a dinner party, the effect is like suddenly having in front of him the magician who has emerged unharmed from the minor explosion which is a part of his act. He bows to the person whom his hostess has named to him as Bergotte whereupon,

> my greeting was returned by a youngish, uncouth, thickset and myopic little man, with a red nose curled like a snail shell and a goatee beard.

> I was cruelly disappointed, for what had just vanished in the dust of the explosion was not only the languorous old man, of whom no vestige now remained, but also the beauty of an immense work which I had contrived to enshrine in the frail and hallowed organism that I had constructed, like a temple, expressly for it, but for which no room was to be found in the squat figure, packed tight with blood-vessels, bones, glands, sinews, of the little man with the snub nose and black beard who stood before me.[11]

One could imagine a similar kind of response for a number of those who, closely familiar with Shakespeare's plays and poems, saw the Droeshout engraving, or the Stratford bust, for the first time. Of course, Proust being Proust, Marcel's first reaction to Bergotte is far from being the end of the matter and he is gradually able to re-associate the man with his work. But this is because he is meeting him in the flesh and can listen to his conversation. The Shakespeare enthusiast is, by contrast, faced with a set of features which do not move and which (as Jonson intimates) might mean anything or nothing.

Appearances, we need constantly to remind ourselves, and especially the single, fixed appearance which is all the portrait usually allows, can be deceptive. There is a cheerfully diverting illustration of this in the autobiography of Ray Milland, a star of post-Second World War cinema. He recalls the praise he received for a scene in which he had to emerge from under water in the company of Dorothy Lamour and regard her lovingly as they kissed. The sequence, he explains, was shot while he had a pressing need to urinate, but was prevented from going to the toilet by the anxiety of his German director who wanted to make the best of the intermittent sunlight. When he was finally told to dive in the cold water, the shock caused him to evacuate automatically so that the blissfully adoring look he was able to direct at his co-star as he emerged, and which the director found so convincing ('That vos vonderful, vonderful. It had a simple extase'), was largely a consequence of physical relief.[12] Out of place though this story may seem here, its important moral is that a single expression is never a reliable guide to either a particular state of mind or, by extension, to character. The great Renaissance portrait artists, the specialists insist, are indeed able to depict character, but whether it is the actual character of the sitter would be hard to establish and, in any case, no one claims that Jannsen and Droeshout, or any of the others responsible for supposed portraits of Shakespeare, were great artists. When even photographs can be misleading indices of the nature of the subject, capturing as they do only one moment, it is difficult to see what useful data about the inner being of Shakespeare can be gleaned from a much-restored bust, a poor engraving or any of the other representations of him. From this point of view, it does not much matter which of the various images of Shakespeare is declared a true likeness since, if one puts to one side the very important question of clothing and other historical details of that kind, all of them are equally uninformative.

Portraits have traditionally played a major role in biographies. One of the most prolific and successful biographers of the 1920s and 1930s was Emil Ludwig, whose life of Kaiser Wilhelm II attracted the serious attention of Freud and Sartre. In an autobiography published in 1931, Ludwig explained that he always began work on his biographies with a portrait he had known for years, 'before I so much as looked at the other documents, and if the painter lied there were others that could be used for comparison' (other portraits, presumably).[13] As remarkable here as Ludwig's confidence in being able to detect a lying painter before looking at other kinds of testimony is his belief in being able to 'read' a portrait biographically: his nineteenth-century confidence in what is predominantly the face as an index of character. There is an example of this confidence in the opening paragraph of his biographical sketch of Baron von Stein, one of sixteen similar pieces, nearly all preceded by a portrait, in his *Genius and Character*:

> The framework of a massive body supports a squared skull with delicately vaulted forehead and thin uncommunicative lips. Yet two clear blue eyes and gigantic nose – evidence respectively of faith and energy – stand out upon this face with an aggressive and commanding prominence. For faith and energy are the fundamental traits of this powerful and simple man.[14]

The modern reader has no difficulty in dismissing this as nonsense, yet the belief that facial characteristics are associated with moral qualities is deep-seated. In reading certain nineteenth-century novels, most of us negotiate with a disturbingly instinctive ease the 'feature code' of weak chins, sensual lips and strong noses, apprehending only if we remain especially alert the intersection points at which a largely spurious folk wisdom can be seen transmogrifying into yet another of the pseudo-sciences of that period. The peculiarities of the Droeshout engraving mean that attention has often focused less on eyes, lips or noses than on the shape of its subject's head, but that can be made to reveal its secrets also, as Washington Irving illustrates when he explains how Shakespeare's 'finely arched forehead' shows 'clear indications of that cheerful, social disposition, by which he was as much characterised among his contemporaries as by the vastness of his genius'.[15]

Most of the recent Shakespeare biographers are rightly wary of the tradition Ludwig illustrates so blatantly, and Washington Irving a little less so, although one can perhaps feel its presence when Park Honan says of the Droeshout engraving that 'if the portrait lacks the "sparkle" of a witty poet, it suggests the inwardness of a writer of great intelligence, an independent man who is not insensitive to the pain of others'; or when the authors of a catalogue for an exhibition intended to advance the claims of the Cobbe portrait describe it as showing 'the face of a good listener, as well as of someone who exercised a natural restraint'.[16] More redolent of the nineteenth century is A. L. Rowse, who, in discussing Shakespeare's appearance, refers to the 'mobile, flexible features we know so well, the sexy nose and sensuous lips, the large luminous eyes and dome of a cranium'.[17] This was in *Shakespeare the Man* but in an earlier essay Rowse had said of this same 'sexy nose' that it had 'sensibility indicated in the flare of the nostril' and exclaimed of the Droeshout portrait, 'What a powerful impression it gives: that searching look of the eyes understanding everything, what a forehead, what a brain!'[18] Peter Ackroyd is also struck by Shakespeare's 'straight and sensitive nose, and his watchful eyes', as well as his 'full lips'; and he quotes a 'professional phrenologist', who has concluded from the shape of the head that 'the dramatist was possessed of "ideality, wonder, wit, imitation, benevolence, and veneration" with "small destructiveness and acquisitiveness".' His cranium, this expert also apparently thought, evinces 'great susceptibility, activity, quickness and love of action'.[19] Here the images which have survived of Shakespeare have been made to yield his personality much in the same way as they would have done to Ludwig, yet the results bear no more convincing a relationship to the man they purport to describe than a horoscope does to the future. Foolish as he may be, Gullio is not wrong to want to hang a picture of Shakespeare in his study because we all need a focus for the admiration his writings inspire. The mistake lies in believing that the qualities which we project on to such a picture somehow emanate from it. I have characterised reading heads and faces as a typically nineteenth-century activity, and it was, after all, in that period phrenology was developed; yet in *The Mill on the Floss* George Eliot rescues the honour of her contemporaries when, in the seventh chapter of the third book, she introduces for the first time Mr Wakem, the lawyer whom we have previously heard Mr Tulliver denouncing as a rascal. 'The lines and lights of the human countenance are like other symbols', Eliot wisely notes, '– not always easy to read without a key.' And she goes on,

> On an *a priori* view of Wakem's aquiline nose, which offended Mr. Tulliver, there was not more rascality than in the shape of his stiff shirt-collar, though this too, along with his nose, might have become fraught with damnatory meaning when once the rascality was ascertained.

When once Shakespeare's character has been ascertained, the meaning with which his portraits are then fraught is almost always laudatory.

# PART II

# 17

## Gossip

THE INFORMATION ON WHICH Shakespeare's biographers chiefly rely can usually be defined as gossip: stories about the subject which have never been picked up first-hand (or, indeed, second- or third-hand). The truth of this claim is illustrated by a rapid glance at four major sources for any account of his life in Stratford. The earliest of these dates from 1662, when John Ward became vicar of Stratford and its most famous resident had been dead for almost fifty years. He gathered what information he could, so that it is from Ward that we learn that Shakespeare was able to spend £1,000 every year and that his death was hastened by that 'merry meeting', or drinking bout, with Jonson and Drayton, a notion discounted by some on the grounds that these last two disliked each other so much. It was probably also in the early 1660s that Aubrey made those enquiries in Stratford which led to his being told, by 'some of the neighbours', that Shakespeare's father had been a butcher and that he himself had earned a reputation for acting in his youth. Around the 1690s, Thomas Betterton, a famous actor who had largely made his name in Shakespearean roles, visited Stratford. It is the stories he heard then about Shakespeare's poaching which were passed on to Nicholas Rowe for eventual use in his 1709 biography. The first notice we have of the epitaph on the Stratford tombstone dates from 1673 but, twenty years later, a visitor called John Dowdall also copied the words down, reporting at the same time that they had proved effective, even though Shakespeare's 'wife and daughters did earnestly desire to be laid in the same grave with him'. This may well be the origin of Frank Harris's interpretation of the epitaph's real meaning, although, if it is, he conveniently forgot about the daughters.[1]

Philosophers tell a joke about Socrates and gossip which may have some relevance here. An acquaintance came up to him one day and asked whether he had heard the latest news about Diogenes. Socrates stopped the man in his tracks and said that he did not want to hear what he had to communicate before it was subjected to three tests. The first was whether he knew the information to be true and the man had to admit that, since it was something he had only *heard* (it was, after all, gossip), he did not. The second was whether it was to the credit of Diogenes, a possibility the man had quickly to dismiss. The third test was whether what the man had to say would be useful to Socrates. The man gave this some thought before deciding in the negative. Well, said Socrates, if you want to tell me something that is neither true, good nor useful, why tell it me at all? And this, the joke concludes, is why Socrates never discovered that Diogenes was sleeping with his wife.

The message in this invented anecdote might seem to be that we ignore gossip at our peril and this is a view which has been taken by some of the more sober of Shakespeare's biographers. Halliwell-Phillipps, for example, while characterising Aubrey as 'one of those foolish and detestable gossips who record everything they hear or misinterpret, and without so much as giving a thought to the damage they may inflict on the reputation of their victims', none the less protested against the 'indiscriminate expulsion of the traditional stories'. The main burden of his argument was that, in Shakespeare's day, provincial towns such as Stratford were much more isolated than they subsequently became.

> The oral history of local affairs [he therefore concluded] thus became in former days imprisoned, as it were, in the districts of their occurrence; and it is accordingly found that, in some cases, provincial incidents have been handed down through successive generations with an accuracy that is truly marvellous.

There is a hint of a non-sequitur here, in that the degree to which a particular item of gossip is confined to the community to which it relates bears no necessary relation to whether or not it happens to be true. But Halliwell-Phillipps supports his case by referring to a story which had been current in Worcester 'from time immemorial', and which concerns the robber of the sanctus bell having had his previously flayed skin nailed to the cathedral door. These details were recently confirmed, he says, by scientific analysis of fragments still hanging to an ancient door in the crypt. This is his single, general illustration of the 'accuracy that is truly marvellous' but, as far as the particular case of Shakespeare is concerned, he notes that Rowe's reference to the straitened circumstances which obliged John Shakespeare to withdraw his son from school was a claim about the early life of his subject which was only shown to be justified by subsequent research.[2] He presumably means that it was only much later that details about John Shakespeare's debts or failure to attend council meetings came to light, but these have, of course, subsequently received varying interpretations. Peter Ackroyd, for example, believes that what seem like debts were only a Catholic's way of protecting his money from the government, while no one has yet been able to establish when Shakespeare stopped going to school and whether, at the time he did so, he was, in fact, withdrawn by his father or simply left. The marvellous accuracy which Halliwell-Phillipps implicitly attributes to Rowe, that is, does not in this case take one very far.

A far more cautious defence of gossip was mounted by E. K. Chambers, in the most unlikely of places. Introducing the section in his book so tellingly entitled 'The Shakespeare-Mythos', he writes, 'It is, I think, possible to underestimate the value of biographical tradition,' although he then immediately adds, 'where it is not inconsistent with other evidence.' 'Provincial memories', he goes on (echoing faintly the case made by Halliwell-Phillipps), 'are long-lived, and so are those of professions which, like that of the stage, are largely recruited as hereditary castes.' Having made this concession, Chambers then retreats to his default position by adding:

> There is, of course, a tact to be exercised in taking the gist of a statement, without laying too much stress on the details. And it must be admitted that after all there is much [in the following section] which throws less light upon Shakespeare than upon the mental processes which lead to the development of myths.[3]

The suggestion here that in the gossip which people like Ward, Aubrey, Betterton or Dowdall picked up, and which then hardened into tradition, there is a valuable 'gist' is repeated by Schoenbaum, although he cites Edmond Malone as being the first to insist that the traditional stories 'may harbour golden kernels of truth'. What is important, Schoenbaum writes, is that these stories should not be dismissed out of hand and he quotes in support some thoughts on the matter which Chambers articulated fifteen or so years after *William Shakespeare: A Study of Facts and Problems* had appeared. In these, Chambers proposes again that 'tradition cannot be altogether disregarded,' and he goes on to repeat Halliwell-Phillipps's point about a country neighbourhood being 'self-contained and tenacious of outstanding local personalities'. But, he then continues,

> Our attitude towards tradition must therefore be one, neither of credulity nor of complete scepticism, but of critical balance. There are criteria to be borne in mind. Does the tradition arise early or late? Does it come from more than one independent source? Does it help to explain record or contradict it?[4]

Few would disagree with Chambers when he says that, in dealing with gossip which has hardened into tradition, there have to be criteria. But what are these to be? Only the first of those which are attributed to Socrates in the joke about Diogenes would seem to have any relevance, although to demand that purveyors of gossip should be certain of the truth of what they say might seem to set the bar too high. In any case, someone can firmly believe what they report is true and still be mistaken. A lot depends on who the someone is. Halliwell-Phillipps was clearly inclined to be sceptical of most of what he found in Aubrey, and when Edmond Malone was attempting to deal with Shakespeare's putative flight from Stratford, after being caught poaching in the grounds of Sir Thomas Lucy, he decided it was one of those stories which he was only prepared to consider seriously if he knew that it had 'been handed down, by a very industrious and careful inquirer, who had derived it from persons most likely to be accurately informed concerning the fact related, and subjoins his authority'.[5] The poaching episode occurs in a record which slightly pre-dates Rowe, but it is from him that most subsequent accounts derive and one might reasonably speculate that his informant, Betterton, was as 'industrious and careful' as Malone might require. But we have no idea of the individuals from whom he gathered his data, a whole century after the supposed events took place. The time gap is crucial, as Chambers recognises when he first of all suggests we should always consider whether any tradition arises early or late, one problem then being that all we can usually know is when it was first *recorded*. As far as Shakespeare's alleged poaching is concerned, the fact that there is a report of it before Rowe's which the latter cannot have seen might seem to answer Chambers's second demand for 'more than one independent source'. Yet, as I said in discussing the Manningham anecdote, that two people hear and then independently repeat the same story is no necessary proof of its veracity. Chambers's final criterion or test is that hardened items of gossip should be in accord with the historical record. For many years, the historical record indicated clearly that Shakespeare's father was a glover, someone who signed Council records with the insignia of that trade, and that therefore Aubrey's claim that he was a butcher must be false. It was then discovered that on two occasions he was accused of dealing in wool without a licence and the thought therefore arose that, like many Elizabethan businessmen, he may have dabbled in several trades. Putting aside, therefore, Duncan-Jones's suggestion that the neighbours meant to speak of Shakespeare's *god*father, it is not beyond the bounds of possibility (very few phenomena are) that Aubrey could have been right, even if being a butcher is not the same as doing the occasional butchering. There is, however, nowhere near enough surviving evidence to be sure and this is so with nearly all the other suggestions thrown up by the mythos. How can we explore, as Chambers invites us to in the final criterion he offers, whether a particular detail is in accord or contradiction with the historical record when that record is so meagre and sparse?

It would be good to have solid criteria, but the example of Chambers shows how difficult they are both to frame and to apply, especially when the information involved is so miscellaneous. Yet by any normal standards, those (for example) to which an academic historian might appeal, the four sources for Shakespeare's life in Stratford which I have cited must surely be regarded as unreliable and therefore unusable without some kind of genuine corroboration. Dowdall is perhaps the most trustworthy in that he clearly identifies his source, an old man of 'above eighty' who showed him round the parish church. But whether such a person could be authoritative as to the desire of Shakespeare's wife to be buried in the same grave as her husband must be doubtful. It might be suspected here that I have chosen these four examples because of their special vulnerability to criticism, but this is not the case. All the other items which Chambers gathered together in the section of his book called 'The Shakespeare-Mythos' are at least as vulnerable or more so, which is presumably why he chose to give them that name. Duncan-Jones's anxiety to establish that someone close to Shakespeare was a butcher, even though this has no close relation to whether he ever pretended to kill a calf in a mumming play, appears to derive from the feeling that, if Aubrey is shown to be wrong in one particular, his whole testimony becomes suspect. Other biographers have been less concerned with consistency, happily deciding that the poaching episode, for example, deserves credit while Shakespeare's £1,000 a year does not. The impression they may be seeking to give in choosing one story rather than another is of discrimination, or that 'critical balance' to which Chambers refers. But when it is only very exceptionally that the odd detail in one of the stories can be verified, all that the exercise of choice will tend to exemplify is the convenience of fluctuating rigour. In so far as it is truth which is at issue here, the plain fact of the matter is that the four sources I have mentioned are like all the others which Chambers collected in his mythos section and would never have received the degree of attention they habitually do were there anything better available.

In addition to calling for criteria, Chambers endorses an idea which Schoenbaum traces back to Malone: that although many of the details of the gossip-based stories may be false, they none the less enclose a 'kernel of truth'. The adoption of this notion by Shakespeare's more recent biographers is usually more implicit than explicit, but Ackroyd says that 'behind all local legends, there lies a modicum of ascertainable fact,' while Weis claims that 'Stratford stories about Shakespeare have a way, sooner of later, of turning out to be true, or very nearly so.'[6] The problem with these two statements can be suggested by noting that both might reasonably be paraphrased with the motto of the tabloids, that there is no smoke without fire. It is perhaps the case that, in many instances, although by no means all, gossip has a genuine historical source, but the difficulty lies in identifying it correctly. Everyone knows from their own experience how quickly a story which concerns themselves becomes distorted as it passes from mouth to mouth: that its transmission is like a game of Chinese whispers. Tracing such a story back is difficult when it is contemporary and those involved are still living; but separating fact from fiction becomes immeasurably more so when, as in Shakespeare's case, the source or origin that is sought lies at least fifty and often almost a hundred years in the past. Whether Shakespeare died after over-indulging himself with Jonson and Drayton, had a father who was a butcher and a wife who would have dearly liked to have joined him in the grave, or was forced to leave Stratford after being caught poaching, are in any case such different claims that they would require different modes of enquiry; yet quite how any of these would allow one to identify the 'golden kernel of truth' which each supposedly contains, and separate it off from the falsehood which might well have accompanied the process by which the story was passed on, is very difficult to imagine.

Since another name for gossip is hearsay, and there have always been intense discussions in English law about hearsay evidence, the standards by which it should be judged are not unreasonably forensic. This may be the reason for a nightmare from which those who spend time with these matters sometimes suffer. The dreamer, who is here male for convenience, has committed some serious but unspecified offence and finds himself mounting the steps to the dock. As he enters into the light of the court and looks across at the members of the jury, he discovers with dismay that every one of them is a Shakespeare biographer and is then invaded with a feeling of utter hopelessness as to his future prospects. Hopelessness may well seem to some an inappropriately severe response to the way the authors of lives of Shakespeare deal with the surviving gossip, especially as (to pursue the legal analogy) it is a well-known provision of English law that it is impossible to libel the dead. When Halliwell-Phillipps complains of Aubrey's indifference to the effect his stories might have on the 'reputation' of his subjects, he not only appears to be dealing more in terms of respectability than truth, but also thinking of those subjects as if they were still living. How, in the end, does it matter what we say about the dead, especially when they have been as long dead as Shakespeare? He is certainly not going to read what is said about him. And yet it ought surely to be one of the iron rules of biography that any story about the subject should be treated with the same care and scepticism as one which related to a contemporary, and with an awareness of how much damage can be done to the living by idle and ill-informed gossip. There is a moral imperative here, but also the practical one of being able to distinguish a biographer from a gossip columnist.

# 18

## *The post-modernist challenge*

BECAUSE THE RECORD IS so inadequate, Shakespeare's biographers are constantly involved in speculation. But then so too, they might well insist, is any other writer who sets out to write the life of another human being. There is enough truth in this defence to give pause to any critic of their work. If numerous occasions occur when biographers find themselves obliged to make conjectures about the lives of subjects as well documented as those of Byron or D. H. Lawrence, why should Shakespeare's biographers not be entitled to their conjectures also? Speculation or conjecture is an inevitable part of *any* biography, so that the only question is just how big a role it plays, and how responsibly it is undertaken. When Stendhal compared memory of the past to a damaged fresco, sections of which had become detached from the wall, he was thinking of autobiography.[1] Writing biography is more like trying to complete a jigsaw puzzle. Although the board is full of gaps, the shape of what is missing can, in the more favourable cases, be indicated by the surrounding pieces. As far as Shakespeare is concerned, however, there are huge areas of empty space and no parameters to keep speculation in control. With so few records and no personal documentation (the point has to be made repeatedly), most of his biographers only feel themselves limited by what might have been possible and what cannot be disproved, and that, as I have tried to show, is no limitation at all.

The reason biographers of Shakespeare cannot legitimately defend their speculation by saying that it is part and parcel of all life-writing is because they indulge themselves in it so much

## The post-modernist challenge

more wildly than others. But my repeated insistence above on the absence of documentation could prompt another and sometimes much more sophisticated form of defence. This consists in pointing out how easy it is to make a fetish of the surviving archival record. One not at all sophisticated aspect of the danger of doing this has been well described recently by an American journalist, commenting on the acquisition by Harvard of a huge cache of papers from the estate of John Updike:

> All those boxes, their contents neatly filed and numbered and alphabetized, in all their exquisite order! But anyone who has spent time poking through a writer's archive ... will realize that the apparent intactness masks what is not there. The letters that got torn up, the drafts that were burned – you can agonize in frustration over what was lost. But for all the diary entries and recipes and Christmas cards that your subject saved, there might have been an equal number which he or she threw away.[2]

This is, of course, quite true. However abundant the record a biographical subject leaves behind, it will always be partial and to that extent inadequate. Thousands of the letters D. H. Lawrence wrote have survived, but the ones he sent to his mother every week over three years, while he was a schoolmaster in Croydon, have disappeared completely.

The perils of the partial record can be illustrated from Shapiro's *1599*, a book which, when it first came out, quickly gained a reputation for speculative sobriety.

> Just because Shakespeare was able to write plays that appealed to audiences across a wide social spectrum [Shapiro asserts] didn't mean that he wasn't frustrated by the limits this imposed on what he could write. As his understanding of drama continued to deepen, his desire to experiment ... jarred with the demands for writing plays that had to please all.

This unjustified and unjustifiable claim to knowledge of Shakespeare's inner life is in accord with the traditional view of the progress of his career; but Shapiro provides his own gloss by adding, 'Those intricate, brilliant sonnets he kept writing provided an outlet, certainly, but that wasn't enough.' Shakespeare's difficulty was compounded, he feels, by 'how he was seen as an artist'. It was only in the year or so before 1599, he writes, that 'contemporary critics' finally began to acknowledge his talent. The problem was that, when they did so, it was invariably because of 'his more sexually charged work – the two long poems *Venus and Adonis* and *Lucrece*, his love tragedy *Romeo and Juliet* and those sonnets that only a privileged few had seen or heard'. Shapiro's evidence for this claim is no more than a few phrases in two contemporary short poems by Richard Barnfield and John Weever, and the testimony of the inevitable Francis Meres (these are his 'contemporary critics'). Meres was the former Cambridge graduate who, in 1598, published what now seems like an idiot's guide to contemporary English literature, *Palladis Tamia: Wit's Treasury* (the English roughly translates the Greek), a work so comprehensive and undiscriminating that any practising writer of the time who was excluded from it would have had every reason to feel aggrieved. Mostly Meres deals in lists of titles, which have certainly proved very useful for scholars. In Shapiro's view, no contemporary comes out better from the book than Shakespeare, although he laments that, once again, 'it's Shakespeare the honey-tongued poet that commands attention', citing in support Meres's famous remark about the 'the sweet witty soul of Ovid' living 'in mellifluous and honey-tongued Shakespeare, witness his *Venus and Adonis*, his *Lucrece*, his sugared *Sonnets* among his private friends'. A little later Shapiro adds, 'We know too little about the reading and book buying habits of the Elizabethans, but what evidence we have confirms that, especially for the younger readers, it was Shakespeare's amorous writing that held the greatest appeal.'[3] The context makes clear that he means a greater appeal than Shakespeare's other writings but, in so far as this statement refers exclusively to books, it makes little sense since the only two non-dramatic works which Shakespeare had himself published by 1599 were both about love, or at least sex, and the first *play* with his name on the front only appeared in 1598. To the extent it is meant to indicate how his subject's general reputation stood at that date, Shapiro's claim is based on a startlingly small number of references to Shakespeare, mostly from people whose social and educational background might incline them to pay more overt attention to his poetry than his plays. To take this handful of brief allusions as representative, and able to tell us anything worthwhile about Shakespeare's general literary standing in 1599, is a prime example of over-reliance on a partial record, the inadequacy of which Shapiro himself partly admits ('we know little . . .'). The evidence available is far too exiguous to allow any conclusions to be drawn from it, even if it is far more substantial than anything that can be adduced in support of the idea that this supposed reputation among his contemporaries, conjured up for Shakespeare by Shapiro, was one which left him feeling frustrated and upset.

## The post-modernist challenge

It might seem possible to defend the way Shapiro uses 'contemporary critics' by insisting again that all biography offers only a partial account, but that would be to ignore vital questions of degree. There is all the difference in the world between the gaps in the documentary record which relate to Byron or Lawrence, and those which relate to Shakespeare. In the first two instances, enough remains to give biographers at least a chance of working out what is missing, of becoming aware of what they do not know. And yet it is not so much those documentary gaps that constitute an unavoidable condition of dealing with the past which have preoccupied some commentators recently, but rather the status of documents themselves. One aspect of that general current of thinking which is very unsatisfactorily known as post-modernism involves a challenge to the naïve assumption that documents allow us direct access to the truth of former events. 'The technical structure of the archiving archive also determines the very structure of the archivable content even in its very coming into existence and its relationship to the future,' writes Jacques Derrida. 'The archivisation produces as much as it records the event.'[4] Whatever the precise meaning of all these words, most biographers may well feel that they can acquit themselves of being too naïvely accepting of archives in their own treatment of, for example, a private diary or a batch of letters. They will insist how they understand that there are often conditions which make it impossible for individuals to tell the truth about themselves, or that to be properly understood a letter always needs to be fully contextualised. But the scepticism which has been encouraged by that way of thinking I refer to is much more radical than this suggests, and extends to documents which are not personal in the sense of diaries or letters, and which have often in the past been assumed to carry an objective, impersonal value. What this means can be at least partly seen in the way Leeds Barroll treats the papers associated with Shakespeare's purchase in 1597 of New Place, the building traditionally described as the second largest house in Stratford.

Leeds Barroll characterises his *Politics, Plague, and Shakespeare's Theater: The Stuart Years* as an 'essay in Shakespearean biography'. Subverting in the course of it the common idea that the accession of James I led to years of plain-sailing for Shakespeare, and challenging the belief that James's adoption of the Lord Chamberlain's Men as his own King's Men has any great significance, Barroll also issues a well-argued challenge to the usually accepted chronology for plays like *Othello, Macbeth* and *Antony and Cleopatra* and thus makes life even more difficult for the biographers. This is because finding Shakespeare in his writings, and associating the latter with key episodes in his life, becomes harder when even previously accepted and familiar dates for certain plays begin to look suspect. It is in his first, introductory chapter that Leeds Barroll deals with the New Place purchase and his treatment says much about his general approach. 'If Shakespeare signed a business document purchasing New Place in 1597,' he asks, 'what are we to think?':

> A current assumption might view this purchase as a desire for respectability or even gentility, but Shakespeare could have bought the large house in Stratford-upon-Avon for any number of reasons. He may have wished to compensate his wife for his absences. The purchase of New Place on the other hand, could have been the least important thing, emotionally, ever to have happened to Shakespeare and Anne Hathaway. The size, concreteness, or expense of New Place as a physical building does not qualify it as the avatar of an equally massive psychic event. . . . Domestic and business records need not inevitably melt together into one canonical account of peace and prosperity.[5]

The chief point here is that, in Leeds Barroll's view, documents – what he calls the 'recorded signs of past human activity' – are not 'univocal' (not many people have ever thought they were); and that, more importantly, they are always 'inevitably appropriated by a history into some ideology'. His concern is to challenge the 'canonical account' which sees the purchase of New Place as a major step on Shakespeare's road to prosperous gentility and provide – eventually, if not in this particular case – alternative narratives, even though 'no single narration can rise above the theoretical problems inherent in the structuring of narrative itself'. The problem of documents for him is, therefore, not so much the partiality of the record they provide, but that our preconceptions in approaching them ensure that they can never yield the truth of the past. Why, then, bother so much about the irresponsible speculation of Shakespeare's biographers when history itself is no more than a collection of alternative narratives and an area where, as Leeds Barroll at one point puts it, 'traditional standards of verification can lay equal claim to relevance, but they cannot appropriate hegemony'?[6]

Had he chosen to discuss the record of Shakespeare's baptism in 1564, Leeds Barroll might have had more difficulty in making his case about documents, although that particular one is also no doubt susceptible to 'alternative narratives'. His focus is on the *interpretation* of the New Place purchase and he exaggerates the extent to which that has been univocal. Mild surprise has often been expressed that it took place before the Globe was up and running, and its relatively early date has opened the way to conjectures about (for example) a gift from Southampton or the success of Anne Shakespeare's business affairs. But our inability to confirm or deny these alternative explanations of how Shakespeare was able to buy New Place has less to do with 'the theoretical problems inherent in the structuring of narrative' than the absence of other supporting documents which would throw light on Shakespeare's financial position at the time, and perhaps also on his motives. It is not my aim here, however, to dispute Leeds Barroll's approach but rather to examine what relevance it might have for Shakespeare biography, both theoretically (as a defence) and in practice.

In so far as practice is concerned, it is useful to consider here the attack by Margreta de Grazia on the folly of Malone's biographical methodology, and by implication, therefore, that of all those who might be inclined to express dissatisfaction with today's biographical writing. De Grazia is chiefly interested in criticising the tradition of textual scholarship which Malone may be said to have founded and which has resulted in the habit of calling certain quartos of Shakespeare's plays 'bad' or 'corrupt' when (as witty commentators have sometimes pointed out) all they really are is textually challenged. But she sees the same bad habit of continually wanting to go back to the source or origin in the study of a Shakespeare text as also vitiating investigation of his life. 'The same preoccupation with authenticity', de Grazia writes, 'characterized Malone's account of Shakespeare's life as it did his treatment of Shakespeare's text.' A case in point for her is the anxiety Malone felt about the poaching episode, a manifestation of which has been quoted above (p. 148). In her view, the very fact that this story was so improbable shows that it was really concerned 'not with recording facts but with commemorating "the occasion" that introduced Shakespeare to his brilliant theatrical career'. It indicated 'not an historical and datable event but a significant occasion'. Other items in the mythos, she believes, were also not concerned with 'actual and verifiable occurrences' but were rather methods which people in the seventeenth and eighteenth centuries employed to meet the 'peculiar problem posed by Shakespeare's art' (in particular, how plays which broke all the classical rules came to be so impressive). According to her, therefore, by 'linking Shakespeare to a past defined by facts and documents Malone cut him off from the traditional context that made his life relevant to those who discussed it'; 'by rejecting the traditional tales in favour of the authentic documents, [he] abstracted the life from the broader social and moral concerns and sealed it in an historically remote past constructed of authentic papers.'[7] He set a bad example, she implies, not merely by perversely refusing to base his own endeavours on the traditional tales in Rowe and others, but also by attempting, with his criticisms, to inhibit other people's enjoyment of them.

De Grazia's attack on Malone represents such an extreme case of that denial of a history which Leeds Barroll implies is in any case unreachable that it is hard to see how a biographer of Shakespeare could either be influenced by it or independently take a similar line. Yet one or the other is what Stephen Greenblatt does when he also comes to consider the poaching episode. 'The question, then,' he writes, 'is not the degree of evidence but rather the imaginative life that the incident has, the access it gives to something important in Shakespeare's life and work.'[8] This is a statement with implications so startling that most readers would no doubt be right to ignore it. The premise of the text which is being presented to them is, after all, that Greenblatt will discover 'the actual person who wrote the most important body of literature of the last thousand years',[9] and this actuality can hardly be arrived at by ignoring degrees of evidence. The question which Greenblatt therefore needs to answer is not so much whether he thinks the poaching episode, or something like it, really happened (as many of his remarks would suggest that he does), but whether he believes its happening matters one way or the other. In so far as he toys with the idea that it does *not* matter, he is implicitly admitting that all the interesting information he goes on to provide concerning Sir Thomas Lucy, as a local magnate and 'relentless persecutor of recusancy',[10] is gratuitous. Why tell us that, in his youth, Lucy was tutored by Foxe of *Book of Martyrs* fame, or that, in 1584, he introduced a bill in Parliament against poaching, if the possibility of him and Shakespeare having come across each other is unimportant compared with what has been, and still can be made of their supposed encounter? If Greenblatt's readers chose to take him seriously when he says that what matters about the poaching episode, and presumably, therefore, many others like it, is not 'the degree of evidence' but rather 'the imaginative life that the incident has, the access it gives to something important in Shakespeare's life and work', they would then wonder why, for much of his book, he argues and behaves like a traditional biographer or historian, quoting documents and making inferences from them. They would wonder (that is) why elsewhere he shows the usual concern for degrees of evidence and elected – and this is the same point – to write a biography in the first place. One could choose to study all the stories which have circulated about Shakespeare for their 'imaginative life' rather than their probability, but the result then would need to have a different name. When de Grazia criticises Malone's methods, or what might here be called (using Leeds Barroll's terminology) 'traditional standards of verification', she casts him as the personification of unhelpful 'Enlightenment' values. She regrets that, in advancing her own views, she has been forced to rely on 'such positivistic mainstays as logic and evidence', but believes that, if these procedures, and others like them, 'can be used to disclose their own past construction in history, they can also be used to accelerate their eventual dismantling in history'.[11] Her critics are likely to feel that, as far as evidence or logic is concerned, she has less to apologise for than she thinks, but her remarks do nevertheless provide some explanation for the contradiction which she finds herself living. It seems to me that Greenblatt has no comparable account of how he can offer to write the kind of history which biography is and at the same time repudiate it by saying that he values a particular report, not for its authenticity but its 'imaginative life'.

Since many post-modernist ideas are inimical to traditional biographical practice, it is perhaps not surprising that the only other of Shakespeare's biographers to flirt with them is Jonathan Bate. This is in the first of his books, *The Genius of Shakespeare*, which is only partly biographical. The version of post-modernism Bate provides might be described as domesticated, or at least adapted to a non-academic public. Quoting the anecdote already discussed above, in which Shakespeare says that, in his capacity as godfather to Jonson's newly born son, he would give the child a dozen Latin / latten spoons so that Ben could then translate them, Bate comments, 'Regardless of its factual origin, this story has the authentically *representative* truth of anecdote.' To understand quite what this means the reader has to go to the introduction of Bate's book where he says,

> Most of the records we have concerning Shakespeare as an actor-dramatist are anecdotal, but the representative anecdote, like the horoscope, is precisely a form of which the purpose is to distil someone's characteristic disposition, their 'genius'. The point of the anecdote is not its factual but its representative truth.[12]

It is surely not a good idea for biographers to encourage their readers to believe that there could be any connections between what they want to do and writing horoscopes; but the important point here is the impossibility of deciding whether or not anecdotes are genuinely representative in the absence of information about the subject which is non-anecdotal. Bate's championing of representative over factual truth is none the less an obviously useful step for a biographer and, if necessary, de Grazia could always be invoked to justify it. There are, no doubt, important differences between what Bate says here and a non-academic such as Holden who, in a statement so memorable I have used it as an epigraph, is willing to describe the Manningham anecdote as 'one of those unverifiable vignettes too good to discard on the grounds of merely dubious provenance';[13] but whether the reasons for relying on what Chambers called the mythos are crude or sophisticated, the important point is that it has to be brought into play. This is because, were it to be ignored, on the grounds that it consists only of rumour, gossip and innuendo, nearly all of it unverified and unverifiable, there would then be no means of satisfying public curiosity about the kind of person Shakespeare was.

# 19

## *The argument from expertise*

NEITHER THE FACT THAT all biographers speculate, nor what can be very loosely termed the post-modernist approach, justifies the speculations in biographies of Shakespeare. Yet how is it possible to object to these when so many of their authors are eminent literary scholars, with a profound knowledge of the Elizabethan and Jacobean periods? Is there no argument from expertise which ought to inhibit criticism? Someone likely to think so is Ray Monk, whose *Ludwig Wittgenstein: The Duty of Genius* deservedly made him one of the most highly regarded and best-known biographers of his generation.

In an essay entitled, 'Philosophical Biography: The Very Idea', Monk characterises biography as a 'peculiarly Wittgensteinian genre'. This is because the kind of understanding to which it aspires corresponds to that on which Wittgenstein laid great emphasis: 'the understanding that consists in seeing connections'. But what happens when some readers fail to see the connections which the biographer wants to make? This had been Monk's own fate when he had moved from dealing with the life of Wittgenstein to that of Bertrand Russell. After eight years reading 'several thousand documents revealing [Russell's] private thoughts and feelings', he felt he was qualified to conclude that his subject's life was 'dominated by his fears of madness and loneliness', that he had showed the connections between his subject's outward behaviour and his inner life. And yet there were still those for whom Russell was quite a different person, 'kind, generous, funny and happy'. It is, in part, for them that Monk recalls the remarks of Wittgenstein on the art connoisseur who can immediately tell whether a picture is real or fake and yet may not be able 'to explain his reasons to a panel of non-experts'. It is a question of the 'imponderable evidence' on which certain kinds of judgements are based and of the expertise of those who make them. To illustrate what he means by expertise, Monk recalls the story told by Stanley Cavell (a fellow Wittgensteinian) about the time he attended the music theory class given by Ernst Bloch at Berkeley. Bloch would apparently play a piece by Bach, 'with one note altered by a half a step from Bach's rendering', and then play the piece as it was written. After repeating this process, he would challenge the students to hear the difference, tell them that if they could not hear it they should not call themselves musicians, and then remind them that there were, after all, many 'honourable trades. Shoe-making, for example.' For Monk, 'understanding a person', either in life or in a biography, is like understanding music, a matter of seeing connections – 'and of course difference – between the various things people do and say'. When people fail to recognise your connections and differences they cannot be accused of making a mistake, only of missing something, 'suffering, as it were, from a kind of blindness, what Wittgenstein called "aspect blindness"'.[1]

These are intimidating thoughts; although the reference to aspect blindness may seem like a concession, many are likely to feel how, if they had to choose between that and a mistake, they would always take the mistake. Yet the relevance of Monk's case in this context cannot be properly evaluated without remembering the differences between the situation he describes and that of the Shakespeare biographer. There are obviously not, in Shakespeare's case, 'several thousand documents', revealing of 'private thoughts and feelings', and, thanks to the efforts of scholars such as Chambers and Schoenbaum, facsimiles of the few which do relate directly to his life are, in any case, freely available to the non-expert (difficult as they may often be to decipher). The question, then, is presumably how far the reading and interpretation of those documents, the ability to find in them connections which reveal the character of Shakespeare, are dependent on an expertise available to only a chosen few. 'The "Elizabethan" context of the early records is a theme to which I return repeatedly,' writes Honigmann, in the preface to a book in which he offers to show that Shakespeare was a much less pleasant person than people have usually thought, 'since I believe that imperfect knowledge of the by-ways of Elizabethan life and letters has often caused confusion.'[2] The long immersion which results in *perfect* knowledge produces the kind of certainty in connection-making that Monk exemplifies in his remarks on Russell. Whether or not it is justified in that instance is not a matter which could be settled briefly; but its dangers are illustrated in his passing reference to Virginia Woolf as someone who felt that Boswell had succeeded in conveying the true spirit of Dr Johnson, largely through allowing us to hear Johnson's voice:

> When we hear Johnson saying things like 'No, sir; stark insensibility!', Woolf says, then we feel we know what kind of man he was. The example is interesting, I think, as an illustration of 'imponderable evidence'. Why is this exclamation so revealing of Johnson's spirit? It is difficult, if not impossible, to say. If pressed, I would reach for some phrase like 'touchingly bombastic' to describe it, but, in the end, it is imponderable. If someone did *not* find that a whole personality was expressed in that phrase, all one could do is say, à la Ernst Bloch: 'If you do not hear it, do not say to yourself you are a biographer. There are many honourable trades.'[3]

Shoemakers of the world might reasonably unite here and point out that Monk misrepresents what Woolf says. His claim that the phrase 'stark insensibility' expresses the whole of Johnson's personality is one she does not make; but that is a trivial matter compared with the uncertainty of the claim itself. Some sense can be attached to it if we think of 'stark insensibility' as a mnemonic, a kind of Arnoldian touchstone. When Matthew Arnold invites his reader to recall, 'And never lifted up a single stone', it is presumably not because he thinks this single phrase contains the essence of Wordsworth's *Michael* but that, for those who have already read the poem, it can function as a reminder of its moving simplicity and power. *Michael* is a far more homogeneous work than Boswell's biography, so that all 'stark insensibility' can do is recall a certain *aspect* of Johnson, one which provides rather less 'imponderable' evidence of his personality once the context of the remark is recalled. He had been describing to Boswell his tutor at Oxford, 'a very worthy man, but a heavy man', and the nonchalant way he had explained his own absences from tutorials by saying that he had been 'sliding in Christ Church meadow'. 'I had no notion', Johnson says, 'that I was wrong or irreverent to my tutor.' Deliberately setting himself up, as he so often does in his biography, Boswell comments, 'That, Sir, was great fortitude of mind,' and it is to this rather foolish description that

Johnson responds with, 'No, Sir; stark insensibility.'[4] The phrase is striking but it is a mystery why anyone should find it either bombastic or touching. What makes it memorable is, on the one hand, the suddenness of response (the joke element) and, on the other, the somewhat uncharacteristic and yet attractive note of self-criticism.

No single phrase could be taken to represent the spirit of Shakespeare in the way Monk thinks 'stark insensibility' represents Johnson's because, apart from his writings, and leaving aside his will and the Mountjoy deposition, no single phrase has been recorded. The surviving documents being as few as they are, explicit claims for the superior understanding which expertise brings tend to be thin on the ground, and as muted as the example from Honigmann already quoted. The only Shakespeare biographer to play this card as openly as Monk is A. L. Rowse who, in his revised edition of *Shakespeare the Man*, says that 'much of the nonsense that has been written about William Shakespeare, in many languages, comes from ignorance of the Elizabethan age and its conditions'; insists that, for the biographer of Shakespeare, 'a knowledge of the Elizabethan age in depth is indispensable'; and complains that there is 'far too much writing about [Shakespeare] by people with no sense of the age'.[5] It is because he is a historian that he feels he can pronounce so authoritatively on various aspects of his subject's private life. When friends would not agree with him he would become very angry, sometimes breaking off life-long relationships, as he did, for example, that with C. V. Wedgwood. The irony here is that she was herself a distinguished historian, if not of quite the same period. But there were many others who were well versed in the Elizabethan age and who disputed his views. Disagreement among specialists is a body blow to the argument from expertise. Wittgenstein's art expert may not have been able to explain his reasons for thinking a particular painting genuine or fake to non-experts, but would he have always been able to convince his fellow specialists that those reasons were sound? The history of art criticism, with its fierce disputes, suggests that the answer is not necessarily yes.

Rowse is altogether exceptional. Among more recent biographers, the argument from expertise either tends to take a more restrained form or be implicit in the approach adopted. An example of the latter case can be found in James Shapiro's preface to *1599* with its familiar claim concerning the impossibility of talking about Shakespeare's plays 'independently of his age', and his insistence on 'The commonplace that dramatists are best understood in relation to their time'.[6] The efforts of the old historicists, whom Shapiro here represents, to read the plays in their contemporary and cultural setting are, of course, both long-standing and on-going, and they were reinforced by those of the so-called new historicists with their claim to a more sophisticated, interactive concept of the relation between text and context. The challenge to both parties comes from the ideas adopted by Leeds Barroll, the full recognition that, as Terence Hawkes and Hugh Grady put it very simply in the introduction to a collection of critical essays with the self-explanatory title of *Presentist Shakespeares*, 'we can only see the past through the eyes of the present' and 'there can be no historicism without a latent presentism.'[7] This is obviously true, and what is also clearly apparent is that, having seen the past with our ideologically conditioned vision, we then have to represent it (no doubt the two processes are often more or less simultaneous) with tools which are necessarily of our own time. The result might then seem to be that, in the inflammatory words of the American historiographer, Hayden White, 'historical narratives are verbal fictions, the contents of which have more in common with their counterparts in literature than they have with those in the sciences.' But if this is so, that Elizabethan 'age' which historicists want to discover must be lost for ever and critics such as Alan Sinfield, who would like their own work to have some meaningful political impact in the here and now, are justified in arguing that they should be free to 'rework the authoritative text so that it is forced to yield, against the grain, explicitly oppositional kinds of understanding'.[8]

These highly contentious issues are only worth mentioning here because they are implicit in the way, in his *1599* preface, Shapiro extends the historicist claim from Shakespeare's work to his life. He is critical there of those who want to 'sever Shakespeare from his age' and who therefore assume 'that what makes people who they are now, made people who they were then'. In support of his sense of how mistaken this assumption is, he lists a number of important features of Elizabethan life which made it so different from ours today: babies being breast-fed by strangers and then swaddled for their first year, for example; people only living, 'on an average, until their mid-forties'; the relative novelty of marrying for love, and so on. With all these differences, Shapiro says, how can we assume that the 'emotional lives' of people like Shakespeare were like ours or, as he put the same point in a later book, that 'people have always experienced the world the same way we ourselves do, that Shakespeare's internal, emotional life was modern.'[9] To save us from this danger, the implication clearly is, we need experts like himself who are very familiar with the period and able therefore to present a Shakespeare who is of his time, preventing us from thinking of him as (to echo the title of a book which had a great success more than fifty years ago) our contemporary.[10]

The complication of these questions is very considerable. Biographers may strive to make subjects long dead appear as foreign as possible, given that the circumstances of their lives now seem in many ways so alien; but at the same time they want the portraits they offer to be intelligible, or even sympathetic to their readers. In pursuit of this latter aim, they have a natural tendency to emphasise those aspects which are modern in the sense that they exhibit no stark discontinuity between the present and the past. A useful analogy here is with Elizabethan spelling and pronunciation. Original-spelling texts of Shakespeare's plays sometimes appear and issue a strong reminder of difference; but although we know from his rhyming that he must have pronounced many words very differently from the way we do now, there is no great clamour for performances in which the actors baffle the audience by speaking the lines as they would have been spoken in the late sixteenth or early seventeenth century. The effect would be *too* alienating. In biography also there are limits – often at least glimpsed in Shapiro's work – as to how far the biographer is prepared to allow alienation to go. Towards the end of his preface, for example, he comments on the meagre nature of the surviving record and concludes, 'plausibility, not certitude, is as close as one can come to what happened' (the word should surely be probability since it is not for nothing that we talk of 'plausible rogues'). In the following and final paragraph, however, he writes of Shakespeare's life with the Lord Chamberlain's Men and of how his

> mornings were taken up with rehearsals, his afternoons with performances, and many of his evenings with company business, such as listening to freelance dramatists pitch new plays to add to their repertory. He had a precious few hours late at night and early in the morning free to read and write – often by flickering candlelight and fighting fatigue.[11]

The flickering candle is of the age but I am not sure that the reference to other dramatists 'pitching' their plays does not conjure up an image of processes inappropriately modern. Yet this inevitable interpretation of a past life in terms of our own does not necessarily mean that all biography is fiction and that the search for accuracy – Shapiro's account of how Shakespeare spent many of his mornings and afternoons is, after all, deduced from documents – should be given up. We may only be capable of seeing the past through the eyes of the present, but there is a reasonable case for believing that it is at least aspects of things as they actually were which we do, in fact, see.

Most of Shakespeare's biographers would endorse the view that different material circumstances produce different structures of thought and feeling. This is presumably the belief behind Park Honan's criticism, in the introduction to his book, of the idea that, as a young boy, Shakespeare was taken to see the celebrations at Kenilworth. This is a mistake, he claims, because it rests on the supposition that his father 'behaved as modern fathers might', and he backs up his belief that John Shakespeare was not a modern father with the detail of those Tudor households where eleven-year-old boys like Shakespeare knelt before their father every morning for a blessing.[12] Those who fail to take sufficient note of differences which a custom like this indicates are often accused of believing in an 'essential' human nature. Such a phenomenon is no doubt an illusion, and yet human nature is essential enough for us to feel confident that, if Anne Shakespeare had made a cuckold of her husband in the way Stephen Dedalus describes, we would have a reasonable idea how Shakespeare might have felt about it. The vastly different circumstances of Elizabethan and Jacobean life (that is), both physical and psychological, hardly appear to affect our understanding of what it meant to be jealous four hundred years ago, as the directness with which Othello and Leontes are able to communicate their jealousy to us would suggest. There is a rule here which holds good for very many aspects of Shakespeare's life that the biographer might want to examine, but there are some where an understanding of the pastness of the past might well be crucial. In pondering the significance of his homoerotic verse, for example, it might well be relevant to know that men in his time tended to hug and kiss each other more than they do now. As far his religious views are concerned, without necessarily subscribing to Lucien Febvre's famous contention that in the sixteenth century disbelief or atheism was a position which contemporary structures of thought made virtually impossible,[13] it might be important to insist (as Honan partly tries to do in his detail of paternal blessing) that Christianity was integrated into social life to a degree which is inconceivable to most of us now.

A further difficulty in our attempted consideration of that 'age' from which Shapiro believes we should not be severed is that it is far from homogeneous. Among the features which he claims differentiates it from our time is the fact that Elizabethan men and women 'delayed marriage until their mid-twenties'; yet that was certainly not Shakespeare's case. As far as marriage is concerned, it can be proved that he deviated from the norm, but as I have tried to suggest in my chapter on money, in most other instances that is not possible. A major reason why C. V. Wedgwood did not accept Rowe's basic premise in his speculations on the Sonnets, for example, is that she could not believe they were addressed to Southampton. Knowing what she did about the period, it seemed to her impossible that a commoner could have referred to an earl with the frankness and familiarity the Sonnets sometimes exhibit.[14] Yet who can tell what anomalies the Elizabethan caste system was able to accommodate? Another illustration of how difficult it sometimes is both to characterise Shakespeare's 'age' and to fit him into it might be found in my reference in a previous chapter to Dr Simon Forman as a 'quack'. In choosing this word I was thinking not so much of the medicines he administered as of the way in which he used astrological castings in order to locate lost or stolen property for his clients. In the book he wrote on Forman, Rowse insisted that he should not be referred to in this way because the doctor believed in what he did.[15] Another criterion which might be invoked to absolve him from quackery is that there was, in his time, a very widespread belief in astrology, one that extended throughout society and as far as Queen Elizabeth herself. Given that belief, what are we to make, from a biographical point of view, of Edmund's contemptuous dismissal in *King Lear* of his father's astrological musings and his disdain for those who 'make guilty of our disasters, the sun, the moon and the stars'? How characteristic of Shakespeare himself, and the circles in which he moved, was Edmund's scepticism? Although this seems to me a reasonable question to ask, it is also one which, with the passage of time, has become impossible to answer. It will, no doubt, seem mistakenly 'modern' to call Forman a quack but, in that case, Edmund is also a representative of modernity, although the issue is then further complicated by the reminder that half of today's world still believes in astrology.

For most of us today, reading a Shakespeare play is something of a messy compromise. We inevitably approach it from our present, 'modern' point of view, but we allow our response to be inflected by what we already know about the period in which the play was written and by what we learn from (for example) a good annotated edition. Biography involves processes not dissimilar in that biographers also 'read' the subject from the dual perspective of their own place in history and their knowledge of a past time. The comparison can be taken a little further by noting that there is much in even a good annotated edition of a Shakespeare play which is redundant in the sense that it has no effect on the reading of particular lines, that it does not produce, to invoke that Wittgensteinian concept to which Monk indirectly refers, aspect change; and that the same is true of much of the information about the Elizabethan age which Shakespeare's biographers supply. But the reasons for that failure are different in the two cases and indicate why the analogy between reading a Shakespeare play and writing his life cannot be sustained for very long. Despite all the fierce controversies which surround the words that have come down to us from the First Folio and the early Quartos, they represent an astonishingly rich data bank for experts and lay people to quarrel over. The information which survives about Shakespeare's life is, by comparison, so paltry that no amount of expertise could compensate for its inadequacies; there can hardly be a convincing argument from expertise when there is so little material to be expert about. The relevance of Shapiro's insistence on the dangers of thinking of Shakespeare's private life as modern does not, therefore, seem especially acute when the information available hardly affords us the opportunity for thinking about it at all.

# 20

## *Final thoughts*

WHAT HAS NOT PERHAPS been as clear as it should have been in my previous chapters is the genuine interest and value of many of the recent Shakespeare biographies. They are often instructive as well as entertaining, taking their readers into areas where they would be otherwise unlikely to venture. Heraldry, for example, is not the most burningly topical of issues. Duncan-Jones makes it a major focus, describing how, in the late 1590s, William Dethick, the Garter King of Arms, was vigorously attacked for having granted many coats of arms too easily. In a list of twenty-three families whose claims to gentlemanly status were, in the opinion of Dethick's critic, spurious, Shakespeare's own was included. Duncan-Jones's suggestion that this contretemps explains why, in sonnet 111, Shakespeare should refer to his name having received a 'brand' may be far-fetched; but her detailed information about the process whereby Elizabethans became armigerous sheds valuable light on matters which clearly had more interest for them than they do for most of us now, and which it is therefore particularly helpful to have explained.[1]

A related matter, with which contemporary readers are even less likely to be familiar, concerns the *imprese*. These were designs painted on paste-board and accompanied with mottos. In the form of shields, these devices were required by those who wanted to participate in the tilts or jousting which Elizabeth organised every year in celebration of her accession to the throne. At the beginning of *1599*, Shapiro takes advantage of the fact that the Lord Chamberlain's Men are recorded as having performed for Elizabeth

*Final thoughts*

in late December 1598 in order to give his readers a guided tour of her palace at Whitehall. He imagines Shakespeare going from room to room, appreciating the many pictures on display or looking with interest at the Queen's library, until he came to 'the shield gallery, a long hall overlooking the Thames, through which visitors arriving by boat passed on their way to court'. This room, he explains, 'was crammed with hundreds of *imprese*'. Shapiro believes that when Shakespeare entered the gallery, his eye would have been drawn to 'his own anonymous contributions. He was obviously skilled in the genre and would later advertise his talents in *Pericles*, which contains a wonderful scene in which six knights display their *imprese*.'[2] There is a problem here in that the scene referred to (which not many other critics have found wonderful) occurs in that part of *Pericles* now commonly thought to have been written by George Wilkins. It also happens that the only evidence of Shakespeare having been involved in the production of an *impresa* dates from 1613 when he and Burbage, a talented amateur painter, were paid 44 shillings for their joint work on a shield for the Earl of Rutland.[3] The idea that in walking through the shield gallery at Whitehall in late 1598, if in fact he ever did so, Shakespeare would have recognised many examples of his work is therefore highly speculative; but the accompanying details about what must now seem to us a strange practice are intriguing, as is the imaginary trip through a building long since disappeared.

Disputes among the heralds and the money aristocrats were willing to spend for eye-catching *imprese* are both relatively minor and unfamiliar topics, but on those of major historical importance, biographies of Shakespeare often make rewarding reading also. I have already suggested how interesting is the description Shapiro gives of the Earl of Essex's Irish campaign, and that the best, non-specialist account of his unauthorised return to England, and his so-called rising, can be found in Bate's second book. Bate has more detail than the other biographers and corrects their habitually asserted impression that the leader of the group which asked the Lord Chamberlain's Men to perform *Richard II* was Sir Gelly Meyrick, Essex's steward. He also challenges the common assumption that this performance was meant to prepare the way for a revolt which had already been planned for the following day. We may have no evidence that, as a member of the Lord Chamberlain's Men and the author of *Richard II*, Shakespeare played anything more than a passive and subsidiary role in these events, but they are none the less pleasing to read about. Shakespeare biography may often be popular history disguised as life-story, yet the history is invariably worthwhile.

For long stretches, many Shakespeare biographies read like history books, but the other resource to which their authors turn in order to fill their pages is commentary on the plays. The results are largely of a kind which have been exiled from recent academic criticism and may therefore provide an additional explanation of why the books in which they appear are so popular. Reminding their readers of the plot, indicating particular themes, paying particular attention to character, the commentaries are usually interesting and valuable, even if they are always in danger of being skewed by the need to fulfil the biographical obligation and somehow relate aspects of the plays to Shakespeare's life. The lack of critical balance which can then occur is best illustrated by Shapiro's innovative decision to concentrate on a single year. The danger he ran in doing this was that his choice would appear arbitrary, but he protected himself by proposing 1599 as a crucial moment in Shakespeare's life: in that favourite structuring device of biographers, a 'turning-point'. His justifications for assuming that this was 'the most decisive year' in his subject's career include the erection of the Globe, and the replacement of Kemp with Robert Armin as the clown of the Lord Chamberlain's Men. All this was part, in Shapiro's view, of the new leap forward which occurred at this time, one which is signalled most evidently by the writing during 1599 of *Hamlet*. 'Restless, unsatisfied with the profitably formulaic and with styles of writing which came too easily to him', here was the moment when Shakespeare went from 'an exceptionally talented writer to being one of the greatest who ever lived'.[4] It is in this context of the blossoming of the mature Shakespeare that Shapiro deals with the three plays which were first performed during the period he is studying: *Henry V, As You Like It* and *Julius Caesar*. He discusses all of them very well, stressing in particular the new and more mature concept of love which emerges in *As You Like It*; yet there would seem to be a clear critical distortion in implicitly asking readers to assume that *Henry V* represents an obvious artistic advance on *2Henry IV*. The many who would regard it as a cruder work might also find themselves startled by the notion that *Twelfth Night*, which inconveniently post-dates *As You Like It*, is an 'accomplished if somewhat formulaic throwback to earlier Shakespearean comedy'.[5] These are dubious critical judgements forced on Shapiro by his developmental hypothesis and its relation to his decision to base his book on a single year in Shakespeare's life.

Shapiro is interested in *As You Like It* because it appears to support his idea of 1599 as the opening to a new and brilliant phase in Shakespeare's writing life, while, for several of his colleagues, it has a special attraction as a play where the author's own presence is more than usually identifiable. Why this should be so is not clear. Perhaps it is because much of the action takes place in the forest of Arden, an anglicisation of the French 'Ardenne' which Shakespeare took directly from his source; but also, of course, a real place near Stratford and the family name of his mother. Perhaps biographers are drawn to it because of the dubious legend, which they are all reluctant to dismiss, that this was the play in which he played the very minor role of Adam. Those who accept that the character of Jaques in *As You Like It* must be a portrait of Ben Jonson, are also more inclined to find Shakespeare himself lurking in, for example, the character of Touchstone, as Duncan-Jones certainly does. But it is Bate, in his first book, who illustrates best the popularity of this play for biographers when, shortly after having said that discovering details of Shakespeare's youth from his plays is a 'very dubious procedure', he writes: 'William of Arden is surely William of Stratford's wittily self-deprecatory portrait of himself as tongue-tied country bumpkin.' The William referred to here, who is just William as far as the play is concerned, is the simple-minded country youth from whom Touchstone steals his Audrey. The exchange in which this happens is brief but it allows Bate to say, 'The self-representation as tongue-tied William is deliciously ironic because Shakespeare's true wit and verbal facility are amply on display in the character of Touchstone.'[6]

Remarks like these are not so much commentary on the plays as exploitation of them for biographical effect, but there are many fewer of them in Bate's second book than in his first. The attributions in *Soul of the Age: The Life, Mind and World of William Shakespeare*, that is, are more cautious and, in general, Bate seems far more aware in his second book of how thin the ice on which he skates often is. His procedure is still to work back from features in the plays to the man who wrote them, but this time his concern is much more with what can be deduced from the writing about Shakespeare's reading. That is to say that, like Shapiro, he is reliant for a fair proportion of his book on the age-old discipline of source study. There is nothing wrong with this in a biography.

Everyone knows, for example, how heavily reliant Shakespeare is in his Roman plays on North's translation of Plutarch. So close and word-for-word is the dependence in certain passages that one has to believe that Shakespeare had either a copy of North open in front of him, or a memory which was photographic. What then becomes interesting are the changes Shakespeare nevertheless made, what he chose to alter, elaborate or omit. Most of these changes can be attributed to the need to transform a prose narrative into a play but some may be indications of Shakespeare's special interests or temperamental affinities, and a route therefore to a definition of his nature. At the very least, examining what Shakespeare read in order to compose his plays is a way of writing what Bate calls, in the introduction to his second book, 'intellectual biography',[7] and in some of its parts *Soul of the Age* is no more, but also no less than that. There are many others, however, where the book is a much more general attempted justification of the word 'Life' on the title-page of the English edition, although a far more prudent one than the biographical sections of *The Genius of Shakespeare*.

The greater reserve and caution Bate displays in his second book were not always appreciated in the reviews. The problem of reviews of Shakespeare biographies is that their authors so often review each other and there is therefore always a risk of something akin to a conspiracy of praise. But Bate was harshly treated by two scholars whom one might have thought had good reasons for reticence. Writing in *The Literary Review*, Duncan-Jones complained of his 'affable fluency' while pin-pointing a number of scholarly errors. Noting how he endorsed a claim that the biography of Shakespeare can be sought only in his writings but can 'never literally and provably' be found, she correctly observed that the book under review would not have been written if Bate had genuinely believed this, and that his practice shows that he did not. In conclusion, Duncan-Jones accused Bate of too often writing in a playful, explorative manner so that he could never be called to account and the reader was never certain that he meant what he said. A major reason for her disapproval appears to have been the extent to which Bate incorporates into his second book qualifications and disclaimers and it is these which, for Greenblatt, writing in the *New York Review of Books*, suggest a writer 'uncomfortable with what he is doing', one who suffers from 'uneasiness about his own project'. When Bate is writing biography, Greenblatt continued, he finds himself 'in a no-man's land of swirling hypotheticals and self-cancelling speculations'. It is only, therefore, when he abandons the idea that 'there is anything in Shakespeare's life to interest a serious person' that he becomes engaging. As far as entering deeply into Shakespeare's mind or revealing anything significant about his life goes, however, 'the reader is better served indulging in the extravagant fantasies of James Joyce.'[8] It is hard to know what to make of these baffling statements, whether (that is) Greenblatt is implicitly apologising for his own previous biographical endeavours or forgetful of them. His review is different from that of Duncan-Jones because she still clearly believes in the possibility of Shakespeare biography, but in so far as both of them complain of the degree of speculation in *Soul of the Age*, Bate would be entitled to feel aggrieved by strictures which come from two biographers whose own writings are full of the very failings they stigmatise.

In comparison with history and commentaries on the plays, the strictly biographical element may be relatively minor in the lives of Shakespeare I have been considering; but it is always there and it is, after all, *as lives* that the books are marketed. They would not sell as well if they were not. In almost all their prefaces, and occasionally elsewhere, there are hints at the unsubstantial nature of the evidence on which any life of Shakespeare has to be based that could be interpreted as bad conscience. These are strong enough in Bate's second book to make both Duncan-Jones and Greenblatt feel that they undermine what he is trying to do. Usually, however, these hints are ones the implications of which their authors then go blithely on to ignore, so that many of them seem like no more than exercises in plausible deniability. Tucked away at the beginning, they are safety warnings which their authors encourage their readers not to take too seriously by themselves paying very little attention to them. Not that the prefaces do not often exhibit also an exuberant confidence in the enterprise ahead. There is 'a remarkably substantial body of documents relating to Shakespeare's life', Duncan-Jones asserts, while I have already quoted Greenblatt's claim that he aims to discover 'the actual person who wrote the most important body of imaginative literature of the last thousand years'. It hardly modifies the startling bravura of this remark that he then immediately adds: 'Or rather, since the actual person is a matter of well-documented public record, it aims to tread the shadowy paths that lead from the life he lived into the literature he created.'[9]

The bad habits of Shakespeare biographers, their persistence in attempting an impossible task and the sleights of hand this necessarily involves may seem to many hardly a phenomenon worth so much fuss. Of the idea that Shakespeare's father took him to Kenilworth when he was eleven and that the festivities he observed there inspired certain lines in *A Midsummer Night's Dream*, Peter Ackroyd writes, 'It is at least suggestive. And a pretty story does no harm.' Commenting on the authenticity of the so-called Grafton portrait, which is dated 1588, and the objection that this is too early a time for Shakespeare to have been able to afford having himself painted, he says: 'But what if he were already a successful dramatist, what then? It is in any case a glorious supposition.'[10] The tone here recalls Anthony Burgess and his remark on the inevitable 'cadenza' biographers need to supply on first transporting their subject to London; and it is Burgess who writes at one point: 'I find it convenient to imagine that [Shakespeare] knew Anne Hathaway carnally, for the first time, in the spring of 1582.'[11] The casual approach to information which Ackroyd and Burgess here display is perhaps appropriate for biographers who are also novelists and who must therefore understand better than most how thin the dividing line is between biography and fiction. They clearly are not too concerned if they happen to cross that line but academics have different responsibilities and their approach must surely be different also. Given what one must assume is their evident awareness of how little we know about Shakespeare, there remains the puzzle I began with of why it has often been some of the most eminent and gifted among them who have agreed to write his biography. It is true that, as I have already indicated, lives of Shakespeare sell well but their more recent authors mostly come from institutions who can afford to pay them handsomely so that the pecuniary motive, never negligible in human affairs, is unlikely to be very strong. More influential may be the urge many academics feel to come down from their ivory tower and address a more general public. This is wholly laudable and part of the responsibility of academic life, a reasonable exchange for the privileged lifestyle the general public so often supports. When, for example, it was found recently that some parents were refusing the usual vaccines on offer for their children in order to replace them with homeopathic equivalents, it was right and important that academics should come forward and point out that injections of water in which there are only 'memory traces' of certain herbs were not likely to be very efficacious. It was then that they publicly earned their keep, even if in doing so they were telling a sizeable section of the public something they did not want to hear. Although the truth about homeopathy is very different from the truth about William Shakespeare, that anything more than a chronicle of his life is not possible is also something unlikely to be popular with the general public (and with publishers); but if academics do not tell it, who will? To not only fail to do so but also nurture the illusion that a life of Shakespeare is within our grasp, may well be a *trahison des clercs*.

After the recent financial crisis, a great deal of public hostility was directed towards the greed and irresponsibility of bankers. This often came from people who had pestered their own banks or building societies for unsecured loans, determined to acquire what, on any reasonable estimate of the matter, they could not have. Although the providers of Shakespeare biography are not thereby exculpated, its recipients have often exerted a similar pressure to have what is not possible. Accustomed to literary biography as it developed in the nineteenth century, with its familiar staging posts and insight into the private life of the subject, they have demanded something similar for Shakespeare, deaf to the suggestion that such a product is not feasible in his case, or indeed that of most other, non-aristocratic individuals from the early modern period. In the financial world, unreasonable expectations have eventually to be paid for but in the world of letters there is no obvious cost beyond a general lowering of intellectual standards and the degradation of the art of biography. To hope, therefore, that anything could be said which could stop the almost continuous flow of lives of Shakespeare would be as impractical as thinking that the little boy who said the Emperor had no clothes could somehow be transformed into the one who put his finger in the dyke. This book has nevertheless been written in the belief that the world of the imagination would be a poorer place without them both.

# Notes

The following cue titles are used in these notes:

Ackroyd — Peter Ackroyd, *Shakespeare: The Biography* (London: Chatto & Windus, 2005).
Bate (1) — Jonathan Bate, *The Genius of Shakespeare* (London: Picador, 1997).
Bate (2) — Jonathan Bate, *Soul of the Age: The Life, Mind and World of William Shakespeare* (London: Penguin, 2009).
Duncan-Jones — Katherine Duncan-Jones, *Ungentle Shakespeare: Scenes from his Life* (London: Arden Shakespeare, 2001). The revised edition of this book (London: Methuen Drama, 2010) is entitled *Shakespeare: An Ungentle Life*.
Greenblatt — Stephen Greenblatt, *Will in the World: How Shakespeare became Shakespeare* (London: Jonathan Cape, 2004).
Shapiro — James Shapiro, *1599: A Year in the Life of William Shakespeare* (London: Faber & Faber, 2005).
Weis — René Weis, *Shakespeare Revealed: A Biography* (London: John Murray, 2007).

*Chapter 1: Rules of the game*

1. For the details, see David Ellis, *Death and the Author: How D. H. Lawrence Died and Was Remembered* (Oxford: Oxford University Press, 2008), p. 156.
2. E. K. Chambers, *William Shakespeare: A Study of Facts and Problems* (Oxford: Clarendon, 1930), vol. 2, p. 214 (my emphasis).
3. E. A. J. Honigmann, *Shakespeare's Impact on His Contemporaries* (London: Macmillan, 1982), p. 18.

*Notes*

4. Chambers, *William Shakespeare*, vol. 2, p. 188. Shakespeare's line reads 'O, tiger's heart wrapt in a woman's hide'.
5. On this topic, see Brian Vickers, *Shakespeare, Co-author: A Historical Study of Five Collaborative Plays* (Oxford: Oxford University Press, 2002), pp. 140–1.
6. Chambers, *William Shakespeare*, vol. 2, p. 189.
7. Someone who has made a strong case for thinking that they refer rather to Peele is Lukas Erne. See his 'Biography and Mythography: Re-reading Chettle's Alleged Apology to Shakespeare', *English Studies*, vol. 5 (1998), pp. 430–40.
8. Chambers reprints Aubrey's notes in the section of *William Shakespeare: A Study of Facts and Problems* which follows 'Contemporary Allusions' and is called 'The Shakespeare Mythos'. See vol. 2, p. 252.
9. In 1588 Shakespeare's name was associated with that of his parents in a case brought in London against the Lamberts, relatives to whom John Shakespeare had ceded a property which he had acquired on his marriage as part of his wife's dowry (see p. 30 above). For Jonathan Bate there are details of this case which provide 'pretty strong evidence of Shakespeare's presence in London (not Lancashire, let alone abroad) in the Armada year of 1588' (Bate (2), p. 323).
10. *The Poems of A. E. Housman* (Oxford: Clarendon, 1997), pp. 157–8.
11. See the essay on 'Literary Biography' in John Updike's *Due Considerations* (London: Hamish Hamilton, 2007), pp. 4–5.

*Chapter 2: How to make bricks without straw*

1. Bate (2), p. 345.
2. Park Honan, *Shakespeare: A Life* (Oxford: Oxford University Press, 1998), p. 18.
3. Gary Taylor, 'Forms of Opposition: Shakespeare and Middleton', *English Literary Renaissance*, vol. 24, no. 2 (Spring, 1994), p. 298.
4. The same pathologist had originally recorded finding non-lethal traces of antimony in Cook's body and hence the popular rhyme which Graves reproduces on p. 228 of *They Hanged My Saintly Billy* (London: Faber & Faber, 1957): 'In antimony, great though his faith,/The quantity found being small, / Taylor's faith in strychnine was yet greater, / For of that he found nothing at all.'
5. S. Schoenbaum, *Shakespeare's Lives* (Oxford: Clarendon, 1991), p. 277.
6. T. S. Eliot, 'Tradition and the Individual Talent' in *Selected Essays* (London: Faber & Faber, 1932), p. 18; J. O. Halliwell-Phillipps, *Outlines of the Life of Shakespeare* (London: Longmans, Green, 1886 – 6th ed.), vol. 1, pp. vi–vii.
7. Greenblatt, p. 13.

8. Anthony Holden, *William Shakespeare: His Life and Work* (London: Little, Brown, 1999), p. 2.
9. For the sake of convenience, all the quotations from Shakespeare's plays or poems in my text are taken from the revised Arden edition of his complete works, edited by Richard Proudfoot, Ann Thompson and David Scott Kasten (London, 2001).
10. The two scholars referred to are E. A. J. Honigmann and Richard Dutton. See also David Bevington, *Shakespeare and Biography* (Oxford: Oxford University Press, 2010), where the composition of *King John* is described as an matter on which 'the jury is still out' (p. 103).
11. Duncan-Jones, pp. 97–9.
12. Giorgio Melchiori (ed.), *The Merry Wives of Windsor* (London: Arden Shakespeare, 2000), pp. 18–30.
13. Bevington, *Shakespeare and Biography*, p. 103.
14. Weis, pp. 183–4.
15. Ibid., p. 203.
16. Duncan-Jones, p. 99.
17. Weis, pp. 204–5.
18. Holden, *William Shakespeare: His Life and Work*, p. 151.
19. Michael Wood, *In Search of Shakespeare* (London: BBC Worldwide, 2003), p. 166.

## Chapter 3: Forebears

1. John Richardson, *A Life of Picasso* (London: Jonathan Cape, 1991–), vol. 1, p. 16.
2. Peter Ackroyd, *Dickens* (London: Minerva, 1991), pp. 3–4. Both these examples, and the one above concerning Picasso, are taken from the third chapter of my *Literary Lives: Biography and the Search for Understanding* (Edinburgh: Edinburgh University Press, 2000) where the whole topic is explored from a more theoretical point of view.
3. Duncan-Jones, pp. 1–2.
4. Ackroyd, p. 18.
5. Plume's notes are reproduced in Chambers, *William Shakespeare*, vol. 2, p. 247.
6. Duncan-Jones, pp. 8–9.
7. Greenblatt, pp. 67–71 (the italicisation of 'his cheeks burning' is mine).
8. Robert Bearman, 'John Shakespeare: A Papist or Just Penniless?', *Shakespeare Quarterly*, vol. 56, no. 4 (Winter, 2005), p. 416.
9. See R. Glynn Grylls, *Claire Clairmont: Mother of Byron's Allegra* (London: John Murray, 1939), p. 193.
10. Greenblatt, p. 81.
11. Duncan-Jones, p. 83.

12. Ackroyd, p. 70; Greenblatt, p. 41.
13. Greenblatt, pp. 75–6.
14. C. H. Herford and Percy and Evelyn Simpson (eds), *Works of Ben Jonson* (Oxford: Clarendon, 1925–1952), vol. 3, pp. 503–5.
15. Thomas Nashe, *Pierce Penniless* (London: Scolar, 1969), pp. 25–6.
16. See Duncan-Jones, pp. 118–19.
17. Greenblatt, p. 82; Ackroyd, p. 276.
18. See David Wiles, *Shakespeare's Clown: Actor and Text in the Elizabethan Playhouse* (Cambridge: Cambridge University Press, 1987).
19. Shapiro, pp. 39–49.
20. Wood, *In Search of Shakespeare*, p. 264.

## *Chapter 4: The female line and Catholicism*

1. Honan, *Shakespeare: A Life*, pp. 18–19.
2. Bate (2), p. 36.
3. Ackroyd, p. 27.
4. Ackroyd is only the most recent biographer wedded to the idea of Shakespeare having grown up in a Catholic household. There is a description of the so-called 'Spiritual Testament' which has been associated with Shakespeare's father in S. Schoenbaum, *A Documentary Life* (Oxford: Clarendon, 1975), pp. 41–6, and particularly devastating attacks on the reasons which have been advanced for that association in Robert Bearman, 'John Shakespeare's "Religious Testament": A Reappraisal', *Shakespeare Survey*, vol. 56 (2003), pp. 184–202; Glyn Parry, 'The Context of John Shakespeare's "Recusancy" Re-examined', *Shakespeare Yearbook*, vol. 16 (2005), pp. 1–38; and Peter Davidson and Thomas McCoog, SJ, 'Unreconciled: What Evidence Links Shakespeare and the Jesuits?', *Times Literary Supplement* (16 March 2007). For useful potted summaries of the issues that need to be taken into account when considering whether either John Shakespeare or his son was a Roman Catholic, see Stanley Wells, *Is It True What They Say About Shakespeare?* (Ebrington, Gloucestershire: Long Barn, 2007).
5. There is an excellent account of the Houghton will in E. A. J. Honigmann, *Shakespeare: The 'Lost Years'* (Manchester: Manchester University Press, 1985), pp. 15–39.
6. Chambers, *William Shakespeare*, vol. 2, p. 254.
7. See Honigmann, *Shakespeare: The 'Lost Years'*, but also Richard Wilson, *Secret Shakespeare: Studies in Theatre, Religion and Resistance* (Manchester: Manchester University Press, 2004), especially the second chapter.
8. Wies, p. 47 (my italics). For an impressively researched denial that Stratford was the hive of recusants Wies claims it was, see Robert Bearman, 'The Early Reformation Experience in a Warwickshire

Market Town: Stratford-Upon-Avon, 1530–1580', *Midland History*, vol. 32 (2007).
9. See *The Hunted Priest: An Autobiography of John Gerard*, translated by Philip Caraman (London: Fontana, 1959).
10. Greenblatt, p. 105.
11. Ibid., pp. 105–6.
12. Ibid, pp. 109–17.
13. Ibid., pp. 109, 114–15.
14. Ackroyd, p. 200.
15. Greenblatt, p. 116.
16. The notes were made by Richard Davies; see Chambers, *William Shakespeare*, vol. 2, p. 257.
17. Holden, *William Shakespeare: His Life and Work*, p. 237.

## Chapter 5: Boyhood and youth

1. Jean-Paul Sartre, *L'Idiot de la famille* (Paris: Gallimard, 1988) vol. 1, p. 55; Alexander and Juliette George, *Woodrow Wilson and Colonel House: A Personality Study* (New York: Doves, 1964), p. 3. I discuss both these examples in *Literary Lives: Biography and the Search for Understanding*.
2. Schoenbaum, *Shakespeare's Lives*, p. 42.
3. See Bate (2), pp. 79–101.
4. I give the texts of these poems in *That Man Shakespeare* (Hastings: Helm Information, 2005), pp. 43–4.
5. Schoenbaum, *Shakespeare's Lives*, p. 72.
6. Wies, pp. 71, 73.
7. Ibid., p. 70.
8. Greenblatt, p. 153.
9. Ibid., pp. 151–61.

## Chapter 6: Marriage

1. The details can be found in Schoenbaum, *A Documentary Life*, pp. 70–1.
2. Ibid., p. 71.
3. Ackroyd, p. 89.
4. Ibid.
5. See Germaine Greer, *Shakespeare's Wife* (London: Bloomsbury, 2007), p. 100.
6. Halliwell-Phillipps, *Outlines of the Life of Shakespeare*, vol. 1, p. 65.
7. Greenblatt, p. 125.
8. Shapiro, p. 214.
9. Duncan-Jones, p. 17.

*Notes*

10. See Andrew Gurr, 'Shakespeare's First Poem: Sonnet 145' in *Essays in Criticism*, vol. 21 (1970) and Stephen Booth's edition of *Shakespeare's Sonnets* (New Haven, CT: Yale University Press, 2000).
11. Greer, *Shakespeare's Wife*, p. 59.
12. Schoenbaum, *William Shakespeare: A Documentary Life*, pp. 66–9 (with the English modernised).
13. Greer, *Shakespeare's Wife*, p. 220. Robert Bearman has pointed out to me that the simplest explanation of the Whittingham bequest is that it refers to a debt Anne had inherited as a member of the Hathaway family.
14. Ibid., p. 9.
15. There are details of Edmund's funeral in Schoenbaum, *William Shakespeare: A Documentary Life*, p. 26.
16. Greenblatt, pp. 126–48.

*Chapter 7: The theatre*

1. Halliwell-Phillipps, *Outlines of the Life of Shakespeare*, vol. 1, p. 39.
2. Ibid., p. 40.
3. Greenblatt, p. 30.
4. F. J. Furnivall (ed.), *A Letter describing a part of the entertainment unto Queen Elizabeth at the castle of Kenilworth in 1575 by Robert Laneham* (London: Chatto & Windus, 1907), p. 34 (I have modernised the spelling).
5. Greenblatt, p. 48.
6. Chambers, *William Shakespeare*, vol. 2, p. 253.
7. See Douglas Hamer's review of Schoenbaum's *Shakespeare's Lives* in the *Review of English Studies*, vol. 85 (1971), p. 484.
8. Duncan-Jones, p. 15.
9. Katherine Duncan-Jones, *Shakespeare: Upstart Crow to Sweet Swan* (London: Arden Shakespeare, 2011), pp. 1–15 (the emphasis on *great-grandchildren* is mine).
10. Duncan-Jones, pp. 28, 31.
11. Ibid., pp. 279–80.
12. See Chambers, *William Shakespeare*, vol. 2, p. 265.
13. Ibid., vol. 2, p. 278.
14. Ibid.
15. Ibid., vol. 2, pp. 213–14.
16. Ibid., vol. 2, p. 214.
17. See Shapiro, pp. 38–42. In her most recent book, Katherine Duncan-Jones makes a case for Shakespeare being a more considerable actor than is usually allowed, although at one point she appears to contradict the drift of her own argument by endorsing the testimony from Rowe and Oldys that 'Shakespeare's speciality was old men' (*Shakespeare: Upstart Crow to Sweet Swan*, p. 50).

## Chapter 8: Patronage, or who's who in the Sonnets

1. See *William Shakespeare: Complete Sonnets and Poems*, ed. Colin Burrow (Oxford: Oxford University Press, 2002), pp. 173–4.
2. Ibid., p. 239.
3. Chambers, *William Shakespeare*, vol. 2, p. 265.
4. Weis, p. 113.
5. G. P. V. Akrigg, *Shakespeare and the Earl of Southampton* (London: Hamish Hamilton, 1968), p. 223.
6. Bate (2), p. 12.
7. I am aware that his wording would allow Bate to claim that, even if Shakespeare was not integrated into Southampton's household at Titchfield, that process took place elsewhere; but the juxtapositions seem to me to have the effect of turning a possible stay there into a certain one.
8. Chambers, *William Shakespeare*, vol. 2, p. 332.
9. A. L. Rowse, *Shakespeare the Man* (London: Macmillan, 1988), pp. ix–x, 56–7, 88.
10. See *William Shakespeare: Complete Sonnets and Poems*, ed. Burrow, p. 101.
11. Bate (1), pp. 56–7.
12. An impressive enquiry into the rival poet issue was made in 2005 by Macd. R. Jackson in 'Francis Meres and the Cultural Contexts of Shakespeare's Rival Poet Sonnets' (*Review of English Studies*, vol. 56, pp. 224–46). Using computer analyses of vocabulary, he assigned the rival poet sonnets (78–86) to the period 1598 to 1600 and then offered convincing reasons for believing that in them Shakespeare was not only echoing words from Francis Meres's recent survey of contemporary English literature (see p. 154 above), but also responding to the recent publication of Marlowe's *Hero and Leander*, with its continuation by George Chapman. Whether, however, the undoubted strength of Jackson's argument entitled him to endorse Jonathan Bate's claim that Shakespeare 'spent half his working life exorcising the demon [i.e. Marlowe] who had overshadowed the beginnings of his career', and then say that 'Chapman's continuation of *Hero and Leander*, with its overweening claim to have been inspired by the very spirit of Marlowe, reawakened an old competitiveness, with its attendant insecurities,' seems to me doubtful.
13. Ibid., p. 58.
14. Greenblatt, pp. 233, 254–5.
15. *William Shakespeare: Complete Sonnets and Poems*, ed. Burrow, p. 98.

## Chapter 9: Shakespeare and the love of men

1. Chambers, *William Shakespeare*, vol. 2, p. 213.

## Notes

2. See *A New Variorum Edition of Shakespeare: The Sonnets*, ed. Hyder Edward Rollins (London, 1944), vol. 1, pp. 105–6.
3. Walter Scott, *Kenilworth: a Romance*, ed. J. H. Alexander (Edinburgh: Edinburgh University Press, 1993), p. 174.
4. Weis. pp. 165–6.
5. Ibid., p. 167.
6. Ackroyd, p. 118.
7. Duncan-Jones, p. 80.
8. Ibid., pp. 55, 81. In *Shakespeare: Upstart Crow to Sweet Swan*, Duncan-Jones further destroys the credibility of Reynolds as a reliable witness by calling him 'paranoid' and talking of his 'demented tunnel vision' (p. 83).
9. Ibid., p. 80.
10. Alan Bray, *Homosexuality in Renaissance England* (London: Gay Men's Press, 1982), p. 61.
11. *William Shakespeare: Complete Sonnets and Poems*, ed. Burrow, p. 124.

### Chapter 10: Shakespeare and the love of women

1. Rowse, *Shakespeare the Man*, p. 40.
2. Robert Parker Sorlien (ed.), *The Diary of John Manningham of the Middle Temple. 1602–1603* (Lebanon, NH: University Press of New England, 1976), p. 75.
3. Thomas Wilkes, *General View of the Stage* (1759), pp. 220–1.
4. Bate (1), p. 24.
5. Duncan-Jones, p. 131.
6. Ibid., p. 206.
7. Shapiro, p. 45.
8. Chambers, *William Shakespeare*, vol. 2, p. 254.
9. Ibid., pp. 271–2.
10. Ibid., p. 272.
11. Ibid., p. 269.
12. See Schoenbaum, *William Shakespeare: A Documentary Life*, p. 63.
13. Holden, *William Shakespeare: His Life and Work*, pp. 240, 242, 247.
14. Weis, pp. 295, 307.
15. Greenblatt, pp. 331–4.
16. D. H. Lawrence, 'Introductory Note' to *Collected Poems* (London: Secker, 1928).

### Chapter 11: Friends

1. Duncan-Jones, p. 114; Bate (2), p. 156.
2. Bate (2), p. 143; Duncan-Jones, p. 58.
3. Duncan-Jones, p. 115.

4. Greenblatt, p. 195.
5. Duncan-Jones, p. 5.
6. Shapiro, p. 150.
7. Weis, p. 116.
8. Ibid., p. 104.
9. See Chambers, *William Shakespeare*, vol. 2, p. 267.
10. Ibid., p. 245. In his *Shakespeare and the Poets' War* (New York: Columbia University Press, 2001), James P. Bednarz has attempted to trace back Fuller's 'combats' to a period at the turn of the century (c. 1598–1602) when Jonson, Marston and Dekker made satirical comments on each other in their plays. The traditional assumption has been that Shakespeare took no direct part in this 'Poets' war' but Bednarz argues that not only Jaques in *As You Like It* but also Ajax in *Troilus and Cressida* are retaliatory portraits of Jonson. His case is very far from having received general acceptance but, even if it could be proven, the difference it would make to any putative friendship between Shakespeare and Jonson would not be great. Bednarz himself points out that shortly after the Poets' war had ceased, Dekker collaborated with Jonson on an entertainment for James I and Marston dedicated *The Malcontent* to Jonson (p. 51). The bearing, that is, of a public exchange of insults on the private relations of the authors concerned cannot be established without more evidence than we at present possess.
11. Ibid., p. 250 (the vicar was called John Ward).
12. Anthony Burgess, *Shakespeare* (London: Jonathan Cape, 1970), p. 150.
13. The lines attributed to Beaumont are quoted by William Gifford in his 'Memoirs of Ben Jonson'. See *The Works of Ben Jonson* (London: Bickers, 1875), vol. 1, p. lxvi.
14. Chambers, *William Shakespeare*, vol. 2, p. 243.
15. Bate (1), p. 31.
16. S. Schoenbaum, 'Shakespeare and Jonson: Fact and Myth' in *Shakespeare and Others* (Washington, DC: Folger Shakespeare Library, 1985), p. 175.
17. Herford and Simpson (eds), *Works of Ben Jonson*, vol. 8, pp. 583–4. A rough paraphrase of Augustus's remark about Haterius might be 'our friend has got to be gagged.'
18. Schoenbaum, *Shakespeare and Others*, p. 173.
19. Chambers, *William Shakespeare*, vol. 2, p. 267 – Jonson's disparaging remarks about Shakespeare can be found on pp. 202–6.

*Chapter 12: London life*

1. Burgess, *Shakespeare*, p. 65.
2. Ackroyd, p. 105.

*Notes*

3. Greenblatt, p. 173.
4. See Schoenbaum, *Shakespeare's Lives*, p. 468.
5. Charles Nicholl, *The Lodger: Shakespeare on Silver Street* (London: Allen Lane, 2007), p. 4.
6. Ibid., p. 272.
7. Chambers, *William Shakespeare*, vol. 2, p. 92.
8. Holden, *William Shakespeare: His Life and Work*, pp. 217–18.
9. Wood, *In Search of Shakespeare*, p. 246.
10. Vickers, *Shakespeare, Co-author*, pp. 291–332.
11. For these details see Roger Prior, 'The Life of George Wilkins', *Shakespeare Survey*, vol. 25 (1972), pp. 137–52.
12. See Nicholl, *The Lodger: Shakespeare on Silver Street*, p. 198.
13. Duncan-Jones, pp. 208–9.
14. Nicholl, *The Lodger: Shakespeare on Silver Street*, p. 6.
15. Ibid., p. 16.
16. Wood, *In Search of Shakespeare*, p. 243.

*Chapter 13: Politics*

1. See Bate (2), pp. 239–48.
2. Leslie Hotson, *Shakespeare's Sonnets Dated and Other Essays* (London: Hart-Davis, 1949), pp. 4–10.
3. Shapiro, p. 307.
4. Jonathan Bate, *The Sunday Telegraph*, 5 June 2005.
5. Weis, p. 260; Duncan-Jones, p. 127.
6. Bate (2), pp. 281–6; Greenblatt, p. 309. For a cogent account of why Elizabeth might not have been referring to Shakespeare's play, see Paul E. J. Hammer, 'Shakespeare's *Richard II*, the Play of 7 February 1601, and the Essex Rising', *Shakespeare Quarterly*, vol. 59 (2008), pp. 1–35.
7. Duncan-Jones, p. 127; Bate (2), p. 280.
8. Chambers, *William Shakespeare*, vol. 2, p. 189.
9. Duncan-Jones, pp. 129–31. In her latest book, Duncan-Jones has weakened her argument for the significance of Chettle's reproach by making clear that he extended it to nine other poets of the period, including Jonson, Drayton and Chapman (*Shakespeare: Upstart Crow to Sweet Swan*, pp. 181–7).
10. See Leeds Barroll, *Politics, Plague, and Shakespeare's Theater: The Stuart Years* (Ithaca, NY: Cornell University Press, 1991).
11. Chambers, *William Shakespeare*, vol. 2, pp. 270, 281.
12. Shapiro, p. xvi. It must be a hundred years since anyone has made a serious case for a trans-historical Shakespeare.

## Chapter 14: Money

1. James T. Boulton and Lindeth Vasey (eds), *The Letters of D. H. Lawrence*, vol. 5 (Cambridge: Cambridge University Press, 1989), p. 585.
2. Theodore Besterman, *Voltaire* (London: Longmans, 1969), p. 162.
3. Alexander Pope, 'First Epistle of the Second Book of Horace Imitated' in *Poetical Works*, ed. Herbert Davis (Oxford: Oxford University Press, 1966), ll. 69–72, p. 363.
4. Holden, *William Shakespeare: His Life and Work*, p. 7.
5. See Schoenbaum, *William Shakespeare: A Documentary Life*, pp. 179–81.
6. James Shapiro, *Contested Will: Who Wrote Shakespeare* (London: Faber & Faber, 2010), pp. 12, 70.
7. Ibid., pp. 193–4.
8. Greer, *Shakespeare's Wife*, pp. 225–8.
9. E. A. J. Honigmann, 'In search of William Shakespeare: the public and the private man' in *Myriad-minded Shakespeare* (London: Macmillan, 1989), p. 6.
10. E. A. J. Honigmann, 'The Man' in *Shakespeare's Impact on His Contemporaries* (London: Macmillan, 1982), p. 16.
11. Honigmann, *Myriad-minded Shakespeare*, p. 11; *Shakespeare's Impact on His Contemporaries*, p. 22.
12. E. A. J. Honigmann, 'Shakespeare on his deathbed: the last will and testament' in *Myriad-minded Shakespeare*, pp. 225–6.
13. Greenblatt, p. 363 (my italics).
14. See Schoenbaum, *William Shakespeare: A Documentary Life*, pp. 239–40.
15. Honigmann, *Myriad-minded Shakespeare*, p. 224.
16. B. Roland Lewis, *The Shakespeare Documents* (Palo Alto: Stanford University Press, 1940), vol. 1, p. 486.
17. Honigmann, *Myriad-minded Shakespeare*, pp. 226, 223; Duncan-Jones, p. 262. A lot depends here, of course, on how much Shakespeare had to leave. The idea that he was a rich man when he died has been contested by both Germaine Greer and Robert Bearman.
18. Greenblatt, p. 362.
19. Chambers, *William Shakespeare*, vol. 2, p. 149.

## Chapter 15: Retirement and death

1. See Chambers, *William Shakespeare*, vol. 2, p. 254.
2. Bate (2), p. 355.
3. Greenblatt, pp. 12, 374.
4. Bate (2), p. 359.
5. Ackroyd, p. 294.
6. Greer, *Shakespeare's Wife*, p. 305.
7. Duncan-Jones, p. 222.

8. Burgess, *Shakespeare*, p. 214; Duncan-Jones, p. 266.
9. Robert Bearman has suggested to me that Hall kept a record of his *cures* so that the absence of Shakespeare's name from his notes is not at all surprising.
10. Edmond Malone, *Supplement to the edition of Shakespeare's plays published in 1778 by George Steevens and Samuel Johnson* (1780), vol. 1, p. 657.
11. For a description of these arrangements, see Schoenbaum, *William Shakespeare: A Documentary Life*, pp. 220–5.
12. Duncan-Jones, p. 271.
13. Greer, *Shakespeare's Wife*, pp. 315, 304.
14. Chambers, *William Shakespeare*, vol. 2, p. 181.
15. The visitor was a Mr Dowdall; see Chambers, *William Shakespeare*, vol. 2, p. 259.
16. Frank Harris, *The Man Shakespeare and His Tragic Life Story* (London: Palmer, 1909), p. 280.
17. Greenblatt, pp. 147–8.
18. Greer, *Shakespeare's Wife*, pp. 305–6.

## Chapter 16: Post-mortem

1. Chambers, *William Shakespeare*, vol. 2, p. 231.
2. See S. Schoenbaum, *William Shakespeare: Records and Images* (London: Scolar, 1981), p. 158.
3. Schoenbaum, *Shakespeare's Lives*, p. 130.
4. W. D. Macray (ed.), *Pilgrimage to Parnassus, with the two parts of the Return from Parnassus* (Oxford: Oxford University Press, 1886), p. 57.
5. Schoenbaum, *William Shakespeare: A Documentary Life*, p. 169.
6. See Hildegaard Hammerschmidt-Hummel, *The True Face of William Shakespeare* (London: Chaucer, 2006), p. 38.
7. Chambers, *William Shakespeare*, vol. 2, p. 207.
8. The scholar who made this often-quoted remark was John Dover Wilson. See his *The Essential Shakespeare: A Biographical Adventure* (Cambridge: Cambridge University Press, 1932), p. 6.
9. Wood, *In Search of Shakespeare*, p. 132.
10. See Stanley Wells (ed.), *Shakespeare Found! A Life Portrait at Last: Portraits, Poet, Patron, Poems* (Stratford-upon-Avon: Cobbe Foundation and Shakespeare Birthplace Trust, 2009). Since the claim is that this portrait once belonged to the Earl of Southampton and may have been commissioned by him, establishing its authenticity would obviously have important implications; but for indications that this may prove difficult, see Katherine Duncan-Jones, 'Unfound(ed)? – The Real Identity of the Sitter for a "Shakespeare" portrait', *Times Literary Supplement*, 20 March 2009, and Robert Bearman's review of

*Shakespeare Found!* in the *Shakespeare Quarterly*, vol. 60, no. 4 (2009), pp. 483–7.
11. Marcel Proust, *In Search of Lost Time: vol. 2: Within a Budding Grove*, translated by C. K. Scott-Moncrieff and Terence Kilmartin, revised by D. J. Enright (London: Chatto & Windus, 1992), p. 164.
12. Ray Milland, *Wide-eyed in Babylon* (New York: Ballantine, 1974), pp. 177–8.
13. Emil Ludwig, *Gifts of Life: A Retrospect* (London: G. P. Putnam's Sons, 1931), p. 368. The remarks on Ludwig are based on the discussion of him in my 'Images of D. H. Lawrence: On the Use of Photographs in Biography' in *The Portrait in Photography*, ed. Graham Clarke (London: Reaction, 1992), pp. 155–72.
14. Emil Ludwig, *Genius and Character* (London: Jonathan Cape, 1930), p. 31.
15. Quoted by Michael Keevak in *Sexual Shakespeare* (Detroit: Wayne State University Press, 2001), pp. 87–8.
16. Honan, *Shakespeare: A Life*, p. 324; Mark Broch and Paul Edmondson, *Shakespeare Found: A Life Portrait* (Shakespeare Birthplace Trust, 2009), p. 23.
17. Rowse, *Shakespeare the Man*, p. 238.
18. These remarks from the revised edition of A. L. Rowse, *The English Spirit: Essays in Literature and History* (London: MacMillan, 1966), are quoted in Schoenbaum, *William Shakespeare: Records and Images*, p. 170.
19. Ackroyd, p. 380.

## Chapter 17: Gossip

1. See Chambers, *William Shakespeare*, vol. 2, pp. 249–50, 252–4, 259, 264–9.
2. Halliwell-Phillipps, *Outlines of the Life of Shakespeare*, vol. 1, pp. vii–xiv.
3. Chambers, *William Shakespeare*, vol. 2, p. 238.
4. Schoenbaum, *Shakespeare's Lives*, p. 554. The book by Chambers from which Schoenbaum quotes is *Sources for a Biography of Shakespeare* (Oxford: Clarendon, 1946).
5. Edmond Malone, *The Plays and Poems of William Shakespeare: vol. 2. Prolegomena* (London: J. Rivington/L. Davis et al., 1821), p. 119.
6. Ackroyd, pp. 20–1; Weis, p. 5.

## Chapter 18: The post-modernist challenge

1. Stendhal, *Œuvres Intimes (Vie de Henry Brulard)*, ed. Henri Maritineau (Paris: Pléiade, 1966), pp. 113–14.
2. Ruth Franklin, 'Why Author's Archives like Updike's Just Aren't That Useful', *The New Republic*, 30 June 2010.

3. Shapiro, pp. 17–19.
4. Jacques Derrida, *Archive Fever*, translated by Eric Prenowitz (Chicago: University of Chicago Press, 1996), p. 17.
5. Leeds Barroll, *Politics, Plague and Shakespeare's Theater: The Stuart Years*, pp. 13, 3.
6. Ibid., pp. 6, 7, 154.
7. Margreta de Grazia, *Shakespeare Verbatim: The Representation of Authenticity and the 1790 Apparatus* (Oxford: Oxford University Press, 1991), pp. 71–8.
8. Greenblatt, p. 151.
9. Ibid., p. 12.
10. Ibid., p. 156.
11. de Grazia, *Shakespeare Verbatim*, pp. 12–13.
12. Bate (1), pp. 31, 5.
13. Holden, *Shakespeare: His Life and Work*, p. 100.

## Chapter 19: The argument from expertise

1. Ray Monk, 'Philosophical Biography: The Very Idea' in *Wittgenstein: Biography and Philosophy* (Cambridge: Cambridge University Press, 2001), pp. 3–15.
2. Honigmann, *Shakespeare's Impact on his Contemporaries*, p. ix.
3. Monk, *Wittgenstein: Biography and Philosophy*, p. 11. For Woolf's remarks see her *Collected Essays* (London: Hogarth, 1967), vol. 4, p. 230.
4. James Boswell, *The Life of Samuel Johnson*, ed. G. B. Hill and L. F. Powell (Oxford: Clarendon, 1934), vol. 1, p. 60.
5. Rowse, *Shakespeare the Man*, pp. 1–2.
6. Shapiro, p. 16.
7. Hugh Grady and Terence Hawkes (eds), *Presentist Shakespeares* (London: Routledge, 2007), p. 3.
8. The quotations from Hayden White and Alan Sinfield can be found in R. Headlam Wells, *Shakespeare's Politics: A Contextual Introduction* (London: Continuum, 2009), pp. 206, 200.
9. Shapiro, pp. xvi–xix; Shapiro, *Contested Will*, p. 44.
10. See Jan Kott, *Shakespeare our Contemporary* (London: Methuen, 1964).
11. Shapiro, p. xxiii.
12. Honan, *Shakespeare: A Life*, p. x.
13. See Lucien Febvre, *Le Problème de l'incroyance au XVe siècle: la religion de Rabelais* (Paris: Albin Michel, 1962).
14. Richard Ollard, *A Man of Contradictions: A Life of A. L. Rowse* (London: Allen Lane, 1999), p. 246.
15. A. L. Rowse, *Simon Forman: Sex and Society in Shakespeare's Age* (London: Weidenfeld & Nicolson, 1974), p. 6.

*Chapter 20: Final thoughts*

1. See Duncan-Jones, especially pp. 99–103.
2. Shapiro, pp. 29–34.
3. Schoenbaum, *William Shakespeare: A Documentary Life*, p. 220.
4. Shapiro, p. xxii.
5. Ibid., p. 369.
6. Bate (1), pp. 6–7. For a lengthy, elaborate but (for me) not finally convincing argument that Shakespeare not only depicted himself in William but also acted that part, see James P. Bednarz, *Shakespeare and the Poets' War*, pp. 123–31.
7. Bate (2), p. 4.
8. Katherine Duncan-Jones, 'As You Like Him', *Literary Review*, October (2008); Stephen Greenblatt, 'Shakespeare in No Man's Land', *New York Review of Books*, December (2008).
9. Duncan-Jones, p. ix; Greenblatt, p. 12.
10. Ackroyd, pp. 62, 160.
11. Burgess, *Shakespeare*, p. 53.

# *Index*

Ackrigg, G. P. V., 67
Ackroyd, Peter, 21–2, 25, 27, 31, 37, 48 (a Catholic wedding), 77, 100 (London), 128, 140, 147, 150, 176
Addenbrooke, John, 119, 120, 122
Ajax, 186n10
Alfred the Great, 124
*All's Well That Ends Well*, 53, 54, 62, 103
*Antony and Cleopatra*, 23, 85, 156
Arden, Edward, 30, 31, 101
Arden, Mary, 29, 30–3 (quality of her mothering and ancestry); as 'his mother': 38, 101, 173
Arden, Robert, 30
Arion, 56
Armin, Robert, 27, 75, 172
Arnold, Matthew, 163
*As You Like It*, 28, 61, 77, 110, 172–3, 186n10
Aubrey, John, 6–7, 33, 57–8 (Shakespeare's father a butcher?), 84, 85, 126, 145, 146, 147, 148, 150, 151

Bach, J. S., 162
Badger family, 34
Banquo, 87
Barnfield, Richard, 80, 154
Barroll, Leeds J., 114, 155–6 (purchase of New Place), 157, 159, 165
Bate, Jonathan, viii, 11, 30, 34, 35, 44, 67, 68, 72–3 (identifying the dark lady), 77, 82, 83, 90 (Richard Field), 96, 111, 112–13 (Essex Rising), 126, 127, 128, 159, 160, 171, 173, 174 (reviews of his second book), 175
Baudelaire, Charles, 127
Bearman, Robert, 24, 183n13 (chap. 6), 188n17, 189n10 (chap. 15)
Beaumont, Francis, 95
Beeston, Christopher, 6–7
Beeston, William, 6
Belott, Stephen, 11, 102–3, 105, 106, 107, 108, 128, 130
Bednarz, James P., 186n10, 192n6
Bergotte, Proust's, 137–8
Besterman, Theodore, 117
Betterton, Thomas, 61, 145, 147, 148
Bevington, David, 19
Bloch, Ernst, 162
Booth, Stephen, 51
Boswell, James, 163
Bottom, 28
Bray, Alan, 80
Brock, Susan, 123
Brontës, the, 55
Brutus, 53
Bryson, Bill, 87
Burbage, Cuthbert, 65
Burbage, James, 64
Burbage, Richard, 61, 62, 64, 65, 75, 81, 82, 83, 91, 94, 114, 171
Burbages, the, 65, 92
Burgess, Anthony, 95, 129, 176
Burghley, Lord, 66

193

Burrow, Colin, 71, 73
Bush, George W., 82
Butler, Samuel (author of *Hudibras*), 84
Byron, Lord, vii, viii, 87, 89, 125, 152, 155

Campion, Edmund, 15–16 (mission to England), 32, 34, 36–8 (Greenblatt's account of contacts with Shakespeare)
Cavell, Stanley, 162
Chambers, E. K., 5, 6, 7, 10, 23, 49, 61, 147–9 (defence of gossip), 150, 160, 162
Chandos portrait, 136
Chapman, George, 72, 184n12, 187n9 (chap. 13)
Chettle, Henry, 5–6 (on Shakespeare), 59, 113, 121
Clairmont, Claire, 24
Cleopatra, 85
Cobbe portrait, 137, 140
Collins, Francis, 130
Condell, Henry, 94, 124 (his widow)
Cook, John, 15, 179n4 (chap. 2)
*Coriolanus*, 116; references to Coriolanus himself: 26, 27
Cottam, John, 33, 40
*Cymbeline*, 92

Daniel, Samuel, 72 (his sister)
Davenant bust, 137
Davenant, Jeanette (or Jane), 85, 86
Davenant, John, 85
Davenant, William, 67, 84–5 (claim to be Shakespeare's son), 86, 87, 88, 114
Davenants, the, 126
Davies of Hereford, John, 61–2 (references to Shakespeare in his poems), 72–3 (as rival poet), 75, 76
Davies, Richard, 42
Dedalus, Stephen, 53
Dekker, Thomas, 106, 186n10
Derby, 4th Earl of, 35, 59
Derrida, Jacques, 155
Dethick, Sir William, 83, 170
Dickens, Charles, 21–2
Dickens, William, 21
Digges, Leonard, 134
Diogenes, 146, 148

Dowdall, John, 145, 147, 149
Drayton, Michael, 95, 129, 145, 150, 187n9 (chap.13)
Droeshout engraving, 138, 139, 140
Droeshout, Martin, 135, 136
Duncan-Jones, Katherine, viii, 11, 18, 19, 22, 23, 24, 26 ('not without mustard'), 34–5, 44, 50–1 (Shakespeare's marriage), 58–60 (Shakespeare and the acting companies), 67, 71, 78–9 (homosexuality), 83, 89–93 (Richard Field), 106, 112, 113, 114, 121, 124, 129 (syphilis), 130, 131, 149, 170 (heraldry), 173, 174, 175, 185n8 (chap. 9), 187n9 (chap. 13)

Edmonds, Piers, 78
Edmund (in *King Lear*), 168
Edward VI, 31, 109
Eliot, George, 141
Eliot, T. S., 17
Elizabeth I, 31, 56, 64, 68, 72, 79, 109, 110, 111, 112, 113, 114, 115, 168, 170
Erne, Lukas, 179n7 (chap. 1)
Essex, 2nd Earl of, 16, 68, 78, 79, 109, 110, 111–13 (his Rising), 114, 115, 116, 171, 187n6 (chap. 13)
*Every Man In His Humour*, 26, 94, 95, 99
*Every Man Out of His Humour*, 25, 26

Falstaff, 17, 23, 27, 42, 114
*Famous Victories of Henry V, The*, 59
Febvre, Lucien, 167
Feste, 27
Field, Richard, 89–94 (as Shakespeare's friend)
Finch, Herbert, 123
Fitton, Mary, 72
Fletcher, John, 127
Florio, John, 37, 68, 72 (his wife)
Forman, Simon, 104, 105, 168
Forster, E. M., 79
Foxe, John, 158
Freud, Sigmund, 4, 78, 139
Fripp, Edgar, 48–9
Fuller, Thomas, 95

Gerard, Father John, 34
Gobbo, 67
Godwin, William, 24
Grady, Hugh, 165

## Index

Grafton portrait, The, 137, 176
Graves, Robert, 14, 179n4 (chap. 2)
Grazia, Margreta de, 157–8, 159, 160
Greenblatt, Stephen, viii, 11, 17, 23–4 (John Shakespeare's drinking), 25, 27, 35–7 (Shakespeare in Lancashire), 38, 44–5 (poaching episode), 50, 53–4 (Shakespeare's marriage), 56, 57, 73, 80, 84, 86–7 (the Davenants), 91, 101, 113, 121, 122, 124, 126, 127, 132, 158, 159, 174–5 (review of Bate)
Greene, Robert, 5, 6, 59, 121
Greene, Thomas, 124–5 (enclosure), 127
Greer, Germaine, 49, 51, 52, 54, 120, 121, 128, 131, 132, 134
Greville, Sir Fulke, 60
Gurr, Andrew, 51
Gyllom, Foke, 33

Hall, Beatrice (alias Stephen G. Tallentyre), 117
Hall, John, 129, 131, 132
Halliwell-Phillipps, J., 10, 17, 48–9 (Shakespeare's marriage), 55, 56, 132, 146–7 (defence of gossip), 148, 151
Hamer, Douglas, 57, 58
*Hamlet*, 20, 28, 54, 60, 105, 110, 111, 113, 172; references to Hamlet himself: 17, 23, 27, 28, 77
Hamlet's ghost, 61, 62
Harris, Frank, 132, 145
Harvey, Gabriel, 37
Hathaway, Anne, 37, 47–52 (marriage to Shakespeare), 156, 176; as 'Shakespeare's wife': 50, 130, 149; as 'his wife': 30, 32, 44, 50, 51, 54, 73, 81, 130 (the second best bed), 132, 156, 179 n.9
Hawkes, Terence, 165
Hayward, Sir John, 112–13
Hearne, Thomas, 85
Heminges, John, 94
*Henry IV Part One*, 59, 44 (Hal), 62, 107
*Henry IV Part Two*, 27, 59, 62, 107, 172
*Henry V*, 27, 59, 63, 105, 110, 111, 113, 127, 172
*Henry VI*, 5, 43
*Henry VIII*, 127
Henry VIII, 31

Hesketh, Sir Thomas, 33, 35
Hilliard, Nicholas, 78–9
Hobhouse, John Cam, 89
Holden, Anthony, 17, 20, 38, 85–6 (Shakespeare and Mrs Davenant), 104, 105, 118, 160
Holinshed, Raphael, 91
Holland, Hugh, 134
Holland, Peter, 8
Holroyd, Michael, 78
Honan, Park, 14, 29–30 (Shakespeare's early relation with his mother), 140, 167
Honigmann, Ernst, 5, 33, 34, 121–9 (Shakespeare's meanness), 162, 164
Hotson, Leslie, 110
Hotspur, 53, 54
Houghton, Alexander, 33, 35, 37
Houghton, Thomas, 33
Housman, A. E., 9

'I. M.', 134
Iago, 24
Innogen, 92–3
Irving, Washington, 140

Jackson, Macd. R., 184n12
James I, 68, 114, 155, 186n10
Janssen, Gheerhart, 135
Jaques (*As You Like It*), 186n10
Jesus, 55, 131
Johnson, Dr, 89, 97, 163–4 ('stark insensibility')
Jonson, Ben, 8, 14, 17, 25, 26, 72, 84, 94–9 (as Shakespeare's friend), 121, 129, 134, 136 (verses on the engraving),138, 145, 150, 159, 173, 186n10
Joyce, James, 53 (*Ulysses*), 175
*Julius Caesar*, 98–9; (Jonson's criticism), 115, 172

Kemp, William, 27–8 (leaves the Lord Chamberlain's Men), 62, 65, 75, 172
*King John*, 18–19 (Constance's lament), 36 (reference to John himself), 180n10 (chap. 2)
*King Lear*, 27, 86, 105, 168
Knell, William, 59, 60
Knight, Charles, 15, 16
Kyd, Thomas, 8

195

L'Estrange, Nicholas, 95, 96
Lamberts, the, 179n9
Lamour, Dorothy, 138
Lanier, Emilia, 69, 72
Lawrence, D. H., vii, viii, 3, 87, 117, 131, 152, 153, 155
Leicester, Earl of, 56, 59–60 (his 'Men')
Leontes, 53, 167
Lewis, Roland B., 124
Looney, J. T., 120
*Love's Labour's Lost*, 37, 39, 68
Lucy, Sir Thomas, 42, 43, 44, 45, 148, 158
Ludwig, Emil, 139, 140
Luke, Saint (his gospel), 55

*Macbeth*, 38, 87, 114, 137, 156; references to Macbeth himself, 54, 93, 112
Malone, Edmund, 10, 32, 76, 94, 120, 130, 135, 147, 148, 150, 157–8 (his method)
Malvolio, 27, 101
Mann, Thomas, 129
Manningham, John, 81–4 (his Shakespeare anecdote), 85, 96, 114, 149, 160
Mark Antony, 85
Marlowe, Christopher, 6, 8, 14, 72, 94, 184n12
Mary Queen of Scots, 36
Mary, Queen, 31, 57 (as 'Princess Mary')
Meade, Jacob, 123
*Measure for Measure*, 53, 128, 132
Mennis, Sir John, 23
*Merchant of Venice, The*, 67, 79, 120
Meres, Francis, 154, 184n12
*Merry Wives of Windsor, The*, 18, 19, 42, 54
Meyrick, Sir Gelly, 171
*Midsummer Night's Dream, A*, 56, 114, 176
Milland, Ray, 138
*Mirror for Magistrates, The*, 91
Monk, Ray, 161–3 (nature of biography)
Montaigne, Michel de, 68
Mountjoy, Christopher, 11, 102, 103, 105, 128, 130, 164
Mountjoy, Mary, 102, 103, 104–5 (suspected affairs)
Mountjoys, the, 102, 103, 104, 106, 107, 108

Mozart, Wolfgang Amadeus, 55
*Much Ado About Nothing*, 27
Munday, Anthony, 8

Nashe, Thomas, 26, 37
Nicholl, Charles, 102–3, 107–8 (Shakespeare and the Mountjoys), 130
Nietzsche, Friedrich, 131
North, Sir Thomas *see* Plutarch

Oldys, William, 61, 62, 183n17
*Othello*, 104, 156; references to Othello himself, 17, 53, 104, 167
Ovid, 49
Oxford, 17th Earl of, 120

Painter, George, 78
Palmer, William, 14–15
Parsons, Robert, 34
Peele, George, 6, 8, 179n7 (chap. 1)
Pembroke, Earl of, 64 (his Men), 71, 72
*Pericles*, 105, 106, 107, 171
Phillips, Augustine, 94, 113
Picasso, Pablo, 21, 55
Plume, Thomas, 23
Plutarch, 85, 91, 174
Pope, Alexander, 84, 118, 120
Prospero, 49, 127
Proust, Marcel, 78, 127, 137–8 (Bergotte)
Pyttes, Michael, 123

Quiney, Adrian, 119
Quiney, Richard, 119–20 (his letter)
Quiney, Thomas, 119, 123–4 (not mentioned in Shakespeare's will), 129

Raleigh, Sir Walter, 124
*Rape of Lucrece, The*, 66, 68, 90, 110, 114
*Return from Parnassus, The*, 135
Reynolds, William, 78, 79, 185n8 (chap. 9)
*Richard II*, 81, 113
*Richard III*, 76, 81 (reference to Richard himself)
Richardson, John, 21
Robinson, John, 129
Rogers, Phillip, 119, 120, 122
*Romeo and Juliet*, 19, 20, 27, 36, 82, 153

*Index*

Rowe, Nicholas, 43, 44, 60, 61, 62, 67, 94, 99, 145, 147, 148, 158, 168
Rowse, A. L., 69–70 (his self-confidence), 72, 81, 140, 164, 168
Russell, Bertand, 161, 163
Rutland, Earl of, 171

Sadler, Hamnet, 94
Sartre, Jean-Paul, 39, 139
Schoenbaum, Samuel, vii, 15, 40–1 (categories of biographical conjecture), 43, 96, 134, 135, 147, 150, 162
Scoloker, Anthony, 5, 7
Scott, Sir Walter, 76
*Sejanus*, 60
Shakespeare family
  Anne *see* Hathaway
  Edmund, 53
  Gilbert, 53
  Hamnet, 8, 18–20 (his death)
  Joan, 129
  John, 22–3 (early career), 24, 30, 31, 32 (as covert Catholic), 55, 56, 57–8 (butcher?), 90, 147, 167
  Judith, 8, 119, 122–4 (her legacy), 129
  Mary *see* Arden
  Richard (WS's grandfather), 22
  Richard, 53
  Susanna, 86, 122, 129
Shapiro, James, viii, 11, 16, 27–8 (Shakespeare and social status), 34, 50, 62–3 (epilogue to *2Henry IV*), 84, 92, 111, 115, 120, 121, 153–4 (Shakespeare's reputation among his contemporaries), 155, 164–9 (importance of seeing Shakespeare in context), 170–1 (the *imprese*), 172, 173
Shelley, Mary, 24
Shelley, Percy Bysshe, 89
Shylock, 119, 137
Sinfield, Alan, 165
Somerville, John, 30, 31, 101
Sonnets, Shakespeare's
  no. 35, 71
  no. 37, 76
  no. 41, 71
  no. 62, 75
  no. 73, 75
  no. 81, 70
  no. 89, 76
  no. 110, 75
  no. 111, 75–6
Southampton, 3rd Earl of, 66, 67, 68, 69 (his family name), 71, 72, 73, 78 (androgynous?), 79, 88, 90, 110, 112, 113, 114, 118, 157, 168
Spence, Joseph, 84
Stein Baron von, 139
Stendhal, 152
Strachey, Lytton, 78
Strange, Fernando and then Lord, 35, 59, 64

Taylor, Gary, 14
*Tempest, The*, 49, 127
Thorpe, Thomas, 68, 69, 71
*Titus Andronicus*, 99
Tolstoy, Leo, 54
Touchstone, 27, 173
Touse (or Towse), William, 82
*Troilus and Cressida*, 128
*Twelfth Night*, 19, 75, 172
Tyler, Richard, 58
Tyler, William, 58

Updike, John, 9, 153

Vautrollier, Thomas, 90, 91
*Venus and Adonis*, 49, 50, 66, 153, 154
Volpone, 124
Voltaire, 117

Wallaces, the, 10, 102, 118
Ward, John, 145
Warwick, Guy of, 58
Weever, John, 154
Weis, René, viii, 11, 19, 20, 34, 35, 44–5 (the poaching episode), 67, 76–7 (Shakespeare's disability), 80, 83, 86 (Shakespeare as Davenant's father), 93 (Richard Field), 94, 112, 150
Wells, R. Headlam, 191n8 (chap. 19)
Whateley, Ann, 40, 47
White, Hayden, 165
Whittington, Dick, 44
Wilde, Oscar, 9, 79
Wilkes, Thomas, 82, 83
Wilkins, George, 83, 105–7 (his career), 129, 171
Willis, Robert, 56

Wilson, John Dover, 189n8 (chap. 16)
Wilson, Richard, 34
Wilson, Woodrow, 39
Wittgenstein, Ludwig, 80, 161–2, 164, 169

Wood, Henry, 104–5
Wood, Michael, 15, 20, 28, 38, 45, 105, 108, 137
Woolf, Virginia, 24, 89, 163
Worcester, Earl of, 55 (his Men)